The British Country House Revival

The British Country House Revival

Ben Cowell

THE BOYDELL PRESS

First published 2024
The Boydell Press, Woodbridge

ISBN 978 1 83765 058 3

The Boydell Press is an imprint of Boydell & Brewer Ltd
PO Box 9, Woodbridge, Suffolk IP12 3DF, UK
and of Boydell & Brewer Inc.
668 Mt Hope Avenue, Rochester, NY 14620–2731, USA
website: www.boydellandbrewer.com

A CIP catalogue record for this book is available
from the British Library

The publisher has no responsibility for the continued existence or accuracy of
URLs for external or third-party internet websites referred to in this book, and
does not guarantee that any content on such websites is, or will remain, accurate
or appropriate

In memoriam
Tim Schadla-Hall (1947–2023)

Contents

Illustrations

The author and publisher are grateful to all the institutions and individuals listed for permission to reproduce the materials in which they hold copyright. Every effort has been made to trace the copyright holders; apologies are offered for any omission, and the publisher will be pleased to add any necessary acknowledgement in subsequent editions.

1. The monument to Coke of Norfolk at Holkham Hall, Norfolk.

Preface

A monument in the park at Holkham Hall in Norfolk pays tribute to Thomas William Coke (1754–1842), agricultural improver and first earl of Leicester (of second creation). The foundation stone for the column was erected in 1845, three years after the earl's death, to mark his achievements as landowner, farmer, and steward of the family estates. The monument stands on an incline that overlooks the mansion. An imaginary line of symmetry would run, north to south, from the middle of the monument through the centre of the house before continuing beyond to connect with an obelisk built more than a century earlier, the towering grandeur of which the Coke monument replicates.[1]

Four decorated panels make up the base of the monument and relate to Coke's life and work. The first features a scene of farm hands attending to sheep, indicating the importance of livestock to the Holkham estate. The second shows cattle, each of a substantial size and proportion. A third panel depicts the earl himself seated at a table, consulting maps and documents alongside his estate managers and agents. The final panel is a dedication to the earl inscribed in bronze, which recalls "a life devoted to the welfare of his friends, neighbours and tenants". The inscription goes on to note for posterity that Coke "pre-eminently combined public services with private worth", and that the loss of such a "father, friend and landlord" was felt keenly in the worlds of politics, the arts, and agriculture.

Farming, livestock, and land management were the principal sources of the wealth that financed the building of the Palladian-style mansion at Holkham. A visit to the estate today, more than two centuries on from Coke of Norfolk's time, makes clear that its income is now derived from a variety of wholly different sources. On a blazing hot summer's day in 2022, the grass in the park turned yellow by the effects of an ongoing heatwave, the estate is alive with all sorts of activity. Crowds of visitors arrive in a steady stream of cars, which rapidly fill the parking spaces nearest to the house. Soon there will be so many cars that vehicles must be directed towards another section of the park roped

---

[1] The building of the obelisk, begun in 1730, in fact preceded that of the main house, which would be constructed over the course of the subsequent three decades. Christine Hiskey, *Holkham: The Social, Architectural and Landscape History of a Great English Country House* (Norwich, 2016).

off for the purpose. This overflow car park borders onto another fenced-off area, filled with white bell-tents and portable loos: this is the arena for a festival of sport, being built for an event due to take place the following week. Nearer to the house, the adventure playground and woodland rope swings are already busy by ten o'clock in the morning. Brisk business is being done at the cycle hire station, where trail bikes can be rented for a couple of hours or the full day.

As the day progresses the paths and avenues that crisscross the estate fill with visitors, on foot as well as on bikes. They walk the distance from the house to the six-acre walled gardens on the other side of the lake. At the lake, boats can be hired for an afternoon's gentle rowing. Occasionally, visitors need to make way for one of the large green tractors that are busy moving around the estate as the harvest is brought in. Most visitors are in shorts and T-shirts, but a rather more smartly dressed group processes from the car park to the newly refurbished Lady Elizabeth Wing, where an afternoon wedding event is taking place. Those exploring the estate by bike may have reached as far as the Holkham Studios at Longlands Farm, where modern offices are leased to a diverse range of companies from architects and art dealers to luxury jewellery designers. To the north of the park, across the busy coastal road, are the Holkham nature reserves where conservation efforts have led to the return of countless species of plant, animal, and insect life. Between the reserve and the local town of Wells-next-the-Sea spreads Pinewoods caravan park, also owned by the Holkham estate, with more than five hundred static caravans and yet more caravan pitches all booked up for this blisteringly hot summer season.

If, many years from now, a monument was erected to Tom Coke, the eighth and current earl of Leicester, or to his father Edward, the late seventh earl, what activities might be represented at its base? Tractors would no doubt feature, given the ongoing importance of farming on the estate. But alongside them could possibly be cars, boats, bicycles, wedding breakfasts, ice creams, gift shops, tourists, or caravans. These are just a few of the ways in which Holkham generates income today. Indeed, it would be a challenge to isolate just three scenes to emblazon on the base of a modern-day obelisk, such is the diversity of the business activities conducted in and around Holkham Hall.

Since taking over the running of the estate in 2005, the eighth earl has brought a host of new ideas, particularly in relation to sustainability and nature restoration, just as his father before him, a former president of the Historic Houses Association (HHA), had been a pioneer of historic houses as tourist attractions and as places to stay. The Holkham estate is just one example, albeit a remarkably successful one, of a house that has found a new way to exist and prosper in the twenty-first century. Up and down the country there are countless other mansion properties and estates that have done the same thing. This book tells the story of how British country houses, at one point considered to be on the verge of imminent destruction, have been reborn over the last fifty years because of the enterprise and initiative of their owners, and because of improvements to the business conditions in which they operate.

Country houses are in far ruder health today than they were in the dark days of the early 1970s, when so many continued to suffer from the neglect and abandonment faced in the decades that followed the second world war. But if country houses have had a remarkable revival over the last half century, history tells us that it would be unwise to assume that such benign circumstances can last forever. The threats faced in the third decade of the twenty-first century may not be those of demolition and decay, as they appeared to be back in 1974 when an exhibition on that theme opened at the Victoria and Albert Museum (V&A) in London. Without retelling the story of how the improvements of the last fifty years were achieved, the gains that have been made could all too easily be lost.

Acknowledgements

Many people have helped in the preparation of this book. First, I must recognise the contributions of my colleagues at Historic Houses. They been unfailingly supportive and encouraging of me and of this project, and my heartfelt thanks go to them all: Fiona Attenborough, Lois Bayne-Jardine, Natalie Bussey, Madeleine Eagan, Pat Jacobs, Anna Matthews, Rufus Mitcheson, Robert Parker, James Probert, Emma Robinson, Sarah Roller, Tolu Sangowawa, Jane Seymour, Rosie Wang, and Natalie Williams.

Early into my time as Director General of Historic Houses, it was a conversation with Robert Parker, Historic Houses' technical adviser, and the owner of Browsholme Hall in Lancashire, that first alerted me to the story of country house revival over the last half century, and to the agency of those hardworking owners prepared to make personal sacrifices in the interests of keeping heritage intact. I am most grateful to Robert and his family for their kind hospitality on my many visits to Browsholme in recent years. Robert's predecessor as technical adviser, Norman Hudson, has also been very generous in sharing his memories of the Historic Houses Association over the decades. His dedication to the cause of British country house heritage is unrivalled.

I would like to express my thanks and admiration for all those house and garden owners who occupy positions at Historic Houses: members of the board and council, members of the association's advisory committees, and the chairs and members of the regional and country branches. Owners who have been especially generous with their time, thoughts, and hospitality over the years include: Eleanor Argyll, Lucy Arthurs, Hal Bagot, Edward Barham, James Birch, Sarah Callander Beckett, Robert Brackenbury, William Cash, Sheila and Nicholas Charrington, Ursula Cholmeley, Martha and Henry Cobbold, Richard and Lucinda Compton, Charlie Courtenay, Simon Cunliffe-Lister, Martin Fiennes, Susanna Fitzgerald, Sir Richard Fitzherbert, Peter and Iona Frost-Pennington, Phil Godsal, Philip Godsal, Gilbert Greenall, William Hanham, Edward Harley, James Hervey Bathurst, Andrew Hopetoun, Sir Bernard de Hoghton, Robert Hunter, Richard Inglewood, Giles Keating, Jason and Demetra Lindsay, Gavin and Sarah Mackie, Peter and Naomi Milne, Patrick Phillips, Sir William Proby, James Saunders Watson, James Scott, and Harry Scrope.

Special thanks go to those who saw the book in manuscript and kindly offered thoughts and suggestions. Among them were Sarah Callander Beckett,

Ursula Cholmeley, Martha and Henry Cobbold, David Cowell, James Hervey-Bathurst, Norman Hudson, Richard Inglewood, Simon Jervis, and Robert Parker. All errors and mistakes that remain are entirely my responsibility. Above all I am grateful to the board of Historic Houses for its support, as well as for the assistance of Rosie Wang in sourcing the illustrations for this book.

Elena Porter's D.Phil thesis was being completed just as work on this book commenced, and it stands as the only detailed scholarly account of the foundation of the Historic Houses Association. I am grateful to Elena for sharing her thesis with me in full, and to her supervisors at the University of Oxford, Oliver Cox and William Whyte. For its rich detail and incisive commentary, I thoroughly recommend Elena's thesis to anyone interested in the territory I am about to cover. I would also like to thank Susan O'Brien for sharing a copy of her MA thesis, and Neil Lyons for sharing his work on Northamptonshire houses. Leigh Stanford was hugely helpful in showing me items from the archives of SAVE Britain's Heritage. Samuel Hill kindly indexed the back issues of *Historic House* magazine. Henry Bankes at VisitBritain helped with my enquiries about the British Tourist Authority's (BTA) company records. Staff at The National Archives, the British Library, the London Library and Saffron Walden Library have been very helpful in responding to my requests for help.

At Boydell and Brewer, my thanks to Michael Middeke and Crispin Peet for being so supportive of this project. Thanks too to Caroline Palmer, for her early encouragement, and to the anonymous peer reviewers who gave feedback on drafts of my manuscript.

A host of researchers, writers, and thinkers in the field of heritage and country house studies have inspired me, offered new ways of thinking about the subject, and provided encouragement and support in other ways over the years. Among them are: David Adshead, Sophie Andreae, Adrian Babbidge, Ian Baxter, John Beckett, Matthew Beckett, David Cannadine, Oliver Cox, Stephen Daniels, Gillian Darley, John Darlington, Terry Dooley, Eleanor Doughty, Shaun Evans, Jon Finch, John Goodall, Simon Jenkins, Miranda Kaufman, Jamie Larkin, Peter Mandler, Jeremy Musson, Wendy Philips, Martin Postle, Christopher Ridgway, Ken Robinson, Mike Sutherill, Setsu Tachibana, Annie Tindley, Adrian Tinniswood, Charles Watkins, Tom Williamson, and Lucy Worsley. My thanks go too to my friends and colleagues from across the UK heritage sector. My thanks go too to Adam Dant, whose art graces the front cover of this book as well as the walls of Upton Cressett.

A visit to Calke Abbey in Derbyshire when I was fourteen or so, not long after it had been acquired by the National Trust, set me off on a path that would eventually lead to a career in heritage and historic houses. For this, and for so much else, I am grateful beyond words for the support of my parents, Susan and David. I hope I am helping to make similar memories today for my own children, Reuben and Toby, when they too are taken on visits to historic houses, castles, and gardens. To Julie, my soulmate, I must apologise for the delay in the revival of our own historic house – a delay that has been caused, in part, by the writing of this book.

Ben Cowell
Newport, Essex
September 2023

Abbreviations

ATED	Annual Tax on Enveloped Dwellings
BTA	British Tourist Authority (or, before 1969, British Travel Association)
CGT	Capital Gains Tax
CPS	Commons Preservation Society
CTT	Capital Transfer Tax
HBC	Historic Buildings Council
HHA	Historic Houses Association (now known as Historic Houses)
HLF	Heritage Lottery Fund
IHT	Inheritance Tax
ICOMOS	International Committee on Monuments and Sites
NHMF	National Heritage Memorial Fund
NLHF	National Lottery Heritage Fund
PET	Potentially Exempt Transfer
RIBA	Royal Institute of British Architects
TNA	The National Archive, Kew
VAT	Value Added Tax
V&A	Victoria and Albert Museum

Abbreviations

Introduction

'Historic Homes' or 'Roofless Ruins': British country houses after the war

"To our visitors without whose interest
many of Britain's Historic Homes
would be Roofless Ruins"

Lord Montagu, dedication of *The Gilt and the Gingerbread* (1967)

Scratch the stone, stucco, or brick of the walls of any of Britain's estimated two thousand country houses and you will find a multitude of survival stories. The owners and custodians of these houses have found unique and diverse ways for each of them to remain standing into the twenty-first century, when so many other houses have been lost. These owners and custodians have developed coping strategies that have enabled houses not only to weather storms – whether literal, or of fire, flood, war, or pandemic – but subsequently to enjoy renewed strength, vitality, and resilience.

The stories that are told about country houses often begin with the ambitions and achievements of the generations that first commissioned mansions to be built. Such foundational owners may have hoped and anticipated that their descendants would enjoy untroubled lives amid verdant and productive farmland and harmonious local community relations. This was rarely, if ever, the case. All too frequently, the early aggrandisement of landed families, as expressed through the building of country houses surrounded by substantial gardens and parks, would give way at some point to hubris, and occasionally a dramatic fall.[1] By the late nineteenth and early twentieth centuries, the stories that were increasingly being told about the grandest country residences involved themes of decay and decline. Nevertheless, periods of demise might be followed by phases of revival, as owners found new purposes for the houses

---

[1] For examples of 'rise and fall' stories see Marcus Scriven, *Splendour and Squalor: The Disintegration of Three Aristocratic Dynasties* (London, 2009); Catherine Bailey, *Black Diamonds: The Rise and Fall of an English Dynasty* (London, 2007); J. V. Beckett, *The Rise and Fall of the Grenvilles: Dukes of Buckingham and Chandos, 1710 to 1921* (Manchester, 1994).

that they had inherited or acquired. This was certainly the case for some country houses in the 1950s and 1960s, when they opened for the first time to paying tourist visitors. Revival stories involved enterprise, initiative, clever financial management, and sheer hard graft, coupled with benign economic, political, and social circumstances as well as, sometimes, the good fortune of a successful marriage match.[2]

This book attempts to tell some of these stories. In doing so, it shows how an important part of what used to be called 'the national heritage' – the British country house – has been saved in ways that involve far less reliance on direct state support than other categories of heritage. The book therefore asks: how have country houses fared in the fifty years since their imminent demise was prophesied in a research report prepared by John Cornforth for the British Tourist Authority (BTA) (*Country Houses in Britain: Can They Survive?*) and through an exhibition that opened at the V&A in October 1974 (*The Destruction of the Country House*)?

The doom-laden predictions of the 1970s suggested that if the trend to greater and greater taxation of lived-in country houses continued, there might be fewer than a hundred of them left within half a century, outside of those that had already been acquired and preserved by the National Trust. Such predictions have proved shockingly wide of the mark. Far from being on the verge of extinction, country houses in Britain are in a better state today than they have been for nearly a century. It is likely, however, that the harbingers of those gloomy 1970s scenarios knew exactly what they were doing. Armed with apocalyptic visions of a world without country house architecture, landscape, or collections, lobbyists for the stately home cause persuaded first a Labour government, and then a Conservative one, to improve the fiscal environment for the owners of such places. The removal of the risk implicit in swingeing rates of capital transfer tax (CTT), or inheritance tax (IHT) as it became in 1986, coupled with rising affluence and a new-found collective national enthusiasm for heritage and the past, meant that many country houses were well-placed to develop and grow as businesses from the late 1970s through to the early decades of the new millennium.

---

[2] See the stories in Clive Aslet, *Old Homes, New Life: The Resurgence of the British Country House* (London, 2020), and *The Story of the Country House: A History of Places and People* (New Haven and London, 2022). The 'rise and fall' genre was brilliantly subverted by Peter Mandler in the title of his history of the country house in the modern era, *The Fall and Rise of the Stately Home* (New Haven and London, 1997). For 1950s and 1960s revival stories, see also Adrian Tinniswood, *Noble Ambitions: The Fall and Rise of the Post-War Country House* (London, 2021).

The representative body for such houses, the HHA, came into being in the dark days of the early 1970s, when few owners had much hope about the future. Buoyed by the optimism of its founding president, Lord Montagu of Beaulieu, and by general improvements in UK economic conditions, the association ceased to be the handmaiden to decline and instead found itself running conferences and events for its members on topics such as 'new uses for country houses'. The number of country houses being taken over by the National Trust plummeted after the mid-1980s: too many private owners were now able to "live in a stately home and make money", as the subtitle of Lord Montagu's 1967 book on the subject, *The Gilt and the Gingerbread*, had encouraged them to do.[3] What emerged was a unique form of public-private partnership, as private owners got on with the business of managing their houses and in many cases opening them up to public access, within markedly more positive fiscal and regulatory circumstances.

It could still be said, however, that the threat of destruction, as it was flagged by the V&A in 1974, has been postponed rather than entirely averted. New pressures in the twenty-first century serve to undermine the solidity of the country house revival of the last fifty years, almost as much as the wreckers' balls did in the period after the second world war. The ever-increasing costs of running a country house have been the subject of complaint by owners since time immemorial, but the inflationary pressures of the early 2020s have proved an existential challenge to anyone still reliant on oil-based heating systems to keep a many-bedroomed mansion warm. Such houses anyway run the risk of being dinosaurs in a net-zero era. Meanwhile, owners of country houses with connections to the UK's colonial and imperial past face growing societal pressure to account for the activities of their ancestors. This has profound implications for the way a house and its collection might be curated and presented, creating a set of moral and political hazards that were unlikely to have been anticipated by Lord Montagu and his contemporaries in the 1950s.

Defining the country house

Before getting further into such potentially contentious territory, however, it would be as well to address issues of definition. What do we mean when we talk of a 'country house'? The term is inexact, and often used synonymously with phrases such as 'stately home', 'mansion house' or 'country seat'. The country house escapes precise definition in this book too, but generally refers here to

---

[3]   Lord Montagu of Beaulieu, *The Gilt and the Gingerbread* (London, 1967).

a domestic residence of some substantial size and status (architecturally and in every other sense), usually found at the heart of a rural estate comprising parkland, fields, farms, and cottages.

Given the inexact quality of this definition, it may be easier to define the country house by what it is *not*. Clearly, it is not a townhouse – an elegant city residence. Nor is it a rectory or villa – rural seats of some size, yet not quite as big as the country houses to which they may have been satellites.[4] Clive Aslet defines a country house as being simply "a work of domestic architecture in a rural location, surrounded by its own land (although not necessarily a landed estate) and intended to seem a self-contained unit".[5] It is as good a definition as any, and the qualification in parentheses reminds us that the British land market has at times been remarkably fluid. Great estates have been broken up, or in other cases have remained intact even while the houses at their core may have been reduced to rubble. Alternatively, the ownership of a house may have become detached from that of the estate of which it was originally a constituent part. Increasingly in the twentieth century a substantial landed estate was no longer the *sine qua non* of a country house, and yet the impression, if not the reality, of being surrounded by a significant area of contiguous land often remained a defining feature.

Attentive readers may have observed the confident assertion in the first sentence of this chapter that there are two thousand such houses in Britain. This is not, and cannot be, an exact figure. But two thousand is not an unreasonable number, combining as it does the total of privately owned houses in the membership of the HHA (around 1,450), the mansion properties held by the National Trust, the National Trust for Scotland, English Heritage, and Cadw in Wales (collectively, fewer than three hundred in total), and those owned by local authorities or preservation trusts. That leaves just a couple of hundred or so other country houses that don't fall into one of these ownership categories. Two thousand was the number that the Labour peer Malcolm Shepherd used when responding for the government in a debate on historic houses in 1974.[6] And it was the same number that the report of the Gowers committee on country houses in 1950 reckoned as a fair assessment of the number of houses of "outstanding historic or architectural interest". The compilers of the report

---

[4] Giles Worsley, 'Beyond the Powerhouse: Understanding the Country House in the Twenty-First Century', *Historical Research* 78:201 (2005), 423–435.

[5] Aslet, *Story*, p. 5.

[6] HL Deb. 26 June 1974, vol. 352, col. 1490. Shepherd broke the number down geographically: 1,500 houses in England, up to 400 in Scotland, and up to 60 in Wales.

were hampered by the fact that the official listing (designation) of buildings had only been introduced a few years earlier, in 1947, such that the work of listing (under the chairmanship of Sir Eric Maclagan) was running concurrently with the investigations of Sir Ernest Gowers and his committee. The committee's estimate was based on evidence provided by the Ministry of Works and the two National Trusts.[7] But the same estimate appears in other places too. Michael Sayer thought that in 1975 there were around 2,300 traditional country estates owned by the same family for two or three generations, but that this number had reduced to 1,800 by 1992. Of these estates, the principal residence had been demolished in four hundred cases, meaning that the true number of surviving houses was more like 1,400.[8] John Cornforth began his overview of the country house scene in 1998 by saying that "it would be reasonable to guess that there are probably about 1,500 country houses that are still fairly complete entities in private ownership".[9]

These two thousand or so country houses do not have a perfectly equal distribution across the country. The building of country houses tended to proliferate in certain, quite particular, circumstances. Farming counties such as Northamptonshire contained perfect conditions: large, consolidated estates on good farming soil, within relatively easy reach of London to allow for the regular inflow of new sources of capital wealth. Lawrence and Jeanne Stone first noted that county's favourable conditions in their account of early modern social mobility, while a recent study has demonstrated just how resilient many estates here were, such that fewer country house demolitions occurred in Northamptonshire compared with other counties.[10] Locations that were closer to major urban centres would witness the frequent loss of landed estates to development and suburbanisation. Hence, in parts of Essex and Hertfordshire, country houses might more easily be lost than in other counties; certainly, the influence of the metropolis on the property market meant

---

[7] Ernest Gowers, *Report of the Committee on Houses of Outstanding Historic or Architectural Interest* (London, 1950), p. 29. Derek Sherborn claimed to have provided this list of two thousand houses personally to the committee, even though the text of the report only ever acknowledged the authorship of the Ministry of Works. See Derek Sherborn, *An Inspector Recalls: Saving our Heritage* (Lewes, 2003), pp. 140 and 282.

[8] Michael Sayer, *The Disintegration of a Heritage: Country Houses and their Collections 1979–1992* (Norwich, 1993), p. 17.

[9] John Cornforth, *The Country Houses of England 1948–1998* (London, 1998), p. 3.

[10] Lawrence Stone and Jeanne C. Fawtier Stone, *An Open Elite? England, 1540–1880* (Oxford, 1984); Neil Lyon, *'Useless Anachronisms?': A Study of the Country Houses and Landed Estates of Northamptonshire since 1880* (Northampton, 2018).

that they changed hands here with more frequency. The further the distance a part of the country was from the capital, the greater chance there was for large estates to agglomerate, such as in the Dukeries area of Nottinghamshire or the uplands of the Peak District, where aristocratic houses such as Clumber, Welbeck, and Chatsworth were all built. That Clumber no longer survives is proof, however, that even the presence of a substantial estate provided no guarantee of a house's survival.

Destruction, revisited

The immediate starting point for this book is the political and cultural debate in the post-1945 period regarding the fate of country houses. Concern about their future had been brewing for many decades but was exacerbated by wartime experiences, when so many country houses were requisitioned and then suffered further depredations because of the subsequent period of austerity and materials shortages. The V&A's exhibition *The Destruction of the Country House* in 1974 catalogued more than a thousand houses that had been lost in the century since 1875. Since then, research interest in lost houses has grown into an extensive literature of studies into the phenomenon.[11]

Destruction was ascribed to many different causes. Fire, the traditional enemy, claimed a great many houses.[12] The opulent interiors of Copped Hall in Essex had been gutted in a catastrophic blaze in 1917, while Easton Lodge in the same county had been rebuilt twice: first after a conflagration in 1847, and then again after another over seventy years later in 1918.[13] A substantial fire could often be the prelude to a significant phase of rebuilding, but fires could equally leave permanent scarring. The interior of the main block at Vanbrugh's Seaton

[11] For examples see: Tom Williamson, Ivan Ringwood, Sarah Spooner, *Lost Country Houses of Norfolk: History, Archaeology and Myth* (Woodbridge, 2015); James Raven (ed.), *Lost Mansions: Essays on the Destruction of the Country House* (Basingstoke, 2015); W. M. Roberts, *Lost Country Houses of Suffolk* (Woodbridge, 2010); Lyon, 'Useless Anachronisms?'; Philippa Parker, 'Lost Country Houses in Lancashire: Reappraisal and Analysis', *Northern History* 55:1 (2018), 111–123.

[12] Giles Worsley reckoned that at least twenty-five houses were lost because of accidental fires in the twentieth century. See Giles Worsley, 'Country House Fires', *Historic House* 26:3 (Autumn, 2002), 31–33.

[13] Copped Hall also featured in an article that ran in *Country Life* in August 1974 on the threats to landscape parks from road building and other incursions. Marcus Binney and Peter Burman, 'Assault by Motorway', *Country Life*, 15 August 1974, pp. 418–420. Easton Lodge was rebuilt after both fires, only to be demolished by owner Maynard Greville in 1950.

Delaval in Northumberland was never restored following a fire in 1822, while the distinctive domed roof of Castle Howard in North Yorkshire was destroyed by fire in 1940 and left unrepaired throughout most of the subsequent two decades. Without constant habitation and maintenance, houses could succumb all too quickly to a range of other problems, among them damp, dry rot, infestation, and the cumulative impact of excessive wind, rain, sun, and snow.

Fashion played both a destructive and a regenerative role over the centuries, as successive owners upgraded their medieval or Tudor-era manor houses with smart new homes built to the latest architectural styles. Agricultural depression in the 1870s, a result of poor harvests combined with the cheaper prices of grain newly imported from the USA, meant falling rent rolls and a diminution in the wealth of the owners of larger estates. Then, from 1894, estates were subject to new forms of capital taxation, when the Liberal chancellor of the exchequer Sir William Harcourt introduced the first effective estate duty in a bid to appease the more radical political voices elsewhere in his party calling for land reform. Once the principle had been established that the capital residual within landed estates was fair game for taxation, the amounts raised by governments in this way continued to rise. Although the initial estate duty had been no more than eight per cent (on properties worth more than one million pounds), this figure increased to fifteen per cent in David Lloyd George's People's Budget of 1909/10 and was stepped up steadily thereafter.[14] Losses of life in the first world war led to an acceleration in the market for land and estates once fighting was over. It has been estimated that almost a quarter of all land changed hands in the years immediately after 1918.[15] The second world war, meanwhile, saw numerous country houses requisitioned for use as military bases, hospitals, or schools. They would require significant amounts of repair and maintenance when returned to civilian use after the fighting had ended, a time of materials shortages and ever-rising costs.[16]

---

[14] See Martin Daunton, *Trusting Leviathan: The Politics of Taxation in Britain, 1799–1914* (Cambridge, 2001). See also Geoffrey Lee, *The People's Budget: An Edwardian Tragedy* (London, 2008). Geoffrey Lee formerly worked at *Country Life* and served as finance officer to the HHA from 1984 to 2003.

[15] See the discussion in John Beckett and Michael Turner, 'Land Reform and the English Land Market, 1880–1925', in Matthew Cragoe and Paul Readman (eds), *The Land Question in England, 1750–1950* (London, 2010), pp. 219–236.

[16] John Martin Robinson, *Requisitioned: The British Country House in the Second World War* (London, 2014); Julie Summers, *Our Uninvited Guests: Ordinary Lives in Extraordinary Times in the Country Houses of Wartime Britain* (London, 2019).

Decisions by owners to pull down houses were rational choices made in response to the harsher circumstances of the first half of the twentieth century. Sentiment seemed hardly to come into it. Houses were demolished so that the timbers, bricks, and stonework could be sold on to the building trade, and the land developed for other uses. Skreens Park in Essex was just one example, where the collection was sold, the mansion taken down brick by brick, and the estate divided up into separate farms.[17] The wealthiest owners with multiple estates sometimes chose to consolidate their holdings. The duke of Sutherland let Trentham go in 1905 and took the decision to demolish it seven years later once it became clear that no institutional owner was prepared to take on its annual maintenance costs. The duke of Newcastle sold fire-damaged Clumber for the value of its scrap in 1938. The Petre family abandoned Thorndon Hall in Essex in 1920, after its devastation by fire in 1878, and retreated to their ancestral seat at Ingatestone (which had previously been on lease).

At the start of the twentieth century, country houses were significant employers. The two world wars saw the mobilisation of working people, whether for fighting or for working in factories at home. Estates and country mansions were suddenly denuded of the labour forces that had hitherto kept them going. The requisition of hundreds of country houses as military bases, hospitals, prisons, and schools meant that, in some cases for a significant period, owners were separated from their houses and estates.[18] Combat and other losses sometimes left houses without owners or heirs. Audley End in Essex was not the only country house to be requisitioned during the second world war and then handed back in a less than satisfactory condition. Elizabethan Hill Hall, one of the earliest classically designed mansions in the country, was commandeered for use as a prisoner of war camp. A wing of Blake Hall, also in Essex, was adopted for use as an RAF operation base, while the American air force took over Elveden in Suffolk among many others. In some cases, houses suffered collateral damage from German bombing raids. Shortages of building materials meant that problems were left to fester.

What was to be done? The eventual solution for Audley End – outright acquisition by the state in 1947 – was rare, but also occurred in one or two other instances. The extravagant château at Wrest Park in Bedfordshire, which had been one of the first country houses to be used as a hospital in the first world

---

[17] The park meanwhile was then used as a holiday retreat for East End children; it is now a Scout Association campsite.

[18] See also John Martin Robinson, *The Country House at War* (London, 1989), and *idem, Requisitioned*.

war, continued in state hands after 1945 as an agricultural research centre. Ham House, by the Thames in south-west London, was given to the National Trust in 1948, but then leased back to the Ministry of Works and kept for much of the next half century as an outpost of the V&A. The duke of Wellington gave Apsley House in London to the nation in 1947 but reserved the right to remain in occupation in half of it.

There were limits to how far the state would step in. Although significant parts of the economy were nationalised under the Labour government of 1945–1951, the idea of nationalising the nation's stately homes was just far too fanciful. Such was the concern about the 'country house problem' that Labour's chancellor of the exchequer, Sir Stafford Cripps, commissioned a report in 1948 from veteran civil servant Sir Ernest Gowers into the steps that needed to be taken to save other country houses. Gowers, who had overseen the civil defence of London during the Blitz, assembled a committee of experts to conduct his investigations during 1948 and 1949.[19] The committee was asked to explore "what general arrangements might be made by the Government for the preservation, maintenance and use of houses of outstanding historic or architectural interest … including, where desirable, the preservation of a house and its contents as a unity". When its report was published in June 1950, its findings may have been a shock to the socialist administration. The committee concluded that private, rather than public, ownership was the best form of defence for such properties. Government simply could not afford to bring into public ownership more than the smallest sample of the best of the nation's houses. It was far better, the committee's report averred, for houses generally to stay in private ownership, and for the owners to be incentivised to look after their properties through tax concessions and grants.

Over time, these policies would become the standard government approach to the protection of country house heritage.[20] But the Labour government in 1950 could not bring itself to act on the findings of the report: its proposals were quietly parked. The Conservative government that assumed office next, in 1951, followed one of the report's recommendations and established the first historic buildings councils, which were empowered to give grants to private owners of important heritage assets. It was too little, too late. The early 1950s

---

[19] Ann Scott, *Ernest Gowers: Plain Words and Forgotten Deeds* (London, 2009).
[20] This remains the case today. See *Capital Taxation and the National Heritage* <https://www.gov.uk/government/publications/capital-taxation-and-tax-exempt-heritage-assets> [accessed 24 December 2022].

saw the peak of country house demolitions.[21] In counties near to London, such as Essex, it was not untypical for one or two large country houses to be demolished every year, not least where their grounds had been coveted for incorporation into new housing developments. Nationwide, it was claimed that a country house was being lost every five days at the height of this post-war wave of demolition. "Each year sees the decay or disappearance of more great houses", Arthur Colegate told the House of Commons in a debate in February 1953. He went on to explain that "those that remain in private ownership are becoming increasingly difficult to maintain. Only some action by the State – whether by relief of taxation or in some other way – can save them."[22] Coleshill (Berkshire), Kings Weston (Gloucestershire), Blyth Hall (Nottinghamshire), and Marks Hall (Essex) were all cited in the debate as examples of houses that had suffered this fate. Nevertheless, the government declined to implement the sort of tax regime for houses that had been proposed in the Gowers report. Officials reassured ministers that "the number of important houses demolished is small and even then … was agreed because of the high cost of restoration. It illustrates the point that the importance of many of the houses demolished can be easily exaggerated."[23]

'Doing the Statelys'

Although the prevailing experience of the post-war country house could therefore be characterised as that of decay leading often to outright destruction, a countervailing theme was also soon to emerge: that of stately homes as vibrant visitor attractions. Much media coverage in the early 1950s was devoted to the opening of country houses as places to visit and enjoy. Some houses were already in the practice of doing this and had started to reopen as soon as they could just after the war, including houses such as Burghley, Penshurst, and St Michael's Mount.[24] But the true pioneers of the stately home business were those that opened a few years later: Longleat from 1949, Wilton from 1951, Beaulieu from 1952, and Woburn from 1955.[25] Such houses took advantage of

---

[21] For a full list of the casualties, see Sherborn, *An Inspector Recalls*, chapter 11: 'The Destructive Fifties', pp. 170–196. See also Mandler, *Fall and Rise*, p. 360.

[22] HC Deb. 6 Feb. 1953, vol. 510, col. 2192.

[23] TNA, LCO 2/5753.

[24] Mandler, *Fall and Rise*, p. 369.

[25] The story of this boom in country houses open to the public is told in Mandler, *Fall and Rise*, pp. 369–388, and Tinniswood, *Noble Ambitions*, chapter 13. See also Victor Middleton, *British Tourism: The Remarkable Story of Growth* (2007), pp. 73–76.

increasingly affluent post-war conditions. More money and leisure time, and increasing ownership of motor cars, meant that the early 1950s was a boom time for the domestic tourism market. With no Sunday sports fixtures, and no Sunday trading at the shops, country houses filled a gap in the market as 'somewhere to go' with the family. From just seventy houses open in around 1950, half of them National Trust properties, Mandler estimates that the number exceeded two hundred by 1955 and had reached around three hundred open houses by the early 1960s.[26] Citing British Travel Association (BTA) figures, Lord Montagu reported that as many as six hundred houses were open to the public in 1966: a doubling of the number within just six years.[27] Montagu described this as a 'revolution', but one that was absolutely necessary if aristocratic owners were to move with the times: "If we fail our houses will inevitably become a further burden to the State."[28]

Montagu's principal contention was that owners needed to professionalise their operations. Drawing on what he had seen of American tourist attractions, he was convinced that Britain's tourism industry, including its country houses, needed to raise its standards. He had inherited his own house, Beaulieu in Hampshire, in 1951. Here, the ruins of a monastic abbey had long been open to public visits, of which there were around forty thousand a year.[29] Having discounted the idea of turning Palace House into a retirement home for clergymen, or a commercial hotel, Montagu alighted on the idea of copying Lord Bath at Longleat by opening the house as an attraction. If visitors were already willing to pay a shilling to see the ruins, he calculated,

> then most of them would be prepared to pay 2s. 6d. to be allowed inside an historic home full of family heirlooms. Public access would be restricted to the rooms in the old part of the house so that the privacy of my personal apartments in the Victorian wing would be preserved. It sounded practical, manageable and even rather exciting.[30]

His problem was that the house was rather modest by comparison to Longleat or Blenheim and had little to compare with the Canalettos on show at Woburn, or the van Dycks at Wilton.[31] But Montagu's particular strength was

---

[26] Mandler, *Fall and Rise*, p. 371.

[27] Montagu, *Gilt and the Gingerbread*, p. 17.

[28] *Ibid.*, pp. 10–11.

[29] Lord Montagu of Beaulieu, *Wheels Within Wheels: An Unconventional Life* (London, 2000), p. 144.

[30] *Ibid.*

[31] *Ibid.*, p. 146.

in public relations. His father had been a pioneer of motoring, so Montagu decided to establish a display of historic motor vehicles in his honour as part of the attraction. Opening in a blaze of publicity in April 1952, Beaulieu proved an immediate success. "The doors opened at eleven o'clock", he recounted, "and by twelve-thirty the hundredth visitor had arrived. We had champagne for lunch."[32]

In Montagu's opinion, a commitment to public opening was an obligation for all owners who wanted to hold on to their homes in an era when the country house was otherwise facing extinction. To mark Beaulieu's opening, he offered a memorable quote, which was printed in numerous newspapers: "I would rather keep my home and surrender my privacy than have things the other way round." Alongside this was a much-reproduced photograph of Montagu in shirtsleeves, scrubbing the floor of the entrance hall of Palace House, which was given a tongue-in-cheek headline: "It's enough to bring a peer to his knees."[33] Montagu was nothing if not the showman, appearing alongside the duke of Bedford and Lord Bath on the BBC's *Tonight* with Cliff Michelmore to sing a rendition of Noel Coward's 'The Stately Homes of England'.[34] But beyond the frivolity there was a deeply serious commitment to growing the country house business at Beaulieu and across the nation at large.

Other house owners shared Montagu's enthusiasm for public opening – such as the duke of Bedford, for whom the future of his family and his position was bound up with the reopening of Woburn, his Bedfordshire seat, as a major tourist attraction complete with safari park.[35] But not all owners agreed. Elena Porter notes that some owners resented Montagu and Bedford, for presenting a model (of the 'open' stately home) "that many other aristocratic owners would rather did not exist".[36] Differences of opinion among historic house owners were all too evident to Montagu. For *The Gilt and the Gingerbread*, he surveyed around a hundred and thirty of the most visited houses. He received sixty-six replies and was clearly put out that almost half of his fellow owners

[32] Montagu, *Gilt and the Gingerbread*, p. 55. He had promised champagne at dinner if at least a hundred visitors had arrived by the end of the day.

[33] Montagu later admitted that the picture showed him holding the brush the wrong way round. *Wheels Within Wheels*, pp. 250–251.

[34] Montagu, *Wheels Within Wheels*, p. 129.

[35] John Russell, duke of Bedford, *A Silver-Plated Spoon* (London, 1959); John Russell, duke of Bedford, *How to Run a Stately Home* (London, 1971).

[36] Elena Porter, 'National Heritage in Private Hands: The Political and Cultural Status of Country Houses in Britain, 1950–2000' (Unpublished D.Phil thesis, University of Oxford, 2022), p. 66.

2. Lord Montagu scrubbing the floors of Palace House Beaulieu, Hampshire prior to its opening to the public in April 1952 (Motoring Picture Library / Alamy Stock Photo).

had ignored him altogether. Drawing on the endless press coverage of annual visitor statistics, Montagu divided the owners of the nation's country houses into two imaginary cricket teams: the Gentlemen and the Players. The Gentlemen were "owners of essentially amateur status, usually the occupiers of naturally attractive properties, but with no inclination for the cruder aspects of professionalism". Among them were such aristocratic houses as Chatsworth, Blenheim, Hever, Berkeley Castle, Harewood, Hatfield, Inveraray, and Luton

Hoo. Montagu had a measure of disdain for the duke of Devonshire at Chatsworth, who refused to respond to the survey, despite attracting a quarter of a million visitors annually.[37] Montagu decried what he knew of the Chatsworth visitor experience: "I do know that it is impossible to purchase even a glass of water at the house, that the car parks and lavatories are adequate, and that there are a few souvenirs offered for sale."[38] The Players meanwhile were those country houses where a more professional approach had been taken. Led by Beaulieu, naturally, this group also included Woburn, Warwick Castle, Longleat, Arundel Castle, Castle Howard, and Burghley.

Lord Montagu's talent for marketing and publicity also translated into a keen sense of the need for a clear political articulation of the country house cause. As early as 1952, the year of Beaulieu's opening, he began discussions about how stately homes might "present a common front to Government". But he knew from the outset that he had a challenge on his hands, given that the landed classes were "virtually by definition, fully paid-up members of the 'awkward squad'. It was frustrating to find them so averse to discipline, coordination, mutual self-interest and everything else that might have turned them into a coherent, effective fighting force." He began by joining a meeting of fellow owners at the Dorchester Hotel, where the idea of a new association was discussed. It would have a joining fee of £25, with a discount for smaller houses. The idea was not new: it was a revival of a concept first explored in the mid-1930s, when leading lights at the National Trust had started to conceive of a 'Country Houses Association' in which the Trust would act in unison with private owners to attempt to secure fiscal concessions from the government.[39] Now, two decades later, the idea of such an association was revived, this time with the endorsement of the BTA, an early representative body for the tourism industry, and of Sir Harold Wernher, owner of Luton Hoo in Bedfordshire. But without clear National Trust endorsement this time around, the idea of a country house owners' association once again failed to take off. Elena Porter notes the recollections of some of those who attended as being that: "nothing emerged

---

[37] It is possible that some owners refused to respond to Montagu's survey because of his well-publicised, if unwarranted, criminal record. Montagu was imprisoned for homosexual acts in 1954, a charge he denied even while he made no secret of his bisexuality. Many have speculated that the high-profile nature of the case did much to influence the recommendations made by the Wolfenden Committee in 1957, and the eventual decriminalisation of homosexuality in 1967.

[38] Montagu, *Gilt and the Gingerbread*, p. 91.

[39] Merlin Waterson, *The National Trust: The First Hundred Years* (London, 1994), p. 108.

from this meeting because those present were divided into two groups – the larger houses who were satisfied with a good record of attendances and the smaller owners who were financially unable to contribute towards any joint approach to the problem."[40] Montagu recorded in his memoirs that the Dorchester Hotel meeting ended in "disarray and disillusion" – it was an idea for which the time had still not yet come.[41]

The idea of an owners' association was put on ice for the time being. Private owners would continue to draw support from the National Trust, which lobbied ministers in 1959 for exemptions from estate duty for owners in charge of important heritage buildings.[42] In the early 1960s, the Trust continued to complain to government that "there have been architectural losses which we cannot but deplore and buildings of national importance continue to decay through lack of money for their repair and maintenance." The Trust called for a new Gowers-style committee to be assembled to make recommendations about what could be done. The National Trusts would be among those who would be invited to give evidence to such a committee, along with bodies such as the historic buildings councils and amenity groups such as the Society for the Protection of Ancient Buildings and the Georgian Group. The aim was "to help private owners themselves to preserve and maintain important houses rather than pass them on to the Trust, either directly or by way of transfer to the Treasury in payment of death duties".[43] In the meantime, some private owners took out direct membership of the BTA, which received an annual grant from government to further its work in promoting tourism. Fifty houses had joined the BTA by the mid-1950s, a number that had doubled again by the end of the decade. Ross Geddes, BTA chairman from 1964, noted that the strength of the country house contingent among BTA members meant that in 1965 a small working party was established to consider how their collective needs might best be met. This working party's conclusion was that "the B.T.A. should set up a committee of historic house owners." This met for the first time in 1966 under the chairmanship of Hugh Wontner, managing director of the Savoy hotel group.[44] Wontner would continue in this role for some years after being awarded his knighthood in 1972.

---

[40] Porter, 'National Heritage', p. 83, quoting records held at Castle Howard.

[41] Montagu, *Wheels Within Wheels*, pp. 153–154.

[42] TNA, T 218/524.

[43] *Ibid.*, Letter Crawford to Selwyn Lloyd, 19 Dec. 1961.

[44] HL Deb. 26 June 1974, vol. 352, col. 1559. Porter notes that this committee continued to meet until July 1977, when it was replaced by the BTA's Heritage Committee,

It seemed that tourism held the key to the survival of country houses. This was the message taken from a survey carried out jointly by the newly created Countryside Commission and the BTA in the summer and autumn of 1968.[45] The survey, based on interviews of visitors to Castle Howard, Ragley, and Tatton Park, revealed the popularity of these places as tourism destinations. Although demographically the visitors tended to be more skewed towards managerial and higher social classes, the majority of those interviewed saw country houses as places to take their holiday. Moreover, those surveyed showed high levels of satisfaction with the offer that they found when they visited and were often repeat visitors to these and other houses.[46]

The Tourism Act of 1969 led to the creation of a new government agency for tourism promotion, the British Tourist Authority.[47] It happily shared the same acronym as its predecessor body, the British Travel Association, which wound up its affairs and transferred its operations to the new entity. The first chairman of the thus newly reconstituted BTA was Sir Alexander ('Sandy') Glen, a voluble advocate for the benefits of tourism. After a career in shipping and subsequently as director of British European Airways, Glen was a sensible choice to become a government-appointed cheerleader for the tourism industry. Glen's enthusiasm for the country house cause may have owed something to the fact that he had been a close friend and contemporary of that chronicler of mid-twentieth-century country house life, Evelyn Waugh.[48] It was perhaps ironic, therefore, that Waugh's preface to a new edition of his *Brideshead Revisited* in 1959 was so crushingly dismissive of the effects of tourism in creating "the present cult of the English country house".

The establishment of the BTA in 1970 demonstrated that tourism was a serious enough industrial force to have direct sponsorship and leadership from

---

which had a wider remit also featuring the major museums and galleries. Porter, 'National Heritage', p. 105.

[45] The Countryside Commission was established in 1968 as a replacement for the former National Parks Commission, but with a remit that covered the wider countryside in England and Wales in addition to national park areas. The survey of country houses was therefore a demonstration of the new commission's wider remit.

[46] TNA, COU 3/676: Historic Houses Survey: a joint publication by the Countryside Commission and the British Tourist Authority.

[47] See the account in Alexander Glen, *Footholds Against a Whirlwind* (London, 1975), p. 246.

[48] In 1934, Glen had taken Waugh, and Hugh Lygon, possibly the inspiration for Sebastian Flyte in *Brideshead Revisited*, on an expedition to the Arctic. Waugh nearly drowned on this trip because of a thawing glacier. Waugh and Glen would later serve together in wartime Yugoslavia.

government. The new BTA remained as willing as its predecessor to wield cudgels in defence of country houses. In March 1971 Glen wrote to the chancellor of the exchequer, Anthony Barber, to make the case for tax concessions for country houses, given the contribution that private owners made to the UK's overall tourism offer. The BTA's support for private owners was welcomed, but owners like Montagu could not be active members of a government agency in the same way that they had individually joined the former British Travel Association. Although the BTA's Historic Houses Committee continued to meet under the new arrangements, there grew a much warmer reception among owners once again to the idea of an independent consultative body that might directly represent their interests – including, if necessary, offering direct criticism of the government if it was deemed to be not doing enough to save and protect houses. As we shall see in the next chapter, this led eventually to the formation of a dedicated association for owners – the Historic Houses Association or HHA – in November 1973, at a time when the future for such houses looked uncertain at best.

As Peter Mandler has noted, "The story of the country house's rise to prominence in and after 1974 is an absorbing one and deserves a book of its own."[49] Whether or not this book does enough to meet this challenge, it attempts to tell the story of how British country houses have survived into the twenty-first century. It is a story told in two parts. The first part is an account of the survival of these houses following their post-war nadir. The chapters here follow in a loosely chronological order, rehearsing the events that led to the formation of the HHA in November 1973 and the 1974 V&A exhibition, before tracing the story of how public policy towards country houses developed until the mid-1980s. The second part of the book considers the revival of country houses in a more general sense over the last fifty years. The chapters here are thematic rather than strictly chronological, looking for example at how houses have benefited from different sorts of business diversification, considering the different options for how houses of significance could be saved for posterity or 'for the nation', and looking at case studies of how buildings and their landscapes have been rescued and restored. The book seeks to assess the role of country houses in British cultural life today and to ask what a modern-day Sir Ernest Gowers might make of the situation, more than seventy years after his seminal report. At all times, the focus is on the houses themselves, rather than on the lives and fates of their owners, who have in any case tended to regard themselves as merely the temporary custodians of the country seats that they have inherited.

---

[49]   Mandler, *Fall and Rise*, p. 401.

Part One
Survival

Part One

Survival

1

On the brink

The alarms started clanging at 2:30am that Sunday morning. Each of the volunteer firemen in the village had a bell fitted in their house, to alert them to when they were needed at the station. In a rush, Barry Heaton got himself ready; within minutes he was out of the front door and running to join his crewmates at the fire station on Debden Road. Eric Byford was already there, having switched on the station lights and started up the communications equipment. Barry heaved open the metal concertina doors and started to put on his gear.

At first, Barry couldn't believe it when Eric shouted that the fire was at Shortgrove Hall. Shortgrove was a constant backdrop to village life. Built in 1684 for Giles Dent, it stood at the top of a hill to the north of the village, reached through ornate iron gates and across a classically designed bridge over the river Cam.[1] The house was now empty, the Butler family having sold it a few years earlier to a Mr Geoffrey Allen. Barry remembered that Mr Allen lived at Duddenhoe End and had not yet moved in to Shortgrove. It must be a false alarm, surely?

It wasn't. "We drove through the main gates past the Lodge and over the old bridge", Barry later remembered, "and then in front of us, between the oak trees, was a scene we shall never forget." The entire house was ablaze, and it was serious. "On every storey flames were pouring out of every window, with very little smoke." Arthur Butler, the son of the previous owners, was staying that evening at his parents' new house in the grounds of Shortgrove Hall. He vividly recalled the conflagration: "A huge ball of flame was shooting out of the front door and was curling upwards and backwards over the roof. The heat was intense, but the really terrifying thing was the noise of the flames – like two express trains passing simultaneously through a station."

Immediately the fire crews set to work, connecting the hoses to the water mains. As well as Barry Heaton and Eric Byford, up to sixty firemen and a

---

[1] Anthony Tuck *et al.*, *Victoria History of Essex: Newport* (London, 2015), pp. 45–49. Pevsner speculated that it might be even earlier in date: *Essex* (Harmondsworth, 1954), p. 279.

dozen pumps were called to the house from across north-west Essex and east Hertfordshire, from Thaxted, Stansted, Bishop's Stortford, and Harlow. "We jumped up and down and cheered them as they flashed past us through the village," recalled one Newport resident later, a schoolgirl at the time.[2] The mains water having insufficient pressure for the task, Barry went around to the back of the house to investigate the use of the swimming pool and the fishpond. Water from the fishpond was subsequently targeted at the blaze. The fish all died.

It took nearly four hours for the firemen to get the blaze under control. The chief fire officer in control of the operations focused on saving the two wings of the house rather than the main block. It was sufficient to ensure that at least some of the rare bricks of this 1680s mansion could be rescued. But the fire – one of the hottest that any of the firemen had ever attended – was enough to spell the end of Shortgrove's nearly three-hundred-year history. Its interiors, including the "fine staircase with delicate wrought iron scrolls" that had been noted by Pevsner, were all gone.[3] The only person in the house at the time was Clifford Carrick, the caretaker, who was rescued from a smoke-filled ground-floor bedroom by four of the firemen, after throwing his bedding out onto the lawn. The house was not so lucky, being "destroyed down to its foundations" although the outer walls continued to stand, smouldering, on the hilltop.[4]

The local newspaper carried a quote from the hall's new owner, Mr Allen. He had not been at Shortgrove that evening. Instead, he had been in London at the Colony Club, "discussing the future of the hall and other matters with Mr George Raft, the film star". Mr Allen had bought the house with the intention of converting it into a twenty-nine-bedroom luxury hotel. The damage to the house and its interiors was now estimated at thousands of pounds. "This has been a considerable setback", admitted Mr Allen, "but we shall carry on with our original plan."[5]

Alert readers, however, may have already begun to harbour suspicions. George Raft, the drinking partner of Geoffrey Allen on the evening of the fire, was best known for his portrayal of gangsters in films such as *Gold Diggers of Broadway* (1929), *Quick Millions* (1931), *Scarface* (1932), and *I Stole a Million*

---

[2]   Rachel Morris, *The Museum Makers: A Journey Backwards* (Tewkesbury, 2020), p. 26.

[3]   Pevsner, *Essex*, p. 279.

[4]   The eyewitness accounts of the fire are from *Newport News* 35 (Summer 1991), pp. 42–43, and Morris, *The Museum Makers*.

[5]   '10 Pumps Fight Mansion Blaze', *Herts & Essex Observer*, 10 June 1966, p. 1.

(1939). The regularity with which Raft was cast in such roles mirrored the constant gossip about his alleged real-life links to the criminal underworld. In the 1950s he dropped out of the cinema business altogether for a while before being tempted back to a role – as a gangster, naturally – in *Some Like it Hot* (1959). He appeared as a casino owner in *Ocean's 11* (1960) before life imitated art once more when he moved to London as the co-owner and manager of the casino at the Colony Club. In 1967 he would be refused entry back into the United Kingdom because of his undesirable criminal connections.

Geoffrey Allen was himself far from being innocent of such nefarious connections. It was known locally that he had invited the East End gang leaders Ronnie and Reggie Kray to Shortgrove sometime before the fire. When Mr Allen's next historic property acquisition, Briggate Mill in Norfolk, also burned down in unexplained circumstances in 1975, criminal investigators made the link. Geoffrey Allen was sentenced to seven years' imprisonment for insurance fraud. The fire at Shortgrove had been one of the most spectacular of Allen's achievements, although the insurance company refused the £150,000 payout that he had claimed.[6]

In this way, Shortgrove became one of the houses that would later feature in the V&A's *Destruction of the Country House* exhibition in 1974. A single entry in the volume accompanying the exhibition read 'Shortgrove (1968) F S', which meant that Shortgrove was lost in 1968 to a fire but that the shell of the house still stood at the time of the exhibition in 1974. The fact that the fire had occurred two years earlier, in June 1966, did not diminish the significance of the loss, nor the criminal circumstances of its demise.[7]

The burned-out shell of Shortgrove Hall was not the only house on the brink of disappearance by the early years of the 1970s. All over the country, mansion properties appeared to be in a state of terminal decline. Twenty years earlier the report prepared by the Gowers committee had described the familiar process by which this happened. "Sooner or later," the report had said, "the house becomes decrepit and the garden runs wild; the park timber is cut down and the beauty of the setting destroyed." The inevitable consequence was the sale of the property, but only if a buyer was available. Often this would lead to

---

[6] 'Insurance Fraud Alleged Over Burned Properties', *The Times*, 8 September 1976, p. 4. I am grateful to Chris Ridgway for the reference.

[7] This was not the only entry in the *Destruction* exhibition that required correction. For example, J. D. Jones, curator of Carisbrooke Castle on the Isle of Wight, wrote to the V&A to point out that East Cowes Castle had been demolished in 1956, not 1950. Letter J. D. Jones to Roy Strong, 2 Oct. 1974, V&A Archive, MA/28/243/1.

the house being ruined through conversion to an alternative institutional or commercial use, or else it would be demolished and sold for its lead, timber, and fittings. "The process is gathering alarming momentum", the report had warned in 1950.[8] Things had not necessarily got any better by the early 1970s.

Three examples, from three different corners of England, illustrate the sorts of situations that owners experienced in the decades after the second world war: Combermere Abbey in Cheshire, Browsholme Hall in Lancashire, and Heveningham Hall in Suffolk.

Combermere Abbey, on the border between Shropshire and Cheshire, had been bought by the industrialist Sir Kenneth Crossley in 1919. Crossley's company, Crossley Motors, produced cars, buses, and aeroplanes. Combermere Abbey was not only a convenient distance from the factory but was also a suitably grand statement of Sir Kenneth's social standing. The house had been through several transformations by the time of Sir Kenneth's acquisition. Originally a Cistercian monastery, it was converted to a mansion property by Sir George Cotton after 1538. A 1586 panegyric to Sir George's son Sir Richard Cotton – an early instance of a country-house poem – celebrated Combermere as "a stately seat, whose like is hard to find". The poem likened the estate to a beehive: "This is the hive; your tenants are the bees: and in the same, have places by degrees."[9] The house continued to grow, organically, bearing the impress of its worker bees. When Dr Johnson visited two centuries later, he saw a rather incoherent mixture of architectural features: "built at different times with different materials, part is of timber, part stone or brick, plaistered and painted over to look like timber." He added, generously, that "it is the best house that I ever saw of this kind."[10] Sir Richard's descendant, Sir Robert Salusbury Cotton (1739–1809), made the next significant intervention at Combermere, dressing the exterior in what architectural historian John Martin Robinson has called "pretty, lightweight, 'pointed' Gothic".[11] His son, Stapleton Cotton (1775–1863), had a military and colonial career that meant he was often away from the estate. Despite this, Stapleton contemplated the wholesale reconstruction of the house on two occasions, in the 1820s and 1830s. Not pursuing either scheme, Stapleton instead added a dining room (to host a visit by the duke of

---

[8]   Ernest Gowers, *Report of the Committee on Houses of Outstanding Historic or Architectural Interest* (London, 1950), p. 6.

[9]   Kathryn Hunter, 'Geoffrey Whitney's "To Richard Cotton, Esq.": An Early English Country-House Poem', *The Review of English Studies*, NS, 28:112 (1977), pp. 438–441.

[10]   Quoted in John Martin Robinson, 'Combermere Abbey, Cheshire', *Country Life*, 6 Jan. 1994, pp. 40–43.

[11]   *Ibid.*, p. 40.

Wellington in 1820) and an armoury to display the weaponry he amassed while on service in India.[12]

Encircling the wide expanse of water that gave the house its name, Combermere's parkland setting was evocative of the landscape ideals of the early nineteenth century. But the later decades of that century were not kind to the house. With the family increasingly in debt, land was sold from the estate in 1893 and the house was rented out, first to empress Elizabeth of Austria and then to the duchess of Westminster. The purchase of estates by industrialists is a common theme of the history of the British country house. It could mean the injection of new capital and thereby help to prevent a property's untimely demise, even while it might mean the end of a property's connection with a particular landed family, as happened at Combermere in 1919. For Sir Kenneth Crossley, however, the dream of a stately seat at Combermere soon became a nightmare of financial liabilities. Sir Kenneth's only son died in a plane crash in 1939, while his heir, Sir Kenneth's grandson, died of polio in 1953. Sir Kenneth lived on at Combermere until 1957, but further land sales had been necessary to meet tax liabilities. Sir Kenneth's great granddaughter, Sarah Callander Beckett, recollected, "Death duties on these unexpected deaths had reduced the landholding to the parkland and some outlying farms, making its viability tenuous without external income sources and trust income."[13]

Sarah's mother, Sir Kenneth's granddaughter, inherited the house in 1959. By this time the estate was fraying at the edges. The park was used as a dairy farm, and maintenance had plummeted to unsustainable levels. Estate buildings were left empty and decrepit, while the main house succumbed to damp and decay. Sarah Callander Beckett evoked the era vividly: "I remember growing up with buckets and pans tactically placed to catch the rainwater pouring through the roof; newts and frogs joined us in the bath as we only got public mains water supply in 1961." By the middle years of the 1970s, Sarah's mother felt she had little choice but to consider a radical overhaul, perhaps even replacement, of the main house. The dry and wet rot was so extensive that the north wing had to be vacated and closed. Two other wings were demolished along with part of the second floor. Architects Raymond Erith and Quinlan Terry were engaged to devise a plan for a smaller modern gothic house on the

[12]   Sir Stapleton was granted the title viscount Combermere in 1827 following the siege of Bharatpur.

[13]   Sarah Callander Beckett, 'An Inheritance Restored: A Private Owner's Experience', in David Cannadine and Jeremy Musson, *The Country House: Past, Present, Future* (New York, 2018), pp. 69–73.

site of Combermere. In May 1974 a planning application was made to Crewe and Nantwich District Council for the partial demolition of the south wing of the house and the entire demolition of the north wing.[14]

Browsholme Hall in Lancashire was another example of the kind of substantial gentry mansion for which the future looked distinctly uncertain in the middle years of the 1970s.[15] Here, the Parker family had made their home in the royal hunting grounds of the Forest of Bowland. The family name derived from their role as custodians of the forest lands, Edmund Parker being the fourteenth-century keeper of Radholme Park. His son took a lease on land in Nether Browsholme in 1425, and by the early sixteenth century a fine house had been built to display the family's status among the county's gentry. Over time the house was added to and augmented. Its asymmetrically positioned front door was embellished with an architectural frontispiece, probably derived from the much grander Elizabethan model at nearby Stonyhurst, the Shireburn seat.[16] J. M. W. Turner depicted the house in 1799, by which point the antiquarian Thomas Lister Parker was in residence. Thomas introduced a new round of improvements in 1805, engaging Jeffry Wyatt to create a drawing room and John Buckler to add a new gallery.[17] The surrounding park landscape was made picturesque by new plantings. Well could Parker write, in 1804, to his friend, the painter James Northcote, "My old place looks delightful, & everyone is now surprised at what I have done."[18]

An interest in the antiquarian and the picturesque did not necessarily pay the bills. Thomas Lister Parker's overspending led to the sale of Browsholme to his kinsman Thomas Parker of Alkincoates, which was another of the Parker family estates in Lancashire. The Alkincoates estate was eventually sold in 1910, and the family consolidated their assets at Browsholme. Grazing and livestock farming were not affected as harshly as arable during the agricultural depression that began in the 1870s, yet money remained tight. A plan to add a new chapel to the house in the 1890s had to be abandoned owing to the need to

---

[14] 'Proposals to Carry Out Works for Partial Demolition and Alteration to Combermere Abbey, Near Whitchurch', *Crewe Chronicle*, 23 May 1974, p. 34.

[15] Browsholme was in Yorkshire until boundary changes in 1974. See Simon Jervis, 'Five Early Inventories of Browsholme Hall', *Furniture History* 22 (1986), 1–24.

[16] I am grateful to Simon Jervis for this insight.

[17] Christopher Hussey, 'Browsholme Hall, Yorkshire: The Seat of Colonel Parker', *Country Life*, 13 July 1935, pp. 38–43.

[18] Quoted by Robert Parker, John Cornforth Memorial Lecture, 'Browsholme Hall, Lancashire' (8 Feb. 2023), given at Christie's, London.

fter the fire, but died in 1965. The Finance Act of that year also created a fis-
al problem for the house. The introduction of capital gains tax (CGT) was
designed to ensure the fair taxation of sums made from increases in the capi-
al valuations of assets. Porter notes that CGT was part of a deliberate policy
within the Labour government to shift a greater degree of the tax burden onto
wealth, rather than income.[21] Heveningham had not been sold, of course. But
the application of CGT to discretionary settlements meant that a liability arose
every fifteen years on a revaluation of the assets.[22]

Andrew Vanneck's successors knew that they did not have the financial
wherewithal to sustain the house or to cope with further fires or tax liabilities. Since Heveningham's settlement had been made in 1955, the first CGT
charge would fall in 1970. Vanneck's daughter, Margita Wheeler, threw herself
on the mercy of Harold Wilson's Labour government, offering the house and
its collection to the nation. Without government support, Wheeler suggested,
Heveningham had no future. She would have no choice but to sell the contents
and then sell the house itself, either whole or for scrap. In the spirit of the recommendations of the Gowers report, the government accepted the property in
lieu of a tax payment, although this was intended as a holding operation rather
than as a permanent solution. A deal was struck with the National Trust, which
became custodian of the property under a management agreement, in a part of
the country where its only other substantial mansion properties were Ickworth
in Suffolk, acquired in 1956, and Blickling in Norfolk, one of the first houses to
be acquired under the Trust's country houses scheme in 1940. Trust custodianship was perhaps a fitting outcome for a house that could boast of "one of the
greatest of all eighteenth-century interiors".[23] But the whole affair had been an
expensive reminder of the sheer cost of this category of built heritage.

By the late 1960s, it was true, the number of outright demolitions of the
kind that had characterised the preceding decades had dwindled. Repair grants
from the historic buildings councils had helped get some houses back into
working order. But there was a finite amount of grant money to spread around,
and a great many more houses that needed attention than could reasonably be
accommodated. Houses such as Combermere and Browsholme were quietly
sinking into a state of decline with barely any notice. The Heveningham affair

---

[21] Porter, 'National Heritage', p. 91.
[22] John Cornforth, 'The Future of Heveningham', *Country Life*, 18 Sept. 1969, pp.
670–673.
[23] John Cornforth, 'Heveningham Hall, Suffolk', *Country Life*, 17 June 1993, pp.
62–65.

devote funds to save the east wing of the main house from cc
it was clear that not all was well. Colonel John Parker advised h
stick with a career in the army rather than return to Browshol
is nothing for you here".

Robert Parker, who also became a colonel serving with the (
regiment, inherited in 1938. Although the house escaped bein;
during the war, it sustained damage through a chronic lack of n
grant for the roof from the historic buildings council in 1958 [
help, as did income from opening to visitors after 1955. But the h
morrhaged its main source of support after selling land from the
tax liabilities. The sale of ten farms in 1960, leaving just a two-h
sixty-acre Home Farm, was a hammer blow to the long-term sus
the estate. By the early 1970s the house had suffered from such
period of under-investment that the next generation observed that
both "unfit to live in" and "unsaleable in its present condition".[20]

Heveningham Hall in Suffolk illustrated the problems faced by g
when trying to tackle country houses in distress. As houses went, i
niably special. It had been built in the middle of the seventeenth
William Heveningham, one of the members of parliament who ha
executed Charles I. A century later, the house was remodelled by
Taylor as a substantial Palladian mansion deep in the Suffolk coun
its then owner Sir Gerald Vanneck. With twenty-three bays, rooms
Wyatt, and designs for a park by Lancelot Brown, Heveningham w
worthy of the grade I status it had been accorded in 1951.

The twentieth century had been hard on Heveningham. Vanneck
dant, the fourth Lord Huntingfield, died intestate in 1915. There we
ty-four claimants to his estate, and to satisfy them all the house, cont
estate were put on the market. The nephew of the fourth lord, his s
as fifth lord, acquired the house, some of the collection, and only som
estate. He, in turn, sold this to his brother, Andrew Vanneck, in 192{
in 1947 had damaged the dining room, one of the "very fine interio
the historic building inspectors had recorded when they visited a fe
later. Andrew Vanneck did much for the house, including a full rest

---

[19] Susan O'Brien, 'Attitude, Altruism and Adaptability: How Two Gentry
es, Kiplin Hall (Yorkshire) and Browsholme Hall (Lancashire), Survived the Twe
Century' (Unpublished MA thesis, University of Leicester, 2018), p. 16.

[20] Christopher Parker, *Browsholme Hall 1975–1995: A Point of View* (Settle,
p. 19, quoted in O'Brien, *ibid.*

was conspicuous mainly by the uniqueness of its eventual resolution – direct acquisition by the state, albeit on a temporary basis. Not long afterwards, however, another country house property in trouble would also rise to public prominence, in a case that would have far wider repercussions for all those involved in the protection of architectural heritage.

The Grange was an enormous early nineteenth-century neoclassical Greek temple designed by William Wilkin and inserted into the Hampshire countryside, encasing an earlier brick building. The Baring family had sold the house and six hundred acres of surrounding land to Charles Wallach in 1934. Wallach was an industrialist whose money had come from the application of paraffin to medical uses, and he invested heavily in filling The Grange once again with artistic treasures. The American army had assumed wartime use of the house, but thereafter The Grange was left empty and abandoned for twenty years. Charles Wallach died in 1964 and at this point John Baring, the seventh Lord Ashburton, bought back the house and grounds. Baring claimed he was doing so not to move into the house, but rather to protect it in its landscape setting. Baring maintained that his intention was to leave The Grange as "a romantic and impressive ruin", by now partially demolished but still standing proud in its parkland setting.

However, the imitation Greek temple proved to be not as substantial as it first appeared. The stone-like exterior was in reality "lime-mortar bound brick faced with Roman cement", prone to crumble on exposure to inclement weather. Even a partial demolition looked like an undignified end for the building.[24] Baring therefore resolved to demolish the house in its entirety and, as required, gave notice of his intent. The local council confirmed that it would not object to the plan by means of issuing a building preservation order, and thus gave Baring permission to proceed.

Had he gone ahead and demolished the building in 1967 he may just have done so without any further comment or criticism. As it was, he delayed calling in the wrecking ball, and this proved to be a tactical mistake. Within a few years the law regarding the demolition of listed buildings had changed. From 1968, any demolition of a listed building required specific consent from the local planning authority, known as listed building consent.[25] Baring reapplied under the new rules in May 1969 and was granted consent in July 1970. The rear wing of the house was removed. It was as the demolition gear moved into place for the remainder of the building in September 1972 that the public fuss began.

[24] John Baring, 'Why the Grange is to be demolished', *The Times*, 9 Sept. 1972, p. 15.
[25] Wayland Kennet, *Preservation* (London, 1972), p. 77.

Christopher Buxton of the company Period and Country Houses wrote to *The Times* on 6 September to observe that Baring should not have been given the permission to demolish. Buxton maintained that it simply wasn't true that The Grange no longer had a viable economic future. After all, Buxton's company was willing to take on a ninety-nine-year lease of the property and restore it. Buxton asserted that Baring was motivated more by a desire simply not to have anyone living at The Grange: "It is clear therefore that the impending demolition turns, not on practical and economic considerations, but on a personal preference to keep an adjoining estate completely private."[26]

Baring maintained that the house was too decrepit for any restoration to be viable. The timbers were full of dry rot and would need to be completely replaced. The decaying brickwork would need treatment. Whereas Baring's plan had been to demolish everything apart from a smaller ionic portico, which would be left "as a sort of memorial folly", he conceded that he would look again at whether more of it could be left standing.[27] Meanwhile, the interiors of the building were being removed for reuse elsewhere.

The case of The Grange divided opinion in a way that few other proposed country house demolitions had done. Not everyone came down on the side of preservation. The country house designer and restorer Michael Toone preferred to see the building removed altogether. A neoclassical temple of this kind might work in London, but in its rural setting it was "the most monstrous eyesore ... hopelessly out of keeping, poised like a multi-legged prehistoric monster on a hilltop surrounded by some of the most beautiful countryside in Hampshire". Christopher Knight agreed in part, writing that it was an "ugly and ill-proportioned building, though interesting to architectural historians". However, he conceded that the main portico should be preserved.[28] For the conservation lobby, however, this was a clear case of an owner being allowed to get away with far too much. Lord Kennet, whose book *Preservation* was published in the same year, used the example of The Grange to observe how more powers were needed for amenity groups to offer their expert counsel on the significance of buildings and offer options for their rescue.[29] The clamour of voices speaking up for The Grange was sufficient to halt any further demolition

[26] Christopher Buxton, 'Why the Grange is to be destroyed', *The Times*, 6 Sept. 1972, p. 15.

[27] Baring, *ibid.*

[28] Michael Toone and Christopher Knight, 'The Grange is an eyesore', *Sunday Times*, 10 Sept. 1972, p. 13.

[29] Lord Kennet, 'Protecting houses like the Grange', *The Times*, 13 Sept. 1972, p. 13; Kennet, *Preservation*.

and led Baring to think again. Out of options, he offered the house to the government as a guardianship site. As at Heveningham, the government agreed to step in and take responsibility for the property, although little was done to it physically in the short-term: its future continued to hang in the balance.

With cases such as Heveningham and The Grange suddenly in public consciousness, house owners concluded that they needed to show a more unified front for their cause. After all, the government was unlikely to be able to step in as rescuer at last resort for very many other houses. Instead, owners would have to devise their own methods for ensuring the longevity of their properties. Consequently, the idea of an independent association for historic houses and their owners was once again revived. The suggestion, which as we have seen was first explored at the Dorchester Hotel in 1952, was initially brought up again at a BTA meeting at Mansion House in 1970. It led to the creation of the BTA's Standing Conference for Historic Houses, which brought together a cross-section of house owners to discuss matters of mutual relevance. The Standing Conference met for the first time at the Royal Automobile Club on Pall Mall in February 1971, with the duke of Grafton in the chair.

An informal forerunner association to the Standing Conference had been founded by Brian Thompson of Puttenden Manor in Surrey, a house owner who was somewhat improbably described by a feature in *The Times* in July 1972 as both an "Irish ex-paratrooper" and an "ex-yoghurt maker".[30] After buying Puttenden in 1966 and opening it to the public shortly afterwards, Thompson had recruited forty-five houses in his area for the purpose of mutually supportive marketing and as a lobbying force to apply pressure on local councils for things like tourism-related road signage.[31] It showed what could be done when owners banded together. Thompson's success led to his appointment to the BTA's historic houses committee. Now, the Standing Conference was being given formal endorsement as an independent national body that could report to government through the BTA.

For Sandy Glen, representing the BTA at the meeting, the case for a Standing Conference was clear. "Tourism, and the country's earnings from tourism, were continuing to expand, and historic properties open to the public played a very great part in assisting this development." As the meeting unfolded it became evident that a great many issues vexed the minds of country house owners. These included threatened motorway developments (as at Levens Hall

[30]   Victoria Brittain, 'Struggling in the second division of the stately homes league', *The Times*, 8 July 1972, p. 14.

[31]   See 'Union for owners of historic homes', *The Times*, 17 Nov. 1970, p. 4.

in Cumbria), the prospect of new levels of taxation, and the cost of advertising. The duke of Atholl complained about the performance of his local planning office. The owner of Glynde in East Sussex raised the issue of how difficult it was to secure adequate road signage to direct visitors to his property. Lord Leicester, of Holkham Hall in Norfolk, asked for advice regarding unauthorised aerial photographs of his house and the correct scale of fees to charge film and television companies when using the house or park for location work. Lord Montagu promised to seek legal advice on the first point, and to recirculate the guidance on levels of charging for film and television work that had already been shared among owners in 1969.[32]

From the outset, the Standing Conference was political as well as practical in its perspective. Along with peers, several members of the House of Commons were present, including Robert Cooke MP, owner of Athelhampton in Dorset. Cooke called for the conference to press strongly for "sensible regulations on the protection and financing of independently owned properties". He also suggested there ought to be a regional flavour to the conference, with owners meeting informally to share notes. Tom Driberg, the Labour MP who lived at Bradwell Lodge in Essex, was also there and lent his support to the idea that separate regional meetings would be needed in addition to gatherings in London clubs. Driberg hesitated, however, at the idea that the Standing Conference needed its own paid secretariat to represent its interests.[33]

All these issues would arise at subsequent meetings of the Standing Conference, in 1971 and 1972. But there were limits to the freedom of discussion that could be enjoyed by an entity that, ultimately, was sponsored by a government agency, in this case the BTA. At the end of the meeting in November 1972, Lord Montagu proposed that a statement should be prepared and issued to the press to alert them to what the Standing Conference had discussed, except that any reference to discussions about "estate duty and tax concessions" should be removed entirely. It was a shrewd move to expunge such politically sensitive topics from the public record, but it highlighted how the Standing Conference was still not yet a fully independent voice for owners.[34]

---

[32]   HHA Archive, Minutes of Inaugural Meeting of the Standing Conference for Historic Houses, 2 Feb. 1971.

[33]   The minutes record that "Mr Driberg thought that [a paid secretariat] was an interesting suggestion."

[34]   HHA Archive, Minutes of the Second AGM of the Standing Conference for Historic Houses, 9 Nov. 1972.

The Standing Conference of historic house owners met for its third and final AGM in November 1973, once more with the duke of Grafton in the chair. Baroness Young was guest of honour, representing the government, and the BTA once again committed its full support. Sandy Glen remarked on "the essential part played by historic houses and castles in the success of Britain's tourism", warning that "a country like Britain would only be pleasant to visit if it remained pleasant to live in". Robert Cooke MP agreed, saying that there was "no excuse for wrecking historic buildings or for spoiling them with motorway or industrial developments close at hand". It was at this meeting that the conference formally reconstituted itself as an independent association of historic house owners, to be known as the Historic Houses Association, or HHA. It was felt that the Standing Conference met too infrequently to be an effective force representing owners. Owners needed an association of their own, "able to speak and act strongly and effectively" on behalf of its members, which at the time numbered just ninety-three (although seventeen more had expressed an interest in joining).[35]

The HHA began its first year with a secretariat on loan from the BTA, the offices of which it initially shared. Effectively, the creation of the HHA delivered the vision that Ernest Gowers had set out nearly a quarter of a century earlier, of a group of private owners who were taking responsibility for the care of a slice of the national heritage by opening their doors to the public.[36] It was an act of assertion on the part of country house owners in the face of political pressures. At the association's first AGM its patron, the duke of Grafton, raised the question of whether the association could seek charity status. The deputy president, George Howard, explained that charity status was simply not possible for "a political pressure group with political origins".[37]

In 1972, a quarter of a century on from Stafford Cripps' commissioning of Ernest Gowers' report into country houses, the historic houses committee of the BTA engaged John Cornforth, *Country Life*'s architectural correspondent, to update Gowers' seminal study. Cornforth's research was to be "an immediate enquiry into the future of country houses", to be carried out "with the co-operation of owners, by an appointed expert".[38] Cornforth's report appeared in early

---

[35] HHA Archive, Minutes of the Third AGM of the Standing Conference for Historic Houses, 8 Nov. 1973.

[36] Mandler, *Fall and Rise*, p. 399.

[37] HHA Archive, Minutes of the First AGM of the Historic Houses Association, 23 Oct. 1974.

[38] HHA Archive, Minutes of the Second AGM of the Standing Conference for Historic Houses, 9 Nov. 1972.

THE
HISTORIC
HOUSES
ASSOCIATION
JOURNAL

3. First edition of the *Historic Houses Association Journal*.

Country Houses in Britain-
can they survive?

By John Cornforth

4. Front cover, John Cornforth, *Country Houses in Britain: Can They Survive?* (1974).

October 1974, with the apocalyptic-sounding title *Country Houses in Britain: Can They Survive?*[39] Its front cover reproduced a bleak John Piper sketch of Rousham in Oxfordshire in a wild and unruly setting. The report would define the agenda for the first decade or so of the HHA's existence, by highlighting the burning platform on which the association had been founded.

A dwindling in the level of public support for private houses could perhaps be discerned from the sagas of Heveningham and The Grange. By the early 1970s, it was true, there were far fewer of the disastrous cases of country houses in distress that had been seen two decades earlier. When cases did arise, they were therefore even more noticeable. The Wedgwood family sustained criticism in 1973 for their decision to apply for permission to demolish Barlaston Hall in Staffordshire. Barlaston stood on coal seams and suffered subsidence, a fact which the National Coal Board was reluctant to concede. Such was the financial liability represented by the house that the family felt they had little choice but to pull it down. Cornforth was less critical of the decision than he was weary of those who did not appreciate the difficult situation in which owners found themselves. There was diminishing public sympathy for owners, which meant the HHA had a challenging public relations role to play.[40] The public mood was more likely now to insist that owners needed to take responsibility for looking after the heritage in their care, or else step aside for others to take their houses on and open them up to new uses.

Perhaps the pervading sense of imminent catastrophe was overplayed. After all, Cornforth highlighted the positive contribution that country houses had made to UK tourism since the war.[41] Fundamental to this was the end of petrol rationing in 1950, and the significant increase in the number of cars on the roads in the 1950s and 1960s. Where the number of cars on the road had been two million in 1939, this had risen to 12.75 million by 1971, and whereas only around a quarter of holiday trips had been taken by car in 1951, this proportion had risen to over two-thirds by 1971. Such trends were sufficient to encourage many owners to open their houses for the first time. Up to two hundred heritage sites were open by 1954, which had increased nearly threefold by the mid-1960s. These places, not all of them country houses, attracted more

---

[39] The title was an echo of the ecologist Teddy Goldsmith's *Can Britain Survive?* (1971). For the general sense of doom and paranoia experienced during the 1970s, see Francis Wheen, *Strange Days Indeed: The Golden Age of Paranoia* (London, 2009).

[40] John Cornforth, *Country Houses in Britain: Can They Survive?* (London, 1974), p. 19.

[41] It was significant that the BTA was given the credit for commissioning the report, rather than its historic houses committee.

than four million visits every year. Domestic tourism had hit boom time, with visits to eight hundred historic sites in 1972 estimated at forty-three million. These sites included monuments, museums, and gardens as well as country houses, but around a hundred and seventy-five of them were houses in private ownership which were open regularly to members of the public.

Visitor numbers were, however, heavily skewed towards the larger houses. The seventy-two houses reported as being open in 1972 for more than fifty days of the year received most visits: nearly four and a half million in total. Nearly half of these, almost two million, went to just six places. Other houses received far fewer visitors, reflecting their reduced opening. Meanwhile, if the visitors to the safari parks at Woburn and Longleat were counted, by 1972 visits to privately owned historic houses exceeded ten million annually. Even if safari hunters were excluded, the most visited historic houses in 1972 were predominantly privately owned. Of thirteen houses that welcomed more than 100,000 visitors that year, ten were privately owned.[42] The other three belonged to the National Trust (Chartwell and Tatton) or to its Scottish counterpart (Culzean).[43]

Simply being open was no guarantee of profit – indeed, the opposite was often the case. Still, Cornforth recognised that tourism had given country houses "a new kind of life". Owners had been prompted to fund restoration schemes and to invest in visitor infrastructure. Not all houses were now open, but Cornforth reckoned that fewer than a dozen of the most important mansions were closed to public access, and even then it might be possible to visit them for charity opening events or on special request. Owners of country houses found themselves presented with enormous opportunities because of the unparalleled increase in demand for "recreational facilities in the countryside".[44] Yet the future for these houses remained uncertain. Private, domestic residences could not always cope with also being popular visitor attractions. The contradictions inherent in trying to be both things meant that one of these identities was likely to win out over the other in the end. Moreover, individual owners no longer had the retinues of servants, gardeners, and maintenance staff that their parents or grandparents might once have enjoyed.

In many ways Cornforth went beyond Gowers, both in the depth of his understanding of the situation facing private owners and in the gloominess of his prognosis for the future of the country house. In his conclusion, he did not

[42] They were Beaulieu, Warwick, Longleat, Harewood, Blenheim, Dodington in Gloucestershire, Sudeley, Blair, Inveraray, and Berkeley.

[43] Cornforth, *Country Houses in Britain*, pp. 99–100.

[44] *Ibid.*, p. 16.

pull his punches: "there is the distinct possibility of destruction on a scale not seen in this country since the sixteenth and seventeenth centuries." Although he was careful to avoid being drawn into party political arguments, Cornforth noted that changes to the tax code, such as the introduction of CGT in 1965, had significant implications for the owners of historic buildings. With the threat of a wealth tax and a capital transfer tax looming in 1974, Cornforth felt there was a very real possibility that many more houses would join his list of three hundred and forty from across Britain that had been demolished since 1945. Reflecting on the Heveningham Hall case, Cornforth foresaw a scenario in which the state might need to step in to save perhaps up to fifty houses in this way. Any more than this would be simply unaffordable. A tsunami of destruction was destined to continue, as private owners ran out of options for ways in which they could continue to protect their inheritance. The future looked "full of gloom", Cornforth wrote in his concluding sentence, and this was made all the worse "because of the senselessness of bringing it about: no one will be any better off, and the nation will be greatly the poorer".[45]

[45]   *Ibid.*, p. 19.

2

Apocalypse then

In October 1974, on the day before the polls opened in that year's second general election, an exhibition opened at the V&A museum in South Kensington, London. The exhibition's alarmist intent was clear from its title, printed in a bold red capital type slanted across the black and white imagery of the promotional poster. The effect was akin to a piece of agitprop of the sort that railed against fashionable contemporary causes such as the Vietnam war, nuclear proliferation, or pollution. This exhibition, however, drew attention to an altogether different problem. *The Destruction of the Country House* brought to the public gaze a list of significant country houses that had been eradicated from the British landscape over the course of the preceding century, many of them surprisingly recently. The exhibition averred that a wholly new phenomenon now beset the country houses of Britain. Mansions were no longer subject solely to the effects of fire and the elements, or to the familiar rhythms of building, rebuilding, and then decline according to the financial fortunes of their owners. Instead, something different was now happening. The market for country houses had, since 1875, completely collapsed.

As John Cornforth completed his investigations into the state of the nation's country houses over the course of 1973 and early 1974, his emergent findings added weight and purpose to the mission pursued by the curators of the *Destruction* exhibition: John Harris of the Royal Institute of British Architects (RIBA), Peter Thornton of the V&A, and, joining a few months after the other two, Marcus Binney of *Country Life*. Together, they sought to convey the horrors of the losses that they believed the nation had witnessed. The *Destruction* exhibition opened just a week after John Cornforth's report was published in October 1974, and it by and large continued Cornforth's line of argument. *Destruction* delivered its message with the showmanship and flair for communications that had come to be associated with the V&A's new director, Roy Strong. Strong had been one of the youngest-ever directors of the National Portrait Gallery when he was appointed to that role in 1967, a time when London was at its most 'swinging'. With his colourful ties and stylish fedora hats, Strong cut a dandyish figure which was also reflected in the subject matter he chose for his exhibitions. His Cecil Beaton show at the National Portrait

Gallery had drawn huge numbers and had demonstrated how a Victorian institution could continue to have relevance to experience-seeking modern audiences. Was Strong about to pull off the same trick again?

The *Destruction* show was one of the very first to open during Strong's tenure at the V&A after he joined the museum in January 1974. He had started to sketch out his concept for the exhibition some time before his arrival in South Kensington, following conversations with John Cornforth.[1] In the autumn of the previous year, in response to an offer of commercial sponsorship for his new museum, Strong had begun to conceive of an exhibition that focused on the conservation of historic interiors. As the idea developed, he decided to search for a way to link such an exhibition to the forthcoming Europe-wide Architectural Heritage Year in 1975.[2] By October 1973 he had landed on the idea of using the V&A as an active heritage campaigning force. "I feel so strongly that the V&A represents the quintessence of our aesthetic heritage," he wrote to Lady Dartmouth, "and that we should be seen to be deeply involved in what has been lost, and what will be lost, if we do not act immediately." He went on to explain that he envisaged the V&A as being "deeply associated with new movements at present in hand to save these things", and not merely fall into the role of being "a mausoleum ready to receive odd bits that can be salvaged from these demolished beauties". He therefore anticipated "an explosive, controversial, exciting and dramatic exhibition", which he dared to imagine could be pulled together for the autumn of 1974, as a "fanfare" to the Architectural Heritage Year.[3] The show would consist mainly of depictions of lost houses but could also encompass displays such as projections of period rooms comprising furniture now held in American museums, or shelves of country house sales catalogues from the preceding century. His original title for the show was "Gone, Going, Going", and it was to be a clear statement of intent, showing how the V&A would in future be much more closely involved "in what is actually happening to things at the moment". The show would need to combine "scholastic integrity and political immediacy".[4] Strong envisaged that it would be

---

[1] Roy Strong, Marcus Binney, John Harris (eds), *The Destruction of the Country House* (London, 1974), p. 6.

[2] Letter from Roy Strong to Glendevon, undated, V&A Archive, MA/28/243/1.

[3] Letter from Roy Strong to Lady Dartmouth, 15 Oct. 1973, V&A Archive, MA/28/243/1.

[4] Letter from Roy Strong to Christopher Gibb, 1 Nov. 1973, V&A Archive, MA/28/243/1. The exhibition was trailed in a House of Lords debate in June 1974 with a slightly different title: "The country house: Going, Going, Going?". HL Deb. 26 June 1974, vol. 352, col. 1486.

followed by similarly crusading exhibitions, for example about churches and town houses.[5]

First, though, Strong had to contend with the institution that he joined in January 1974. "The first three weeks at the V&A were HELL", he recorded in his diaries, a combination of "the dreary Civil Service-ness of it all, the terrible forms, files, signing, the filth, the smell of Jeyes fluid, the dirty loos". He faced resistance to his ideas from some of the staff, but remained undaunted: "I swiped them down," he claimed, "which is the only thing to do." Soon he was in his stride, implementing his new vision for the museum:

> I want to get the twentieth century into that place and make it alive and a comment on our times, to make the Museum symbolise the care of a heritage in all its richness ... I want provocative exhibitions ... happenings in the quadrangle ... huge catalogues to appear ... publications to take off ...[6]

Most of the research for the show was carried out by Binney, Thornton, and Harris, building on the material assembled by John Cornforth, who had declined personally to be involved in making the exhibition because of pressure to get his report finished.[7] But the look and feel of the show, and the punchy way in which it was launched onto the national consciousness, owed much to Strong's skills as a communicator and showman.

Dandyism was in short supply here. Rather, *Destruction* made its point with all the subtlety of a clenched fist. It brought to the world of the national museums the same anger and energy that punk rock would soon unleash on popular music. Once again Strong was anticipating the public mood and, by so doing, was helping to shape it. It was a project conceived in passion and delivered with determination. Much of the show's impact derived from the flair of its designer, Robin Wade, and its confident, bold messaging. An initial schema, conceived by V&A curator Simon Jervis, envisaged an exhibition laid out as if it were the basilica of an early Christian church. Visitors would enter via a narthex, where they would be pummelled with facts about the losses of the preceding century. This section would have a "bleak gloomy deadpan presentation". Proceeding into the nave, visitors would then learn about the current situation, with side chapels revealing the truth about present-day dangers and risks facing country houses. Finally, in the choir, they would be sent off with a "rallying cry and an

---

[5] 'Notes of the first committee meeting on the country house exhibition', 16 Jan. 1974, V&A Archive, MA/28/243/1.

[6] Roy Strong, *The Roy Strong Diaries 1967–1987* (London, 1998), pp. 140–141.

[7] Memo: 'Country Houses Exhibition', 5 Feb. 1974, V&A Archive, MA/28/243/1.

injunction to action". The exit would, naturally, be through a bookshop, where "suitably inspiring texts would be on sale".[8]

The precise ordering of the various elements of the show would go through several iterations over the course of the following months, as might be expected for an exhibition of this kind. As early as February 1974, Strong was alert to the dangers that the show could be interpreted as having "political implications". "We cannot afford to convey an impression (false or otherwise) that we are advocating the return to a way of life that is now defunct and unacceptable", he wrote to Harris and Thornton. It would be "political dynamite" to open the show with an "Arcadian vision" of houses in their heyday, before then subjecting visitors to the brutal reality of how Arcadia had been obliterated by successive tax-raising governments. Setting aside the politics, for Strong the exercise had a clear, irreducible core: the fate of the built heritage. "It is a conservation exhibition; it surveys the past vicissitudes, sums up the present situation, and attempts to look to the future." Nevertheless, he was conscious that he was treading "a dicey political path". He emphasised therefore the need for impartiality in the way the show demonstrated how owners and their families might continue to care for this slice of the national heritage while making it "fully available for public participation".[9]

Initially, Strong and Wade envisaged that the centrepiece of the exhibition would be a newly commissioned set of a dozen drawings by Osbert Lancaster, hung in a rotunda room. Lancaster had collaborated with Strong in a show at the National Portrait Gallery the previous year, *The Littlehampton Bequest*, a parodic recreation of the portrait collection of a fictional landed family accompanied by a pseudo-scholarly commentary. Strong was impressed, declaring that "Osbert Lancaster has done more for the heritage of Britain through wittily sending it up than most of the people who have spent their lives writing enormously learned tomes on British painters and architecture."[10] For *Destruction* he proposed a similar idea: that new drawings by Lancaster would trace "the trials and tribulations of a great estate", from late Victorian grandeur to the ignominy of its late-twentieth-century condition. In between these two points, the fortunes of this imaginary estate would be sketched through a chronological series of tableaux. In an early scene, the heir apparent would be shown to have been killed in action in the first world war. Soon after this "the tax man

[8]   Initial designs by Simon Jervis, V&A Archive, MA/28/243/1.

[9]   Memo: 'Country Houses Exhibition', 5 Feb. 1974, V&A Archive, MA/28/243/1.

[10]   James Knox, *Cartoons & Coronets: The Genius of Osbert Lancaster* (London, 2008), p. 165.

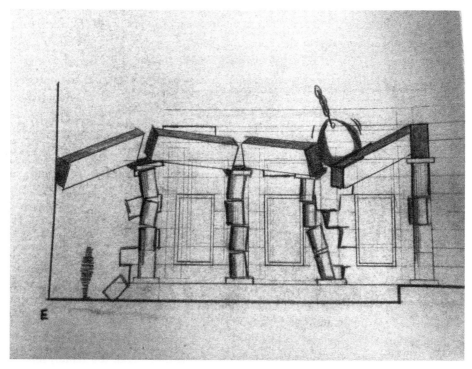

5. Designs by Robin Wade Associates for the *Destruction of the Country House* exhibition at the V&A, 1974.

6. Publicity image for the *Destruction of the Country House* exhibition at the V&A, 1974.

cometh", clutching his demand for estate duties. By the time of the next scene, it would be apparent that the household servants had departed or died: we were to see the countess herself sweeping in the long gallery. The east wing would soon fall, and the west wing would be blown up. The Van Dyck would be sold at auction; in its place the best that could be found would be an Augustus Egg portrait of Aunt Maud. In the second world war, there would be the dual invasion of American troops and evacuees; the ornate gardens would become allotments for vegetables. After the war, everything would be up for sale. The park would be bisected by a motorway and half of it covered in suburban housing. The house would become either a police college or local council office. By then, the full panoply of modern-day horrors would be in place: "caravan rallies – motor museum – safari park – state robes on show – water skiing on the lake – mass catering etc etc."[11] The commissioning brief was indicative of where Strong felt the country house faced its greatest problems.

In the end, however, the exhibition's power derived not from fancies by Osbert Lancaster, but rather from the power of photography. The more they looked, the more Binney, Harris, and Thornton found black and white images of houses that simply no longer existed. The pictures themselves did much of the emotional work of the show, as the relics of a world that was all-too-rapidly slipping away. At the heart of the exhibition when it eventually opened was a room called the 'Hall of Lost Houses'. Like a stage set, blocks were arranged as if they were part of a portico that was being smashed by a wrecker's ball. Images of lost houses appeared on some of these blocks. Having been assembled in architectural formations, the blocks were caught mid-air as they tumbled down. Their use was an echo of the acrylic photograph cubes that could be found on coffee tables in suburban living rooms in the early 1970s as the latest way of displaying polaroid snaps of holiday scenes or family members. Here, they were expanded to the size of pieces of masonry and captured in the freeze frame of the moment of demolition. Over a speaker system, meanwhile, against a background of the sound of crackling flames and falling timbers, John Harris intoned a list of the fallen houses, like a recitation of the fatalities of a recent war.

Looking back after forty years, Harris declared the show to have been "sensational". This was not just because of the dramatic style in which the information was presented but also because of the sheer scale of the losses that were being highlighted. For Harris, this was an "unimaginable" number.[12] It did not seem to matter that the precise number was a matter of some conjecture,

[11]   Roy Strong to Osbert Lancaster, 21 June 1974, V&A Archive, MA/28/243/1.
[12]   Marcus Binney and John Harris, *40 Years On* (London, 2014), p. 10.

even at the time of the exhibition. The exhibition listed hundreds of houses that had been demolished, but the final number was never definitive since new research continued to emerge even while the exhibition was being assembled. The bestselling book that accompanied the exhibition included an appendix, compiled by Peter Reid, that detailed 1,116 houses destroyed since 1875. By the time the book was rolling off the printing presses, this number was already out of date. Another of the exhibition's curators, Marcus Binney, wrote in *Country Life* in November 1974 that the list could have included "two or three hundred more had there been time to check the necessary details before going to press". He noted too that the figures in the book also included houses that had been "gutted or substantially reduced".[13] Binney later claimed that by the time the exhibition closed in December 1974, the number had reached 1,600.[14]

Strong described the impact of the *Destruction* exhibition as "overwhelming". "Many was the time I stood in that exhibition", he reminisced two decades later, "watching the tears stream down the visitors' faces as they battled to come to terms with all that had gone."[15] One such visitor was a leading financier who wrote to Strong to say that "the hall of destruction was so painful that I could not bear to remain there more than one minute."[16] A sharp political intent, however, lay behind the tear-jerking of the crowds. The coincidence of the exhibition opening in the same week as the general election may not have been a deliberate piece of planning, but for Strong the exhibition had an obvious subtext. The minority Labour government under prime minister Harold Wilson that came to power in the election of February 1974 campaigned in October 1974 during the second election campaign of that year on a manifesto that committed the party to new forms of capital taxation in the interests of promoting social justice. The party promised, if re-elected, to begin "the redistribution of wealth by new taxation on the better-off". Specifically, it stated its view "that taxation must be used to achieve a major redistribution of both wealth and income". In March of that year the new government had already announced that a capital transfer tax (CTT) would succeed the old estate duty,

[13] Marcus Binney, 'How Many Country Houses Have Gone?', *Country Life*, 21 Nov. 1974, pp. 1596–1599.

[14] Binney and Harris, *40 Years On*, p. 4. The website lostheritage.org.uk, compiled by Matthew Beckett, keeps a tally of the number of lost country houses in England, which has now reached 1,936. 'Complete list of lost English houses', at <http://www.lostheritage.org.uk/lh_complete_list.html> [accessed 9 Sept. 2023].

[15] Roy Strong, *Diaries 1967–1987*, p. 140.

[16] Quoted in Marcus Binney, *Our Vanishing Heritage* (London, 1984), p. 15.

making it "an effective tax on inherited wealth". Going further, the October manifesto promised an annual tax on wealth above £100,000.[17]

Roy Strong was appalled. Writing to his confidant and collaborator Jan van Dorsten, he foresaw that further disaster was about to be heaped on any remaining country houses:

> The threatened Wealth and Inheritance Taxes if applied to historic owners will see ... the end of a thousand years of English history and culture, as pell-mell the contents are unloaded into the saleroom, the houses handed over to the Government or demolished. I can't tell you the horrors looming unless one fights and intrigues at every level behind the scenes.[18]

This intrigue extended, then, to mounting the *Destruction* exhibition, which was as blatant a political statement as might be imagined for an institution that was, after all, an outpost of the department of education and science.[19] Not for nothing did Strong later describe the show as being "a brave exhibition to mount with a Socialist Government in power", though for reasons of probity he placed an embargo on any press reporting of the opening gala dinner, supported by the sponsors of the exhibition (the wealthy Heinz family).[20] Robert Cooke MP, a Conservative backbencher and a founding member of the HHA by virtue of his ownership of Athelhampton House in Dorset, took a group of MPs of all parties to visit the exhibition. The aim, he said, was "to educate ... his political opponents". He could not resist adding that it was only the Conservative party that recognised "the unique contribution to the arts and to tourism made by historic houses".[21] Marcus Binney acknowledged that although the intention had been polemical, the show ran the risk of being "perceived as political". The need to avoid being seen to take a party-political line led to no representative of the V&A appearing on the evening news programme, *Nationwide*, when presenter Sue Lawley carried a feature on the exhibition.[22]

---

[17] *Britain Will Win with Labour* (October 1974 Labour Party Manifesto), retrieved from <http://www.labour-party.org.uk/manifestos/1974/Oct/1974-oct-labour-manifesto.shtml> [accessed 26 Dec. 2022].

[18] Strong, *Diaries 1967–1987*, p. 141.

[19] The V&A was only established as an independent charity and a non-departmental public body through the National Heritage Act of 1983. At the time of the *Destruction* exhibition in 1974, therefore, its activities were directly supervised from Whitehall.

[20] Strong, *Diaries 1967–1987*, p. 140.

[21] HHA Archive, Minutes of the First AGM of the Historic Houses Association, 23 Oct. 1974.

[22] Binney and Harris, *40 Years On*, p. 4.

Media reviews of the exhibition divided on predictable lines. William Gaunt of *The Times* accepted the general argument of the show, repeating its claim that "hundreds" of houses had been destroyed in the preceding century, including two hundred and fifty since 1945.[23] Gaunt praised Strong for sounding the alarm and for drawing "public attention to the many tragic losses, as well as the efforts made to stem the tide of destruction in recent years". He argued that there was "a clear case for preserving the historic homes of Britain as collective works of art, in their examples of architectural style, richness of interior design and relation to surrounding landscape". The exhibition therefore pointed to the need for a further easing of the tax burden, as well as direct grant-funded support from the historic buildings councils. A sombre review in the *Sunday Telegraph* likewise agreed with the assessment that "a major part of our architectural heritage is in very serious danger".[24]

By contrast, *The Observer* called the *Destruction* show "the most emotive, propagandist exhibition ever to grace a public museum's walls". Its editorial objected to the text of the wall panels, which it declared to be loaded with class prejudice and assumptions.[25] *The Guardian* too had little sympathy for the underlying cause of the exhibition. "In a climate of economic crisis," wrote Caroline Tisdall, "we can hardly be expected to have much sympathy for the lord who is forced through economic straits to 'transfer his flag to a smaller house'."[26] The *Daily Mirror* meanwhile offered a light-hearted left-of-centre comment on the exhibition, in an article by Roger Todd with the headline "Gad..Our Stately Homes Are Grim". The piece took satirical pleasure in reporting that "life in Britain's stately homes is becoming simply too awful for the coronet set. Dukes, baronets and earls have to use buckets to catch rain dripping through the roofs." The thought of titled folk shivering in front of electric fires evidently did not find sympathy with Todd, who pointedly ended his piece with the observation that the whole thing was a bid by "aristocratic slum-dwellers" for tax advantages.[27]

Newspapers were not short of commentators ready to point out that some of the wealthiest people in the country appeared here to be waving shrouds and pleading poverty. Caroline Tisdall had little time for the 'poor rich': "who

[23] William Gaunt, 'Threat to at least 1,000 country houses', *The Times*, 25 Oct. 1974, p. 12.

[24] David Crawford, 'A Lost Heritage', *Sunday Telegraph*, 13 Oct. 1974, p. 15.

[25] Quoted in Ruth Adams, "The V&A, The Destruction of the Country House and the Creation of "English Heritage"', *Museum & Society* 11:1 (2013), 1–18, 8.

[26] Caroline Tisdall, 'Englishmen's Castles', *The Guardian*, 9 Oct. 1974, p. 12.

[27] Roger Todd, 'Gad..Our Stately Homes Are Grim', *Daily Mirror*, 9 Oct. 1974, p. 11.

can raise a tear for the withering of the great estates at a time of land and housing shortage?"[28] Owners were alert to the risk of being inadvertently caught out in this way. Commander Michael Saunders Watson, owner of Rockingham Castle in Northamptonshire and a leading light in the HHA, was visited by a television reporter making a programme entitled "The Suffering Rich". The reporter was made to traipse across several wet clay fields so that Saunders Watson could be filmed in action on his tractor, rather than be shown shooting pheasants (which had been the reporter's original, but rejected, suggestion).[29] Meanwhile, Tisdall's review drew a stiff letter of defence from John Harris and Marcus Binney, pointing out that the exhibition had sought to highlight the loss of important parts of the national heritage, rather than dwell on the "position of privilege" that had produced them. Alongside their letter was another by a schoolboy at Ampleforth College, James Stourton, who astutely observed that "Miss Tisdall is determined to confuse the preservation of England's country houses with the preservation of their owners' standards of living."[30] Needless to say, Roy Strong relished the publicity that Tisdall's review had sparked. "One was, in fact, very pleased about that hostile review", he wrote to Pamela Johnson. After all, "there is nothing like that for bringing people in and arousing public opinion and support."[31]

Ultimately, there was a genuine heritage issue at stake here: the resilience of some of the most significant historic buildings in the country. While the very concept of 'heritage' invariably involves subjective opinions about the relative significance of different aspects of the past, the fact remained that some solution was required for buildings of architectural, aesthetic, or historic importance that seemingly no longer had a viable future. Were they to be left to wither on the vine? As Strong put it, in the book that accompanied the exhibition: "I do not think that we would wish to see them swept away, smashed like the monasteries at the Dissolution, to be looked back upon by some subsequent generation with a nostalgic tear for the 'bare ruined choirs'."[32] Cornforth had brought into play Ruskin's autobiographical observation that

---

28   Tisdall, 'Englishmen's Castles'.

29   Michael Saunders Watson, *I Am Given a Castle* (Hindringham, 2008), p. 96.

30   'In the wake of the greedy bulldozer', *The Guardian*, 14 Oct. 1974, p. 12. James Stourton would go on to be the biographer of Kenneth Clark. Stourton refers to this early foray into heritage campaigning in *Heritage: A History of How We Conserve Our Past* (London, 2022).

31   Roy Strong to Pamela Johnson, 21 Oct. 1976, V&A Archive, MA/28/243/1.

32   Strong, Binney, Harris, *Destruction*, p. 10.

it was probably much happier to live in a small house and have Warwick Castle to be astonished at, than to live in Warwick Castle and have nothing to be astonished at; but that, at all events, it would not make Brunswick Square in the least more pleasantly habitable, to pull Warwick Castle down.[33]

The national mood might not be sympathetic to the owners of these places, but nevertheless the country would regret losing such splendid palaces forever once they had disappeared.

Heritage campaign groups continued to champion the cause of country houses, which added to the afterlife of the *Destruction* show. So too did Roy Strong. He made a BBC2 documentary with David Cheshire, entitled *Going, Going, Going: The Fate of the Country House*, which aired on 2 January 1975. (The filming for it had "dragged me the length and breadth of England through August", he wrote wearily in his *Diaries*.)[34] That year was, after all, the European Architectural Heritage Year, when heritage causes of all kinds were to be highlighted as never before. The *Destruction* exhibition went on regional tour for the year, appearing in Cardiff in June, Dundee in August, and Aberdeen in September.[35] The exhibition continued to tour the country the following year as well, appearing in Birmingham in 1976. This latter destination had the inadvertent result of 'saving' at least one of the houses that had been featured. Douglas Haynes, a senior executive of the Post Office and the owner of thirteenth-century Hanch Hall in Staffordshire, visited the exhibition in the summer of 1976, and was startled to find that his own house had been memorialised. Mr Haynes complained to the museum and reported the mistake to the local newspaper. "The hall is definitely standing and has been lived in for as long as we can ascertain. Far from falling around our ears, we are renovating it", he told the *Lichfield Mercury*. A red-faced representative of the V&A insisted that it was "the only case of its kind which has been drawn to our attention during the prolonged tour which the exhibition has already made during the past year and a half". Dennis Farr, the director of the Birmingham Museum, was able to make capital from the error made by its national museum partner, saying merely that he was "delighted that at least one of the 300 houses so described as having been demolished is receiving care and attention".[36] Although the V&A had a

---

[33] John Ruskin, *Praeterita* (1885), quoted in Cornforth, *Country Houses in Britain*, p. 1.

[34] Strong, *Diaries 1967–1987*, p. 142.

[35] V&A Archive, MA/25/243.

[36] 'The strange case of a hall that "does not exist"', *Lichfield Mercury*, 1 Oct. 1976, pp. 1, 2.

reputation for being "the last word in authenticity", some of the bold claims made by the *Destruction* exhibition could be undermined when closer attention was paid to reality. Indeed, the museum was not telling the whole truth when it claimed that Hanch Hall was the only example of the misattribution of destruction to a standing country house. The owner of Wadhurst Castle in East Sussex was similarly mystified to find that his house featured in the exhibition and wrote to Roy Strong to say so. He was unconvinced by the reply that he received.[37]

The book that accompanied the exhibition carried a list of the houses in England, Scotland, and Wales that had been 'destroyed', yet it was acknowledged that some houses had been included where only part of the building had come down. The example was given of Garnons in Herefordshire, "where almost the entire Atkinson range has gone and yet the mid-Victorian wing forms the new house." The number of houses partially demolished in this way was a reasonably high proportion of the total: of the 747 English houses listed, nearly ten per cent were only partially destroyed. They included the examples of Bowood in Wiltshire, the main part of which was pulled down in 1956, and Settringham in Yorkshire, which suffered a catastrophic fire in 1963. As it happens, both are estates that thrive today: Settringham is a popular wedding venue, and what is left of Bowood House continues to function as a domestic residence at the heart of a busy estate offering days out in the extensive gardens, a well-appointed golf course, and hotel accommodation in a modern purpose-built block at some distance from the historic core of the property.

A further thirty houses in England were listed as having been 'rebuilt', and some of these had many of the same characteristics as those that had been partially destroyed. Wasing Place in Berkshire was listed as being an entirely new house, although in fact it was a restored version of a house that, like Settringham, had been severely damaged by fire in the 1940s. Wasing today also does well, as a wedding venue in the heart of an estate that presents itself as a showcase for sustainability and regenerative agriculture.

The passing of time since the exhibition means that several of the houses listed as being destroyed in 1974 have now been rebuilt, or what remained of them repurposed to new uses. The Grange, included on the list by virtue of being part torn down by its owner in 1972, continues today as a venue for opera and dance. Thorndon Hall in Essex is no longer an empty shell, but is now divided into apartments, having previously served as a golf club. Easton Hall in Lincolnshire was demolished in 1951, but the stables and other buildings were

---

[37]   Personal communication from Susanna Fitzgerald, Wadhurst Castle.

left standing, as were the extensive gardens. These have now been restored and reopened as Easton Walled Gardens, a popular visitor attraction.

Hanch Hall was not alone, therefore. It can be said that as many as one in ten of all the properties that featured in the *Destruction* exhibition continue in use today, albeit often in a diminished or much-altered form. In the case of one county, Northamptonshire, the list of destroyed houses in the 1974 exhibition was wrong by a factor of nineteen per cent.[38] Even those houses listed in the exhibition as being completely ruinated were not, in fact, lost causes. The gothic edifice of Alton Towers in Staffordshire gave its name to the theme park that was created in its grounds. The ruins of Lowther Castle in Cumbria are now a significant tourist attraction. John Martin Robinson was moved to write *The Latest Country Houses*, published in 1984, precisely because of the "wrongheaded" publicity around the *Destruction* exhibition. His motivation was "the dichotomy between the architectural activity I could see all around in the country and the doom-gloom I could read in the newspapers".[39] His book showed examples of where parts of destroyed houses had been reconstructed, materials reused, or ancillary buildings adopted for the principal domestic use (as happened at Bowood). Peter Mandler observed that of the two hundred 'new' houses featured in Robinson's book, eighty-nine were replacements for houses that had been sold or demolished, while eighty-two were alterations of old houses to make them more economic and convenient.[40] Destruction, it seems, was not the final word: many houses were able to find a means of living a half-life even after they had been 'destroyed'.[41]

There was also a sense in which the *Destruction* exhibition was a case of the stable door being closed long after the horse had bolted. The system of listing buildings of architectural and historic significance had only been introduced from 1947.[42] At first, a listing was no more than a descriptive entry on an official list – a tally of the best survivals of Britain's historic structures, and not in itself a means of protecting them. The incidence of a building being on

---

[38] Neil Lyon, *'Useless Anachronisms?': A Study of the Country Houses and Landed Estates of Northamptonshire Since 1880* (Northampton, 2018), p. 59.

[39] John Martin Robinson, *The Latest Country Houses* (London, 1984), p. 6.

[40] Mandler, *Fall and Rise*, pp. 360 and 464, n. 21.

[41] For the debate over 'lost' houses, see Tom Williamson, Ivan Ringwood and Sarah Spooner, *Lost Country Houses of Norfolk: History, Archaeology and Myth* (Woodbridge, 2015); James Raven, *Lost Mansions: Essays on the Destruction of the Country House* (London, 2015).

[42] John Delafons, *Politics and Preservation: A Policy History of the Built Heritage 1882–1996* (London, 1997).

a list may have been a factor in whether the owner of that building was given licence – moral or otherwise – to pull it down. But being listed did not itself prevent demolition from taking place, albeit that local planning authorities had the power to impose preservation orders. It was their failure to exercise this power that was partly responsible for the losses highlighted in the exhibition, according to John Harris and Marcus Binney.[43] The law changed with the Town and Country Planning Act of 1968, which introduced a new system that mandated specific listed building consent to be attained before the alteration or demolition of a listed building. Arguably, the requirement for consent in this way had had the effect of slowing the rate of demolition, almost to a standstill. While Cornforth had reported two hundred and seventy houses demolished in England and Wales after 1945, he noted that just four of these had occurred since 1964.[44] Demolitions of listed buildings were still possible, as shown by the case of The Grange. But destruction was no longer a simple matter of calling in the wreckers and the architectural salvage crew. After 1968, it was something that only happened with the formal agreement of the state. And, as we shall see in the next chapter, it was not the only way in which the government stepped up to rescue the country house in the years that immediately followed the *Destruction* exhibition.

[43] 'In the wake of the greedy bulldozer', *The Guardian*, 14 Oct. 1974, p. 12.
[44] Cornforth, *Country Houses in Britain*, p. 4.

3

Until the pips squeaked

In the summer of 1974, one Welsh estate was in serious trouble. A six-million-pound bill for death duties hung over James, Lord Gethin and his family patrimony, the baronial seat, and many acres of land in the beautiful Trethowan valley. At the age of fifty-eight, Gethin was ready to give it all up and make a new life with his personal assistant, with whom he had started a romantic relationship. But family ties ran deep. The more he was hounded by the tax authorities (there was a particularly zealous official, Mr Mackie, in charge of his case), the more Lord Gethin felt obliged to defend his position.

Gethin's son, Michael, was certainly not ready to let his father head off into the sunset. One day, after all, Michael would inherit the title as well as the estate. Michael knew that the battle was not just with the taxman. The tenants on the estate could cause problems too, as could his father's scheming London lawyer. That six-million-pound bill was a major worry, but so was the discovery that valuable copper deposits lay below the ground. It posed the very real threat that the estate could yet be broken up and then exploited for its mining. Lord Gethin was not averse to the idea if it resolved the tax demand. But it was anathema to his son, who even, horror of horrors, contemplated gifting the estate to the National Trust to protect it from exploitation. Such a drastic step was only considered because a whole way of life faced imminent extinction – a direct consequence of government fiscal policy.

The Inheritors was a six-part television drama that was broadcast on ITV in August 1974. Veteran Scottish actor Robert Urquhart played the lead role of the embattled Welsh aristocrat, while Peter Egan played his son.[1] The series was produced by Wilfred Greatorex, who had a track record of creating dramas that centred on conflict and power struggles among elites. His previous hit for ITV was *Hine* (1971), in which the eponymous hero was an international arms dealer. Before then, *The Power Game* (three series, from 1965 to 1969) focused on high drama in executive boardrooms and was the successor to another corporate drama, *The Plane Makers* (three series, between 1963 and 1965).

---

[1] Much later, Egan would reprise his role as a titled character on ITV screens, in *Downton Abbey* as Hugh MacClare, marquess of Flintshire.

High stakes in the world of industrial espionage were one thing. But could a power struggle be made from the sedate world of the country house? If anyone could do it, Greatorex could. Greatorex lived in Taplow, Maidenhead, where coincidentally he was a near neighbour of Antony Read, who produced the rival BBC series *Mogul* and *Troubleshooters* (1965 to 1972). ("All that lust for power and profit, emanating from one patch", Read later remembered.)[2] The *Daily Mirror*'s television critic was delighted to draw attention to the commercial for Woburn safari park that appeared midway during the first episode of *The Inheritors*:

> Smart move of the night was the commercial popped in with pictures of sleepy tigers urging us all to bustle out to stately Woburn. Quick, that is, before it's been wealth-taxed to dust, given away, dug up for coal, and the inhabitants have been put in a home for the well-heeled down on their luck.

The reviewer had little sympathy for Lord Gethin's fictional plight: "Gawping round the stately homes at their heritage is much like a visit to the zoo. The human dinosaurs, these days, are on view … These days they're out collecting fares on the swings and roundabouts." The review went on to suggest that all Lord Gethin needed to do to solve his problems was procure a tiger or two: "That'll make us put a tiger in our tanks and jog over. There'll be no mining. Nothing will be dug up. He remains the owner. Bingo!"[3]

The drama anticipated the principal theme of the *Destruction* exhibition that would open just a few weeks later – the idea that excessive taxation threatened the viability of stately homes. There was, after all, some truth to this. A minority Labour government had returned to power in February 1974, and a new tax on capital accumulations was one of its flagship policies. The manifesto *Labour's Programme for Britain* proposed not only an increase in the highest rates of income tax, but also a new wealth tax as an "annual levy on the largest concentrations of private wealth".[4] Any of the main political parties might have mooted the idea of a tax on wealth as a means of balancing the public finances, but for Labour the issue hinged as much on the argument for social equity as it did on the efficient operation of the economy. As veteran Labour politician Anthony Crosland had described it in *The Future of Socialism*, "the largest inequalities stem not from the redistribution of earned incomes, but

---

[2] Philip Purser, 'Obituary – Wilfred Greatorex', *The Guardian*, 17 Oct. 2002, p. 26.

[3] *Daily Mirror*, Friday 16 Aug. 1974, p. 16.

[4] Quoted in Martin Daunton, *Just Taxes: The Politics of Taxation in Britain, 1914– 1979* (Cambridge, 2002), p. 329.

from the ownership of inherited capital."[5] He was drawing on a deep well of Labour thinking on the issue, as manifested by books such as R. H. Tawney's *Equality* (1931). The introduction of a tax on capital gains in 1965 by chancellor of the exchequer James Callaghan was deemed to be just the first step to the creation of a more equal society by means of taxation policy.

Nevertheless, the idea was far from new, and was by no means confined to the Labour party. By the mid-1970s the taxation of landed wealth had already been a topic of political discussion for at least a century. The Labour government of the mid-1970s shared some of the same preoccupations about capital accumulations as radical politicians of the second half of the nineteenth century. Land reformists had been mobilised partly because of the publication, in 1876, of the *Return of the Owners of Land*.[6] This was the first serious attempt to quantify landownership in England since the Domesday Book, and hence was sometimes referred to as the Modern Domesday. The idea of collating a statistical digest of data on landownership had first emerged as a response by the landed class to stirring disquiet at the dominance of the larger estates in political life. Landlords had hoped that an examination of the facts would dispel the idea that land was overly concentrated into the hands of a relatively small number of owners and instead reveal its ownership to be widespread and much more equitably spread. The survey proved the exact opposite. It was revealed that four-fifths of the land of England and Wales was owned by just seven hundred families, with the largest landowners, the thirty or so ducal owners, possessing a third of the entire country.[7]

The exposure of such severe concentrations of landed wealth led to a growth in anti-landlord political sentiment in the 1880s and calls for greater taxation of landed property. Factions of the Liberal party, who drew inspiration from the writings of the American reformist Henry George, called openly for the use of the tax system to tackle social inequality. George's *Progress and Poverty* (1879) set out an analysis of the capitalist system, in which the economic rent from land consolidated unfairly in the hands of a relative few. George advocated the taxation of land values as a means of more equitably sharing the proceeds of unearned wealth while also stimulating development

---

[5] Quoted in Martin Chick, 'Taxing Wealth: A Historical Perspective' (2020), p. 11, <https://www.wealthandpolicy.com/wp/121.html> [accessed 28 Dec. 2022].

[6] See Shaun Evans, Tony McCarthy and Annie Tindley (eds), *Land Reform in the British and Irish Isles since 1800* (Edinburgh, 2022).

[7] John Bateman, *The Great Landowners of Great Britain and Ireland* (Leicester, 1971).

and promoting productive activity. George's ideas spread across the Atlantic, and had influence on sections of the Liberal party, the trade union movement, and the early socialists. The clamour for land reform grew, from a relatively minor noise offstage to a much more noticeable anti-aristocratic turn in political life.[8] While the Tories were the party that conventionally represented the interests of the landowning classes, parts of the Liberal party were much more open to anti-landlord thinking. By the early 1890s a faction within the Liberal party called for the burden of taxation to fall much more heavily on land as opposed to falling on incomes or trade. For much of the nineteenth century death duties, if they applied at all, were levied on chattels and personal effects rather than on land. After the publication of the *Return*, a group of nearly a hundred Liberal MPs called openly for "a much heavier assessment upon persons of fortune who do not at present feel the burden at all".[9]

Responding to such pressures, the Liberal chancellor of the exchequer, Sir William Harcourt, implemented the first serious attempt to tax landed wealth. In his budget of 1894, Harcourt introduced a modest duty on the value of estates at death, rising at most to eight per cent on those estates valued at over one million pounds.[10] Although this was a cautious reform, it was interpreted by landowners as a direct attack on their very existence. Harcourt was satirised for pursuing a form of 'second son's revenge', given that he was the second son of the owner of Nuneham Courteney in Oxfordshire and therefore not directly in the line of succession to this country house property. The charge was unfair, as Harcourt later succeeded to the property anyway after his nephew died without issue, leaving him with a double dose of estate duties to pay. (A few decades later, beleaguered by tax demands, the family sold Nuneham altogether.)

Of more importance than the rate at which the duty applied was the principle that landed estates could be burdened in this way at all. Harcourt's Tory successor, Sir Michael Hicks Beach, did not do away with the estate duty, but instead introduced, in 1896, the option for landowners to exempt from estate duty the value of personal effects, such as paintings, books, "or other things not yielding income as appear to the Treasury to be of national, scientific or historic interest". This was a major concession, brought in partly to encourage owners to keep their collections in the country rather than sell them on the international market. The availability of this option was one of the explanations for why the estate duty never raised as much tax revenue as originally anticipated.

[8] Mandler, *Fall and Rise*, pp. 160–191.
[9] Daunton, *Trusting Leviathan*, p. 246.
[10] *Ibid.*, pp. 237–244.

Harcourt referred to the exemption from estate duty as "an enormous present to the richest millionaires in the country".[11]

By the turn of the twentieth century the scene had already been set for estate property – land, country houses, and the collections they contained – to be the focus of intense political debates regarding the relative burdens of taxation. In 1907 Asquith raised the level of estate duty to a new high of eleven per cent. The furore over Lloyd George's 'People's Budget' of 1910 in part hinged around a further increase of the rate to fifteen per cent.[12] The exigencies of war from 1914 led to further calls for levies on capital. The rise of the Labour party as a political force saw a conscious switch to seeing capital taxation as a direct means of addressing social inequalities. Hugh Dalton, who became Labour's chancellor of the exchequer after the second world war, wrote a book in the 1920s which openly criticised "the effects of inherited property in maintaining the inequality of incomes". As chancellor he increased the rate of duty on estates valued at over £21,500 to a maximum rate of seventy-five per cent. One of his successors, Hugh Gaitskill, increased this rate further to eighty per cent.[13]

This, then, was why the Labour government that took power in February 1974 was so committed to continuing its historical mission of raising a greater share of taxation from the assets of the wealthiest in society. At his party's conference the previous autumn, the shadow chancellor of the exchequer Denis Healey anticipated "howls of anguish" from the rich at the prospect of a return to office by Labour. During the first general election campaign of 1974, Healey gave a speech in which he was widely reported as having promised to "squeeze the rich until the pips squeaked".[14] He had said no such thing, of course. Rather, he had in his sights the excessive profits made by "food manufacturers and retailers", while his exact threat was to "squeeze the property speculators until the pips squeak".[15] Landowners, landed estates, and country houses were not mentioned particularly, although he was openly critical of Lord Carrington for making a substantial profit through the accumulation of development land. For those on the left of the party, however, the wealth tax idea was totemic of Labour's commitment to promoting greater social equity. After his appointment, the socialist arts minister Hugh Jenkins made it clear that the

---

[11] *Ibid.*, p. 248.

[12] Mandler, *Fall and Rise*, p. 174.

[13] Daunton, *Just Taxes*, p. 213.

[14] Edward Pearce, *Denis Healey: A Life in our Times* (London, 2002), p. 405.

[15] 'Mr Healey promises action on profits of food manufacturers and retailers', *The Times*, 19 Feb. 1974, p. 4.

preservation of cultural heritage "must take second place to the reduction of privilege and inequality"[16]

The House of Lords debated Labour's proposed wealth tax and its impact on historic houses on 26 June 1974. The debate was initiated by the duke of Grafton, owner of Euston Hall in Suffolk and a devotee of heritage causes, being the chair of the Society for the Protection of Ancient Buildings and a member of the historic buildings council. Grafton also sat on the BTA's historic houses committee. He made clear in his opening remarks that his purpose in calling the debate was to draw attention to the finely balanced accommodation that had been reached between private owners and the state since the report of the committee chaired by Sir Ernest Gowers in 1950. The report had done much to provide a policy rationale for why heritage was best left in private hands, but Grafton thought that the minority Labour government's talk of a wealth tax meant that "this whole delicately poised collaboration between private owners and the Government may be smashed". Grey Gowrie agreed, reiterating one of the central themes of Gowers' report, "that the English country house, in all its aspects, is second only to our literature as a contribution to the Arts of mankind". The need for a wealth tax was disputed not only on principle, but also because of the impracticality of its administration. Both Grafton and Gowrie referred to other European countries where wealth taxes had been introduced, such as in the Netherlands, where, they claimed, owners were given to hiding their artworks behind false paneling to keep them from the prying eyes of the tax authorities. Lord Montagu insisted that instead of threatening a wealth tax, the government ought to be introducing the sort of fiscal framework that Gowers had recommended a quarter of a century earlier.

The leader of the House of Lords, Labour hereditary peer Lord Shepherd, attempted a defence of his government. "We still have a society where great wealth is held in few hands", he argued, setting out the government's intention to reduce conflict in society by working consciously "to even out the position of privilege with the general mass of our people". Speaking in support, the former arts minister Jennie Lee, who had been made a peer after losing her seat to Patrick Cormack in the 1970 general election, was also in no doubt about the need for a wealth tax. Although the green paper had yet to be published, Lee insisted that it was unfair for working people to pay tax on their income, but for the wealthiest not to pay anything in respect of the assets they held. Her vision was for houses to remain in private ownership, but for public access to them to

[16] Hugh Jenkins, *The Culture Gap: An Experience of Government and the Arts* (London, 1979), p. 146.

be hugely expanded. After all, she said, the aim was not for these houses to be preserved "for the exclusive use of any one family". Rather, they should be protected "in order that as many as possible of the people of this country, old and young, can enjoy and have their lives enriched by the contents". Lee set out the Labour party's attitude to heritage, which involved protecting architecture in "the tradition of Morris, of Ruskin and so many others", while not shirking from facing up to "the injustices and cruelties of the past". Her view was not shared by most of her fellow peers, a high proportion of whom were country house owners. The earl of Dundee summed up their view, which was that a wealth tax would "enrich no one and impoverish everyone".[17]

The new government was true to its promise. A green paper published in August 1974 set out Labour's plans for a new wealth tax on assets valued at more than £100,000, as well as a capital transfer tax (CTT) to replace the existing estate duty but this time also covering gifts made in lifetime as well as at death.[18] The implications for heritage were noted from the outset. The government intended to treat "the national heritage, works of art, book collections, and stately homes" as a special case. Exactly how was unclear, but the policy ambition was stated to be "to secure more public display of such treasures in return for deferment of the tax".[19] The green paper proposed that any exemption from the new wealth tax should be conditional on public access being provided to works of art, "with such modifications as might be appropriate for delicate objects or research material". If the tax was deferred for long enough, such artworks might even be taken into public ownership.[20] For the time being CTT, as introduced by the finance bill in 1975, carried the possibility of exemptions not just for artworks but also for land and buildings. As Elena Porter has noted, this transformative step was intended merely as a temporary measure: a stopgap until the wealth tax idea was fully implemented.[21]

Hugh Jenkins recorded in his memoirs the litany of objections he had received to the wealth tax proposals. The National Arts Collection Fund, the Standing Committee on Museums and Galleries, the Reviewing Committee on the Export of Works of Art, and the British Antique Dealers Association all registered their opposition, even before the green paper had been officially

---

[17]   HL Deb. 26 June 1974, vol. 352, col. 1487–1493, 1480–1487, 1502–1507, 1510–1516, 1533–1538, 1562–1566.

[18]   *Wealth Tax*, Cm 5704 (1974).

[19]   'White Paper gives broad outline of liability for gifts', *The Times*, 9 Aug. 1974, p. 6.

[20]   As quoted in Jenkins, *Culture Gap*, p. 141.

[21]   Porter, 'National Heritage', p. 15.

published.[22] Jenkins was unimpressed by the lot of them, as he was with the idea that there might be exemptions from the tax for owners of heritage assets. He was against the idea of exemptions on principle: the wealthiest individuals and organisations in the country did not deserve a get-out-of-jail card in this way. This line of thinking aligned with civil servants' traditional disdain for special pleading. The sorts of reliefs suggested for historic house owners in the Gowers report had traditionally been opposed by officials "on the point of principle that special taxation privileges for a limited section of the community are always undesirable".[23] As one inland revenue official had already noted, any concession given to the owners of historic properties could turn out to be the thin end of a very large wedge. After all, "many other bodies with other special interests could plead equally eloquently" for tax concessions. The official went on to say that:

> without being too fanciful, one can envisage the Federation of Women's Institutes, backed by more specialist bodies, pleading for the practitioners of the various crafts which they encourage, wild life enthusiasts pleading for costly attempts to preserve some near-extinct species, the literary world pleading for would-be poets who spend money seeking inspiration and once got £2 for a verse published in some way-out magazine, and so on. A case could be made on educational, cultural, therapeutic, nutritional, scientific, or artistic grounds, and probably others too. A proliferation of new Cases on these lines, each with its own limitations (such as the Historic Buildings Council approval suggested for historic houses), would be perhaps slightly less damaging than a general admission of relief for losses not incurred in a trade, but not all that much better, and it would add considerably to the complication of both the legislation and its administration.[24]

Jenkins later observed that the inland revenue had originally proposed that the 1974 green paper should contain the words "exemption would not be an appropriate way to help". Before publication, however, one of Jenkins' senior officials had toned down the statement and replaced it with a more equivocal suggestion that there were merely some "forcible arguments against exemption". This subtle change in the wording at the eleventh hour went unnoticed by Jenkins at the time, so the inland revenue's initial opposition to exemptions was not recorded when the green paper was published. Such are the ways in which government policy is formulated: high-minded and sophisticated officials

[22] Jenkins, *Culture Gap*, p. 141.
[23] TNA, T 218/524.
[24] TNA, T 227/4421, 'Fiscal reliefs for owners of historic houses'.

gently steer things in directions of their own choosing, especially if their minister is known to have controversial opinions. Jenkins, the Fabian socialist who went on to become chair of the Campaign for Nuclear Disarmament, was one such minister. His regrets were clear: "in approving the draft as amended I had accepted and endorsed the beginning of the watering down process which ended in the abandonment of the tax."[25]

If left-wing politicians were unhappy that the green paper had pulled its punches, private owners of historic houses were even more unsettled by what was proposed. One such owner, Commander Michael Saunders Watson of Rockingham Castle in Northamptonshire, estimated that the new tax could cost him in the region of £75,000 a year (nearly £700,000 in today's money). Such sums were unimaginable, and left owners uncertain of the future. Saunders Watson recalled his uncle's advice – "if pressed, let the house go but hold onto the land at all costs." The more typical route was first to sell artworks from the house. Even then, Saunders Watson estimated that he had just five years left at the castle, after which it would be emptied of its treasures and the only option left would be the sale of the building itself. Saunders Watson was not to be bowed. Instead, "this 'pip' was going to squeak, and loudly."[26] Others in the heritage world were all too willing to lend support. The National Trust was just one of several organisations to respond to the proposals with a warning about the consequences for private owners. "The National Trust's anxieties arise from the fear that private owners, in whose ownership the bulk of the national heritage at present lies, may be forced by the new taxes and inflation to dispose of their property and that as a result the national heritage will be greatly reduced or dispersed."[27]

With the left wing of the Labour party lined up on one side of the debate, and the establishment of landowners and arts and heritage organisations on the other, Denis Healey found that there was no easy passage for his wealth tax proposal. Given that inflation was shooting up to levels as high as twenty-five per cent, the chancellor in any case had other things on his mind. The option of deferring any final decision until a select committee had investigated the proposals must therefore have seemed a welcome relief. The select committee was chaired by Labour MP and former treasury minister Douglas Jay. It set to work receiving evidence and submissions. A great many organisations sent in

---

[25] Jenkins, *Culture Gap*, p. 142.

[26] Saunders Watson, *I Am Given a Castle*, pp. 90–91.

[27] Evidence given to the Select Committee on a Wealth Tax by the National Trust, November 1975, quoted in Robert Hewison, *The Heritage Industry* (London, 1987), p. 67.

responses to this committee, among them the Historic Houses Association, the Country Landowners Association, the British Tourist Authority, and several of the national museums and galleries. All were in opposition to the tax. Hugh Jenkins meanwhile battled on regardless. His autobiography recorded the efforts he took to press the case for the wealth tax unencumbered by any special exemptions for heritage or works of art, which he saw as a smokescreen for the persistence of privilege and inequality. For Jenkins, this was the contribution that he as arts minister could make to the pursuit of socialism. He ordered Roy Strong, the director of the V&A (and therefore a civil servant), to resign from the ginger group Heritage in Danger set up by the Conservative parliamentarian Patrick Cormack.[28] Jenkins found Roy Strong's views on the wealth tax to be "surprisingly extreme", and no doubt the feeling was mutual.[29]

The newly formed Historic Houses Association had found its cause. Although it had only been constituted in November of the previous year, the fledgling organisation went on the offensive. Under Lord Montagu's leadership, all stops were pulled in the pursuit of influence over policy makers. Day after day, and night after night, the corridors of Westminster and Whitehall were stalked by lobbyists for the heritage cause. One such lobbyist was Michael Saunders Watson, who managed to secure an audience with Healey at a May Day rally organised by Corby District Council following a successful visit by the Labour-led council to Rockingham Castle. ("They were clearly much moved", Saunders Watson wrote of the councillors' experience that day. "They had never seen the estate before and like so many not concerned with land, had little idea of the number of people employed and the costs and sacrifices involved in running a historic house."[30]) Despite anxiety over what he should wear to the rally (he opted, incorrectly, for corduroys and a polo-neck sweater, only to find on arrival that everyone there wore suits), Saunders Watson was able to have a direct conversation with Healey, who encouraged him to write in with evidence. Saunders Watson did so, using it as an opportunity to set out his case for effective heritage maintenance funds.

The Historic Houses Association was among those seeking to mobilise popular opinion in opposition to the wealth tax. In an early publicity stunt for the association's cause, the earl of March was photographed for an article in *The Daily Telegraph* sitting in one of the principal rooms at Goodwood where

---

[28] For which see Patrick Cormack, *Heritage in Danger* (London, 1978), pp. 59–79. (Foreword by Roy Strong.)

[29] Jenkins, *Culture Gap*, p. 149.

[30] Saunders Watson, *I Am Given a Castle*, p. 100.

all the pictures had been stripped from the walls: a not-so-subtle nod towards the consequences of of too drastic a wealth tax.[31] Members of the National Association of Decorative and Fine Arts Societies (NADFAS) were briefed by Marcus Binney, one of the curators of the *Destruction* exhibition, about what they could do to prevent country houses being emptied of contents in this way. They were asked to write letters to their MPs, stage public meetings, adopt a local country house and reach out to local press and radio.[32] A petition was distributed to local NADFAS groups and to HHA member properties open to tourists in the summer season of 1975. The petition was also supported by the National Trust at its properties. By the end of the year, over a million signatures had been gathered, something of a record at the time and indeed rarely equalled in the intervening decades, until, that is, the birth of online polling.[33] The petition was presented to parliament in December 1975 by the double act of Lord Montagu and the Labour MP for Enfield Ted Graham, who was chairman of the all-party parliamentary group on heritage.

The select committee on the wealth tax had by now reached the end of its deliberations. Sub-committees had been established to investigate the details of various aspects of the proposals. But the main committee remained split and was unable to reach a consensus. Meanwhile, the weight of media opinion swung heavily against the idea of introducing a wealth tax, even among left-wing publications such as *The Guardian* and the *New Statesman*. Hugh Jenkins recorded in his memoirs his feelings of isolation and vulnerability as he made his stand against the idea that works of art should be exempted from the new tax. The *Sunday Telegraph* went so far as to brand him a "barbarian". On 18 December 1975, Denis Healey announced to parliament that the wealth tax proposal had been dropped for the rest of that session.[34]

As we have seen, Labour's other tax proposal did come to pass. A capital transfer tax (CTT) replaced the old estate duty in Healey's budget of 1975 and meant a tax on all transfers of wealth whether in life or on death. As also noted, the ability to exempt works of art against this tax was also carried forward to this new regime. But in setting up the CTT, Healey went even further, and introduced the recommendations first made by Sir Ernest Gowers' committee

[31] The picture was reprinted in Cormack, *Heritage in Danger*, p. 64.

[32] Helen Clifford, *Behind the Acanthus: The NADFAS Story* (London, 2008), pp. 27–28.

[33] Specifically, according to Michael Saunders Watson, 1,116,253. Saunders Watson, *I Am Given a Castle*, p. 93.

[34] HC Deb. 18 Dec. 1975, vol. 902, col. 705-6W.

FROM THIS...   TO THIS?

'YOUR HERITAGE IN DANGER'
Britain's Historic Houses and Gardens are
threatened by existing and proposed taxes.
Please sign the Petition to Parliament
and help save your heritage.

PLEASE SIGN NOW

Issued by Historic Houses Association, 64 St James's St. SW1.

7. Early HHA publicity poster, seeking signatures for the petition against the wealth tax, 1975.

8. The petition against the wealth tax delivered to parliament by Lord Montagu and Labour MP for Edmonton Ted Graham, December 1975 (PA Images / Alamy Stock Photo).

in 1950. For the first time, it was now possible to exempt from capital charges not just works of art, but also land and buildings of special historic interest. Perhaps it was not appreciated fully at the time, but this was a completely game-changing moment. All those private owners, the future of whose houses hung in the balance as they wondered how their successors would ever pay the death duties that they owed, now had an entirely new option to consider. Property itself could be offset against tax liabilities, albeit temporarily and conditionally. It meant that places such as Rockingham Castle, or even the fictional Gethin estates as featured in *The Inheritors,* no longer faced the same threats of being broken up. The concession only came after intense behind-the-scenes lobbying. Little wonder that Lord Montagu, in giving his president's report at the annual general meeting of the HHA in November 1975, felt that "some battles had definitely been won this year", the year being "one of constant struggle" in which the association had "played its part".[35]

The following year, Healey went further. The Finance Act of 1976 introduced the option for private owners to create maintenance funds for their properties. This too was one of the recommendations of the Gowers' committee's report. The change in the law enabled landowners to create individual trust funds for exceptional heritage properties, using income-generating assets of their own. These assets – a farm, say, or a collection of let cottages – would enjoy exemption from CTT, but only if the income they produced was devoted solely to the preservation of a connected heritage property, which typically would mean a large country house. The option gave private owners the chance to create the equivalent of the endowments that the National Trust established every time it assumed responsibility for one of its properties. Private owners did not get everything they wanted from the outset in 1976. The maintenance fund option was a one-way street at first, as owners were not able to remove property from funds that they created, and the funds were destined to revert to charitable use if they were ever wound up. Consequently, no estate took up the option in 1976, and it was only with subsequent adjustments that the maintenance fund route became possible for owners to contemplate. Nevertheless, it was a start.

Whereas the imminent destruction of the country house had been predicted by the V&A in 1974, by 1976 the situation had therefore changed quite markedly, following two years of intense lobbying and persuasion on the part of groups such as the HHA. The proposed tax on accumulated wealth had been dropped, for now. Private owners had retained the option of exemption against

---

[35]   HHA Archive, Minutes of the Second AGM of the Historic Houses Association, 4 Nov. 1975.

the new CTT. Moreover, this exemption option had been extended from works of art to property in the widest sense, including the very bricks and mortar of the country houses in which those artworks were hung. Hugh Jenkins was obliged to accept defeat. "My whole struggle had been in vain", he wrote in his memoirs. "I might just as well have gone along with the exemption and had I done so I would still have been everyone's blue-eyed old man."[36] Instead, he was sacked as arts minister in April 1976 by incoming prime minister James Callaghan, who had replaced Harold Wilson after Wilson's surprise retirement that year. Jenkins was convinced that the wealth tax had been defeated by "the most efficient and successful pressure group" working hard behind the scenes. Through gritted teeth he acknowledged that the campaign had been remarkably successful "in recruiting to their side thousands of people, perhaps millions, who would never pay the tax and who could only benefit from its application to the top group of property-owners".[37]

Healey was somewhat rueful in his recollections of the period. In retrospect, he admitted that attempting to levy additional taxes on the richest may have been doomed to fail. Efforts to help the poorest through fiscal policy often ended up being at the expense of the average, "since the very rich do not collectively earn enough to make a difference, and the average man does not nowadays want to punish those who earn a little more than he, since he hopes ultimately to join them". Attempts to use the tax system to promote equality would not succeed, he suggested, because of the complexity of the economy and the "wide variety of need and circumstance in any population".[38] Healey was all-too aware of the susceptibility of a chancellor to be lobbied by special interest groups ahead of every budget. He claimed that he made a point of never meeting these lobby groups personally, although he couldn't resist a delegation led by Margot Fonteyn and Danny La Rue to lobby him about the sales tax levied on theatre tickets, nor a visit from his friend Miles Fitzalan-Howard (later duke of Norfolk) representing the College of Heralds. "I gave nothing away", he asserted, in his defence.

Healey knew too well that the tax system could easily be gamed by those with sufficient knowledge of the technical detail of its many moving parts. "However bad an existing tax," he wrote, "those affected will adapt their behaviour to it in myriads of ways of which no government is aware until the change takes place." He was unapologetic about the replacement of the estate

---

[36] Jenkins, *Culture Gap*, p. 161.

[37] *Ibid.*, pp. 143–144.

[38] Denis Healey, *The Time of My Life* (London, 1989), p. 402.

duty, which had "become a laughing stock, since no one who could afford an accountant ever paid it". Its replacement with a CTT covering gifts in life as well as at death but from which widows were excluded was, he felt, a piece of "natural justice". But he acknowledged that he had conceded too many special cases for exclusion, such that "when I left office four years later, the CTT was still raising less revenue than the avoidable Estate Duty that it replaced." The lesson for future chancellors was clear: never commit to new forms of taxation before taking office, unless it was already clear how they will work in practice.[39] And yet, arguably, his decisions while in office had helped to save numerous country houses.

The success of the country house lobby was partly a result of sheer hard graft, much of which was carried out by Michael Saunders Watson, working with Jeremy Benson. Benson was a conservation architect who did much work for the National Trust before turning his hand to being a professional advocate for heritage in the early 1970s. Benson established the Joint Committee of Amenity Societies Tax Group and made it his business to understand the full complexity of the fiscal framework within which heritage properties operated. Benson made sure he was on top of the detail so that he could bend a sympathetic ear should one be available during his many late-night sessions stalking the back corridors of the Palace of Westminster. The Labour MP Tam Dalyell, a country house owner himself, recorded that Benson "was one of the three most effective lobbyists of Parliament I have known".[40]

Elena Porter has argued, intriguingly, that the successes of 1975 and 1976 were ultimately something of "a fluke of the bureaucratic process".[41] The introduction of full exemption for houses and gardens against CTT was only ever intended to be a temporary fix, while work was underway to introduce a full wealth tax on assets. When the wealth tax policy was dropped, the temporary exemptions remained in place and later solidified into permanent fixtures of the fiscal landscape. "With this sleight of hand," Porter argues, "conditional CTT exemption became the bedrock of government's financial support for privately owned country houses."[42] Yet the positive outcome for owners also reflected

[39] *Ibid.*, p. 403; see also Howard Glennerster, 'A Wealth Tax Abandoned: The Role of the UK Treasury 1974–6' (2011), <http://piketty.pse.ens.fr/files/Glennerster2011.pdf> [accessed 28 Dec. 2022].

[40] 'Obituary: Jeremy Benson', *The Independent*, 7 Dec. 1999, <https://www.independent.co.uk/arts-entertainment/obituary-jeremy-benson-1130783.html> [accessed 9 Sept. 2023].

[41] Porter, 'National Heritage', p. 104.

[42] *Ibid.*, p. 131.

the political realism of Lord Montagu and his associates at the early HHA. Porter notes the importance that Montagu and his colleagues ascribed to winning over key officials in government departments, who were then able to make the temporary provisions permanent without drawing unhelpful or negative public attention. Special effort was made by the early HHA to collaborate with the Labour government of the day, despite the inevitable bias towards support for the Conservative party among the association's membership. At times, this made for some surprising alliances. In November 1976, Labour's chief secretary to the treasury, Joel Barnett, addressed the HHA's annual meeting. Barnett set out a comprehensive account of the measures that the government had taken to save country house heritage. The 1975 Finance Act had first introduced exemptions for outstanding buildings open to public access, and then the 1976 Act had extended exemption to inter vivos transfers, and such property held in discretionary trusts. Montagu reported at the HHA's next annual meeting in 1977 that he had hosted Barnett at Beaulieu, where the minister yet again gave a "sympathetic ear".[43] Montagu even tried to build bridges with the trade union movement, which was then in its pomp and occupying a pivotal role in the governance of the nation. He reported that a meeting in the summer of 1977 with the union leader Clive Jenkins "will, we hope, result in a greater understanding by the TUC of our problems". Montagu personally thanked Jenkins for "all his help and sympathy to our cause". The following year, Jenkins attended the association's annual gathering, held in the Royal Festival Hall, where he set out a surprising manifesto of trade union support for privately owned country houses. Jenkins explained that he thought that "there was enormous merit in state support for this part of our heritage, and also for people still to live in such houses, helping to look after them". His only condition was that owners still needed to demonstrate that they fully deserved their privileged positions. They needed to make "useful and interesting contributions", while also satisfying two further conditions: not selling off their artworks and making special arrangements for promoting school visits. He later recalled that he "was greeted with sustained applause" at this peroration, which preceded the speech given by the Conservatives' shadow spokesman Norman St John-Stevas. For humorous effect, as St John-Stevas took to the stage, he pretended the rapturous response was for him rather than for the trade unionist.[44]

---

[43]   HHA Archive, Minutes of the Fourth AGM of the Historic Houses Association, 1 Nov. 1977.

[44]   Clive Jenkins, *All Against the Collar: Struggles of a White Collar Union Leader* (London, 1990), p. 180; HHA Archive, Minutes of the Fifth AGM of the Historic Houses Association, 29 Nov. 1978.

4

A family affair

When the Conservative minister for the environment, Baroness Young, addressed the inaugural general meeting of the Historic Houses Association in November 1973, she made a point of emphasising the importance of family life to the continuing vitality of country houses. "It is still part of the great appeal of our historic houses that so many are still owned by the families which have played so great a part in their history", she said, demonstrating a shrewd understanding of her audience. The advantage, Lady Young continued, was that lived-in houses remained homes, "rather than merely still-life museum pieces". Lest this be construed as too obvious a swipe at the National Trust and its mansion properties, she went on to emphasise the "immense contribution" made by the Trust and its "high standards of maintenance and display". Yet her preference was clearly for a house, any house, to remain as a domestic residence. Her message in conclusion was to stress the importance of individual owners being "helped and guided in ways of managing and restoring their properties", such that these buildings remained, above all, homes.[1]

Baroness Young was a stalwart defender of the traditional family throughout her career. In this she shared some similarities with her contemporary as a parliamentarian, Margaret Thatcher, who at that time was serving as secretary of state for education in Edward Heath's cabinet.[2] Both women were advocates for traditional, Christian family values, even while they doggedly pursued political power in a manner that was somewhat out of kilter with the housewifely public images that they sometimes sought to project. Lady Young's commitment to the conventional family informed her political positions: later, in the 1990s, she would make bitter enemies when she opposed moves to give equal rights to gay men and women, such as in relation to the adoption of children.[3]

---

[1] HHA Archive, Baroness Young, address to the Standing Conference of Historic Houses, 8 Nov. 1973.

[2] Baroness Young was the only woman ever appointed to a cabinet-level role by Margaret Thatcher: Thatcher appointed her chancellor of the duchy of Lancaster in 1981.

[3] Caroline Jackson, 'Janet Mary Young [née Baker], Baroness Young (1926–2002)', *Oxford Dictionary of National Biography*.

Lady Young's summary definition of privately owned country houses as lived-in family homes was entirely accurate. It was the clear difference that set the HHA's houses apart from those managed by the National Trust or by local or national government. This fact had been highlighted by Sir Ernest Gowers' committee's report in 1950, which listed as a policy recommendation that important country house properties should, so far as was possible, "be preserved as private residences occupied preferably by the families connected with them". The report went out of its way to stress how impressed members of the committee had been when their attention had been drawn to "the struggle made by many owners of historic properties against the fate that threatens their properties". As the report acknowledged, those born into the position of managing a family home often felt a deep sense of responsibility: "For many it is a matter of personal pride to discharge a duty faithfully performed by their families for generations." It was a task that involved not only considerable expense, but also "no small sacrifices of personal comfort", since:

> few of these houses are such as anyone would now choose to live in. The rooms are too vast, too numerous and too scattered; they are difficult to clean, light and heat; generally the house is inconveniently arranged for the life of today, and repairs are a constant burden. In some the owners and their families do much of the domestic work that used to be done by a large staff of servants; we have heard of more than one large house with valuable contents which is being maintained by the owner and his family with no more domestic help than one or two daily women. In some the owners and their families, assisted perhaps by voluntary helpers, devote much time to such tasks as the repair of upholstery and tapestries – a laborious and highly skilled task.[4]

The situation had only worsened by 1974, when John Cornforth published his update of the Gowers' committee's investigations. Cornforth's report contained a whole section on 'The Role of the Wife', which, setting aside its now-dated sexism, foregrounded the ongoing domestic role of many country houses in an era when very few houses could afford staff in the way that they had before the war. Although the wife's role was often "taken for granted", Cornforth stressed how "her sympathy and willingness to tackle a house is of an importance equal to that of the survival of the estate". After all, the house would lose much of its

---

[4] Ernest Gowers, *Report of the Committee on Houses of Outstanding Historic or Architectural Interest* (London, 1950), p. 49, and pp. 6–7.

point if its surrounding estate lands were sold off, yet "if the wife will not accept the challenge of a house, her husband may as well pack it in".[5]

Like Gowers, Cornforth concluded that it made more sense for country houses to remain in private hands, rather than be bailed out by government or the National Trust. Ownership by the National Trust by no means meant the end of a house as a family home of course, since many Trust houses continued to be lived in by the families that had donated them. Despite some internal disagreements, this remained a strong part of the Trust's philosophy.[6] Robin Fedden, the Trust's deputy director general, knew which side of the argument he was on. He wrote in 1968 that the Trust's houses should ideally remain lived in: "They need the breath of life. Built for a family and the life a family creates, they know no better use."[7]

Yet Cornforth and others were alive to the many pressures that bore upon such homes when they remained in private hands, not least the growing costs of maintenance and repairs and ever-tightening rates of taxation. It led house owners to experiment with new forms of public opening as a way of generating additional income, albeit at the risk of destroying the domesticity of their homes in the process. Reconciling the needs of a family residence with the imperatives of a commercial tourist attraction was not always straightforward. "Very easily," explained Cornforth, "a house can become quite intolerable as a family home, for opening can mean loss of space, loss of privacy and loss of peace, as well as a conflict between the way an owner might wish visitors to see the house and the demands of commercial organisation." The example was given of Warwick Castle, where on a fine weekend in July or August the level of noise put a severe dampener on domestic comfort: "it echoes round the curtain walls to such an extent that it can be little pleasure for the owner to live there."[8] Moreover, the sheer size of country houses, and the demands they placed on owners in an era when domestic staff were becoming a distinct rarity, meant such places were increasingly unrealistic as family homes:

---

[5]   Cornforth, *Country Houses*, pp. 65–66.

[6]   For these debates, see Sean Nixon, 'Trouble at the National Trust: Post-War Recreation, the Benson Report and the Rebuilding of a Conservation Organization in the 1960s', *Twentieth Century British History* 26 (2015), 529–550.

[7]   Robin Fedden, *The Continuing Purpose: A History of the National Trust, Its Aims and Work* (London, 1968), p. 119. Quoted in David Matless, *About England* (London, 2023), p. 208.

[8]   Cornforth, *Country Houses*, p. 17.

pulling blinds, closing shutters, the problem of sitting, eating and cooking within a reasonable radius, keeping an eye on the children, putting the cat out or training a puppy, might all sound trivial or silly things to notice, but they can build up into an overwhelming nightmare in a big house just because of the extent of the ground to be covered.[9]

As Kate Retford has observed, "in the domain of the country house, the private and the public have long been interwoven in various and complex ways."[10] Such places were simultaneously houses – formal, sometimes grand suites of rooms, richly furnished and hung with artworks designed to impress upon the visitor the status and position of their host – but also homes, domestic arenas within which private family life unfolded. Retford noted that this disjunction often formed the basis for how privately owned houses chose to market themselves, as 'lived-in family homes' and emphatically not museum-pieces. The success of post-war stately home tourism was in part driven by an awareness that such houses remained the homes of real, living families, whose private lives occasionally made it into the newspapers. Cultural geographer David Matless recalled visiting Woburn Abbey in Bedfordshire on a day coach trip from Norwich at some point in the mid-1970s. A boy at the time, his only memory of the house itself was of "seeing the remnants of the family breakfast on a table left for public view". He even remembered the name of the cereal packet left on show – 'Force' ("then a popular brand," Matless explained, "though not one I ate"). Matless reflected upon how such a detail helped to demarcate a space that was at once "splendid" and "lived in", and that it said "something about an encounter between ordinary publics and elevated lives".[11]

A visit to a stately home might also offer the additional pleasure of an unanticipated brush with celebrity. Perhaps the most famous aristocratic celebrity of the 1980s was Deborah Cavendish, duchess of Devonshire, whose 1982 book on Chatsworth made much of the pros and cons of family life in such a property:

the pros of children being able to roller skate for miles without going out of doors, of being able to walk for hours inside on a wet day; the cons of putting a bag down and not being able to find it again for months, of having

9   *Ibid.*, p. 18.
10   Kate Retford, "'A Family Home and Not … a Museum": Living with the Country House Art Collection', *Art and the Country House* (2020), <https://doi.org/10.17658/ACH/TE582> [accessed 29 Dec. 2022].
11   Matless, *About England*, p. 208.

to trek through corridor after corridor at night to let out a dog being house trained.[12]

On more than a simply practical level, houses and families were almost umbilically connected. There remains even today a proportion of country houses that have been lived in by the same family ever since they were first built. Of these, perhaps the most famous would be the dukes of Marlborough at Blenheim, the earls of Leicester at Holkham, or indeed the Devonshires at Chatsworth. These connections could at times stretch back over even longer spans of time. Earls of Devon have lived at Powderham Castle on the river Exe for more than eight hundred years. The site itself, a strategically important position guarding the access to Exeter by coast, has been inhabited even longer. Archaeological investigation has revealed a Roman villa on the same site as the current estate. This Roman settlement was engaged in much the same mixture of agricultural activity as its present-day successor two thousand years later. Some country houses were therefore indicative of a 'deep history' of enduring and sedimented patterns of settlement within a local landscape, sometimes by the same human genetic pool.

While the fortunes of a family or a title might have fluctuated over time, the urge to remain associated with a particular house that may have been in the same hands for many generations was often overpowering. This reflected the dominance of the legal practice of primogeniture in Britain, or inheritance by the eldest male descendant. The practice of entail meant that the inheritance of an estate was vested in the heir's unborn heirs, making any individual owner merely a transitory link in a genetic chain that insisted on its own replication. A title and a house could in this way pass unopposed or unchallenged from generation to generation, in sharp contrast to the practice in France where the Napoleonic Code meant that estates would be parcelled out between siblings upon the death of a parent, leading to the fracturing of composite landholdings. In British houses, the uncontested succession of titles and properties from one generation to the next, usually from fathers to eldest sons, was commemorated in artworks, memorials, heraldry, and church monuments.[13]

Despite sharp differences in legal practice between Britain and the rest of Europe, the early HHA was surprisingly internationalist in its outlook from the outset, seeing itself as part of a continental family of country house owner

---

[12]   The Duchess of Devonshire, *The House: A Portrait of Chatsworth* (1982), quoted in Retford, "'A Family Home and Not … a Museum'".

[13]   See John Cornforth, 'The Backward Look', in Gervase Jackson-Stops (ed.), *Treasure Houses of Britain* (New Haven and London, 1985), pp. 60–69.

organisations. The issue of whether the UK would join its neighbours on continental Europe in cleaving to the formal structures of the European Communities was as politically divisive in the early 1970s as it would be half a century later. Arguably, it was no coincidence that the HHA was founded in November 1973, in the same year that the UK had formally joined the European Economic Community (EEC) (on 1 January 1973). The existence of independent owners' associations in several other European countries provided a spur for the establishment of the HHA in the UK. British house owners looked with envy across the Channel at organisations like Les Vieilles Maisons Françaises, established as a representative organisation for owners of châteaux and other historic properties. The need for the UK owners to keep up with their European kinsfolk was raised at the founding meeting of the HHA in 1973, when it was noted that a draft European statute for historic houses had been proposed at a recent Council of Europe meeting in Zurich. George Howard claimed credit for improving and enhancing the text of this statute, which he had done in conjunction with the International Castles Institute. But he noted that while a thousand delegates had attended a recent meeting of Les Vieilles Maisons Françaises, the proposed new HHA only had just over a hundred supporters. The HHA would be established on European lines, for example by having a president as its chair (which meant the duke of Grafton, officiating as the founding president, was quickly renamed as the association's patron).[14]

The urgency to keep pace with developments in other European countries was emphasised even more by the fact that 1975 had been declared European Architectural Heritage Year. This was a pan-European campaign to raise public awareness of the importance of built and natural heritage. HHA member properties were encouraged to participate, and the association hosted an international conference of historic house owners in Oxford and York in July 1975.[15] Lord Montagu reciprocated by visiting Germany, Austria, Poland, and Holland to speak to historic house owners there. The European Union of Historic Houses met in Paris and at Château de Beloeil, the home of its president Prince Antoine de Ligne. The executive secretary of the HHA in the UK, Richard Miller, was invited to serve as the secretary general of the European chapter, a recognition that the UK association was one of the few to have its own executive

---

[14]   HHA Archive, Minutes of the Third AGM of the Standing Conference of Historic Houses, 8 Nov. 1973; Minutes of the First AGM of the Historic Houses Association, 23 Oct. 1974.

[15]   HHA Archive, Minutes of the First AGM of the Historic Houses Association, 23 Oct. 1974.

staff. Montagu meanwhile became the president of the European association in autumn 1978.[16]

Montagu was proud of this European activity, which replicated in Brussels what had been achieved in Whitehall and Westminster. In July 1977 he managed to secure a lunch with Roy Jenkins, the British Labour politician who had become president of the European Commission earlier that year. Jenkins recorded in his diary that the lunch, on the rue de Praetère in Brussels, was also attended by George Howard, by Lord O'Hagan, and by Prince de Ligne, although "ironically without Jennifer" (Jenkins' wife, who was the chair of the historic buildings council at the time).[17] At the lunch, Montagu recorded that his idea for a European Heritage Conference to be held in 1979 and supported by the EEC was "enthusiastically accepted" by Jenkins. Montagu was sincere in his support for European heritage causes. When he stepped down as president of the HHA, he initiated a trophy in his own name to mark achievements in the business of historic house conservation. The inaugural Montagu Trophy was awarded posthumously to Anne d'Amodio, founder of Les Vieilles Maisons Françaises. Reaching out to kin across the Channel, just as much as reaching out to representatives of the trade union movement, was all part of Montagu's strategy for reviving the British country house.[18]

At the same time, Montagu knew that British country houses, and the families that owned them, needed to develop their own resilience. For this reason, he emphasised above all else the importance of continuity of ownership and of houses being passed on intact to sons (and sometimes daughters) who would willingly take up the inheritance and continue their parents' missions. Montagu knew that this was not always an easy process. Educated younger generations might aspire to have their own careers. What parent would seek to pour cold water on such dreams, and for their child to sacrifice everything and become "an unpaid custodian living in a semi-public atmosphere"? he asked the HHA's AGM in November 1978. Montagu emphasised the need for future planning, so that owners did not leave things too late before discovering that their heirs had no intention of picking up the reins at the ancestral seat.[19] A few years later, in 1984, the association established a chapter exclusively for

[16]   HHA Archive, Minutes of the Fourth AGM of the Historic Houses Association, 1 Nov. 1977.

[17]   Roy Jenkins, *European Diary, 1977–1981* (London, 1989), p. 127.

[18]   An eyewitness remembers the Montagu Trophy as being a "ghastly-looking thing". Its whereabouts today are unknown.

[19]   HHA Archive, Minutes of the Fifth AGM of the Historic Houses Association, 29 Nov. 1978.

younger, 'successor members'. The first activity for this group would be a "seminar where fathers and sons could discuss the very broad range of problems
associated with the transfer of ownership".[20] The seminar, known as the 'Heirs
and Graces' meeting and held at Goodwood, was also intended as a means of
creating the space in which the generations could at least begin to have conversations about what would happen to family homes. Too often, parents did
not talk to their children about the future of their properties, or about the work
that their management entailed.

Family life has been central to the story of the rescue of the country house.
Not wanting to be the one to 'let it go' has been the driving force behind many
owners who have fought valiant battles to save their houses, whether from
destruction, the sales catalogue, or acquisition by the National Trust. Blood is
thicker than water, and residual loyalty to a family line has often proved sufficient impetus to make sacrifices that few others would make in the interests of
saving a house. Despite the inconveniences involved, the survival and subsequent revival of country houses has often been a family affair.

This was certainly the case with Browsholme in Lancashire, one of the
houses left 'on the brink' earlier. Browsholme's fate hinged on both the change
of generations and the change in the fiscal environment prompted by Denis
Healey's concessions to country house owners in 1975 and 1976. Colonel Robert Parker died in 1975, without children. Six months before his death he had
unexpectedly altered his will to leave Browsholme to his fourth cousin, also
Robert, who was just twenty at the time and a student at the Royal Agricultural
College in Cirencester. The conditional exemption option meant that the post-
war practice of opening Browsholme to informal public visiting suddenly had
a new-found significance. By promising to continue to welcome visitors, the
estate was able, albeit temporarily, to avoid the CCT payment that was due
on Colonel Robert's death. Browsholme may well have been one of the very
first country houses to take advantage of this treatment. It undoubtedly saved
the house from having to be sold, along with its distinctive collections of portraits, arms, and armour. Robert's parents, who were based in East Anglia, left
their comfortable farmhouse and moved to the Forest of Bowland to oversee
the restoration work the property needed. When they got there, they suddenly
realised what they had let themselves in for. Robert's father recorded that:

---

[20]   HHA Archive, Minutes of the Eleventh AGM of the Historic Houses Association, 20 Nov. 1984.

our tour of the Hall did not take long. The East Wing, unused since the war was derelict; the kitchen unsanitary, the water visibly unfit to drink and later to be found severely contaminated; the wiring uncertain and dangerous; the damp and cold penetrating and a general distinctive and unpleasant smell pervaded the whole house: all very disagreeable. As a chartered surveyor I assessed the Hall unfit to live in and unsaleable in its present state.[21]

The family moved into the east wing and set to work transforming the house from its mouldering state into something far more suitable to late-twentieth-century living. They worked hard to make the house habitable, given the semi-derelict state into which it had fallen. With dampness penetrating the very core of the property, and all sorts of problems to address from the water supply to the wiring, they had their work cut out. The Parkers simply got on with it, and turned their hands to anything that needed doing, whether shovelling up rodent droppings or prising damp carpets from the stone floors to which they had become affixed. Mr and Mrs Parker also sold their farmhouse, near Cambridge, and used the proceeds to modernise the east wing. They purchased an adjoining two-hundred-and-fifty-acre livestock farm, which had been sold off by a previous generation, and one hundred and twenty acres of woodland from the Forestry Commission held on a long lease. The estate now extended to six hundred and seventy acres, making it more economically viable. Meanwhile, they dutifully offered the full twenty-eight days of public opening, with various family members acting as room guides.[22] On the completion of his studies, Robert started to build a career in London. But in the late 1980s he and his wife, Amanda, relocated to Browsholme to assume responsibility for the house and estate. The sale of their London home meant more money could be invested in improvements to the main hall. An English Heritage grant for the roof meant that the property was made watertight, at least for the time being. Investment in a biomass boiler was another risk but meant the house could be heated by renewable sources of energy.

Sudeley Castle in Gloucestershire is an example of an ancient house where the desire to keep the house within a single family's ownership has helped to determine the very course of that family's history. Already an important estate at the time of the Domesday Book, a house of some status was clearly in place

---

[21]   Quoted by Robert Parker, John Cornforth Memorial Lecture, 'Browsholme Hall, Lancashire' (8 Feb. 2023), Christie's, London.

[22]   A guidebook to the house was prepared by Simon Jervis, Robert's elder half-brother, who was a curator at the V&A, where he had also been a contributor to the *Destruction* exhibition of 1974.

9. Robert Parker on the roof at Browsholme, Lancashire, 2022.

at Sudeley at the time of the Anarchy in the early twelfth century, when it was captured by followers of Stephen of Blois.[23] By the fifteenth century the estate was owned by the influential and well-connected Boteler family, who oversaw the building of the castle as it is today. Ownership shifted into the hands of the royal family, the Tudors, and from there to the marquess of Northampton before being granted to the Brydges family under Mary I. Garrisoned during the civil wars, Sudeley was greatly damaged by the conflict, which left much of the stonework in ruins. Surviving as a picturesque curio for much of the subsequent century, the property and its wider estate were purchased in the early nineteenth century by John and William Dent. The Dents had made their money from industry as glove-makers, but like many such families were looking to establish their status and credentials through the ownership of a house and estate. The property was next inherited by a Dent nephew, John, who married Emma (from the silk manufacturing Brocklehurst family). The Dent-Brocklehursts have been at Sudeley ever since. Emma and John made Sudeley a lively place once again: the couple were noted for their generous hospitality. To show

[23] James Parry and Elizabeth, Lady Ashcombe, *Sudeley Castle: Royalty, Romance and Revival* (London, 2021), p. 18.

off their restoration of the castle, a historical party was held in 1859, evoking the glory days of when Henry VIII was resident at the castle. A miscarriage had ended Emma's hopes of bearing her husband an heir. Instead, the property passed again to a nephew – this time on Emma's side, a Brocklehurst, who had been christened as Dent-Brocklehurst with a view to preserving the family identity. And so, the property was retained within the family, passing eventually to the stockbroker Mark Dent-Brocklehurst in 1969.

Mark had married an American, Elizabeth Chipps, whom he had met while she was still a design student in New York. The couple moved into Sudeley with their two young children and set about reconfiguring the house as a visitor attraction. Riding the wave of the new public interest in country house tourism was essential to their strategy. Although the house had a chequered ownership, the Dent family had proved its most enduring custodians. "My family have managed to live here longer than any other", Mark used to enjoy boasting. All families have their own tragedies, however. For the Dent-Brocklehurst family it was Mark's sudden death in 1972, of cardiac arrest, at the age of just forty. Attendant on this too was a considerable tax liability on the family property, made even more complicated by Mark dying intestate. As Elizabeth recalled, it all "could easily have seen the end of the Dent-Brocklehurst custodianship of the castle". Her lawyers advised her to sell the castle to meet the family debts. But rather than abandon Sudeley and take her children back to America, Elizabeth resolved to continue Mark's dream of the house remaining with the family. The pull of family loyalty once more prevailed. "I couldn't deny my young children their home and birthright so soon after losing their father", Elizabeth later explained.[24]

With the house in trust, Elizabeth continued to work hard on making Sudeley a viable tourism proposition as well as attending to the urgent restorations that were needed. By the end of the decade, Sudeley was welcoming a hundred thousand visitors annually. Elizabeth's second marriage to the fourth baron Ashcombe, one of Sudeley's trustees, also helped to provide familial stability. Lord Ashcombe sold his own estate – Denbies in Surrey – to focus resources on the revitalisation of Sudeley as a comfortable family home. James Parry observes that Sudeley's business model is "not dissimilar to that of numerous historic country houses in Britain today", being based on a mixed income from rental properties, events such as weddings and concerts, and the day visitor market. Such properties are, Parry contends, "the mainstays of the British heritage industry". Yet for Parry, Sudeley's survival and ongoing success has an

---

[24]   *Ibid.*, p. 149.

added piquancy given Mark Dent-Brocklehurst's untimely passing. The house "retains a special and timeless quality", much of which derives "from the ongoing presence of the family".[25]

Another home connected to a single family was Knebworth House in Hertfordshire. The Lytton family has had a close association with Knebworth since the end of the fifteenth century, when it was purchased, from a relative, by Sir Robert Lytton, under treasurer to Henry VII. The family's association with the house is inscribed on its very walls, in the form of the repeated gothic motif of a bat (or 'lyt' in Old English) against the background of a barrel (or 'ton'). Much of the gothicisation of the building dated from the middle decades of the nineteenth century, when the novelist Edward Bulwer Lytton added turrets and gargoyles to further transform the appearance of the castellated "fair pile of brick" that Sir Henry Chauncy saw in 1700.

When David, heir to Lord Cobbold, first took on responsibility for the house in the early 1970s, its future was far from certain. The costs of maintaining such an ancient building meant that all sorts of ideas were being entertained for its future. Would it become the campus for a proposed new university of Hertfordshire? Or, as had happened to Harlaxton Manor near Grantham, could it become home to an American college? Neither idea took wing. As David's wife Chryssie explained in her memoir of these years, "people had been interested but were frightened off by the state of the building, addled as it was with dry rot and every sort of beetle."[26] The couple, with their young family, made the brave decision instead to open Knebworth as a visitor attraction, in order to make the sort of income that would safeguard the future sustainability of the building.

David followed in his father's footsteps by working as a banker by day, while dreaming up plans for Knebworth at evenings and weekends. (The title of Chryssie's memoirs – *Board Meetings in the Bath* – referred to the couple's habit of updating each other on the business activities of the day while taking an evening bath.) The advantage of being located off a spur road from the adjoining Great North Road (or A1) meant Knebworth was well positioned to enter the stately home business. A start-up £25,000 grant from the newly created Countryside Commission enabled them to lay out a new access road, and they envisaged surrounding the house with car parks, picnic spots, stables for horse

---

[25] *Ibid.*, p. 147.
[26] Chryssie Lytton Cobbold, *Board Meetings in the Bath: The Knebworth House Story* (London, 1986).

riding, and an adventure playground.[27] The adventure playground is still there today, even if the stables proved too difficult (within six months the stables manager and farrier had stopped speaking to each other). Knebworth was successful as a destination from its opening on the Easter weekend of 1971, and Chryssie personally carried much of the responsibility. By the end of Easter Monday, "I could hardly move, my back ached so much. I had carried so many crates of fizzy drinks and cooked pounds of hamburgers … and I was pregnant once again."

The hard work, however, paid off. Knebworth was soon in the top ten of country house attractions. To move to the next level, the couple alighted upon the idea of using the park as an open-air rock music venue. The 'Bucolic Frolic' of 1974 (featuring those two bands of Brothers, Allman and Doobie, as well as Northern Irish troubadour Van Morrison) was followed in 1975 by Pink Floyd. The band "did not mean anything to us at the time," said Chryssie of the English progressive rock group, "but we bought a record and liked the music". A winning formula had been found, and in the years ahead Knebworth would play host to the Rolling Stones, Genesis, Frank Zappa, and Led Zeppelin.[28] Inviting musicians such as these into the mansion was not always a good idea. Brian Wilson of the Beach Boys once ate an entire chocolate cake intended for a children's birthday party and then fell asleep on the sofa just before his 1980 headlining concert was due to start. At other times, having an open house meant that the boundaries between private and public space could be blurred. "The fact that the house is open and that visitors are wandering around is hardly noticed by any of us any more as we are all so used to it and have never known it otherwise", Chryssie consoled herself.[29]

Filling Knebworth House and park with people ensured its short-term survival. The worst of the crumbling masonry and dry rot could be managed, but the burdens and responsibilities were increasingly becoming too much. The income from events and giant rock concerts alone was not going to solve the problem that the house needed restoration from top to bottom. Millions of pounds were needed and were out of reach of the Lytton Cobbold family's diminishing liquid assets. A solution came through David's innovative creation

---

[27] The Countryside Commission for England and Wales was established under the Countryside Act 1968. It was empowered to give grants to private owners as well as public bodies, to promote access to the countryside.

[28] *Knebworth House* (Norwich, 2016), p. 58. For a full account of these concerts, see Freddie Bannister, *There Must Be a Better Way: The Story of the Bath and Knebworth Rock Festivals 1969–1979* (Cambridge, 2003).

[29] Lytton Cobbold, *Board Meetings in the Bath*, p. 126.

10. Knebworth Midsummer Night's Dream: official programme cover, 24 June 1978 (parkerphotography / Alamy Stock Photo).

in 1984 of a special trust, the Knebworth House Education and Preservation Trust, which was granted a long lease over the house and garden. The aim was to put Knebworth on a surer path to a sustainable future, by allowing it to benefit from an endowment established for the purpose of delivering a long-term restoration plan. The family connection with Knebworth continues, in conjunction with the duration of the lease to the trust. This is through three of the nine trustees being family members (not living in the house) working alongside the six independent and ex-officio trustees, who, through a trading company (Lytton Enterprises Limited), remain the motor force behind the financial support to the property through innovative management of the park and wider estate, and enabling development. The non-trustee family members living in the house, and paying rent to the educational trust for the privilege to do so, are the full-time custodians and commercial innovators. Since 2000 it has been driven by David and Chryssie's son, Henry, and their daughter-in-law Martha. A family affair indeed.

A less happy family story provides the backdrop to the revival of Stonor Park in Oxfordshire. On a freezing cold day in January 1976, a hundred-and-twenty-foot-long white marquee was erected on the lawn in front of the red-bricked mansion, parts of which were at least nine hundred years old. The tent's purpose was to host a sale of the contents of the house. Stonor's owners, Lord and Lady Camoys, had recently decamped to the nearby Dower House, taking with them a smattering of the family's treasures (and seven safes within which to keep them). The sale, organised by the auctioneers Phillips, was designed to raise funds for the couple, who complained that they could no longer afford the £20,000 a year running costs of the house. "They are very upset by the whole thing", said Brian Cole, a director of the firm, adding that he thought that they had made "a very brave decision".[30]

Not everyone agreed, including members of Lord and Lady Camoys' immediate family. Although Stonor could lay claim to having the longest history of constant occupation by the same family of any house in the country (even more so than Windsor Castle, as some newspapers were keen to point out), its future now hung in the balance. This time it was disagreements between family members that threatened to undermine the inheritance of more than eight hundred years of family ownership. Lord and Lady Camoys' daughter, Julia, later recalled that she "sat and watched for two days, tears streaming" as the auction proceeded.[31]

---

[30] 'History Goes under the Hammer', *Belfast Telegraph*, 26 Jan. 1976, p. 11.
[31] Julia Camoys Stonor, *Sherman's Wife* (London, 2006), p. 319.

Julia's memoir of her mother did not stint in its criticism of Lady Camoys. According to Julia's account, from the time of the sixth lord's accession to the title her mother's efforts "to disperse the Stonor estate, to acquire more jewellery" only increased. Her intention was to "get the actual deeds of Stonor Park itself, its freehold made out in her name". The sixth Lord Camoys was persuaded to cut his son Thomas out of the will, which instead named his grandson, William, as the co-beneficiary alongside Lady Camoys. Thomas, a banker who lived in his own historic property in Suffolk, had reportedly been willing to buy Stonor from his parents, but they had turned a "deaf ear" to any such entreaties.[32]

The turmoil over the future of the house was a bitter blow after nearly a quarter of a century of renovations at Stonor, when the family had tried to make the house inhabitable again after the war. Stonor had received grants of £60,000 from the historic buildings council for repairs to the roof, which had been matched from the family's own resources after the sale of estate property during the 1950s. The expense of running Stonor had been a constant preoccupation for the sixth lord. He offered the house to the nation, but the government declined to purchase it, on the grounds that "the policy of both the present and previous Governments was only to intervene when a house was in immediate danger of serious deterioration, and there appeared no prospect of saving it except through purchase by the nation." In 1975 Lord Camoys put Stonor up for sale, apparently in the hope that a university or other institution might buy it and open it to public access. At the HHA's annual meeting in early November that year, Lord Montagu acknowledged that many of the two hundred and fifty members attending "would be feeling desperate at this time with the tragic news" that Stonor was on the market, especially given the grants it had secured in the past and the award it had won during the European Architectural Heritage Year. However, putting a brave face on things, he urged that everyone continued "with pride in the past, turned into resolution for the future".[33] Looking to the future, Marcus Binney in the Christmas *Country Life* edition speculated that Stonor might become a regional outpost of the V&A, as a museum of recusant history. Alternatively, perhaps the local council could take it on, following the examples of Tatton and Shugborough.[34]

[32] Geraldine Norman, 'Last-ditch plea to save Stonor Park', *The Times*, 26 Jan. 1976, p. 1.

[33] HHA Archive, Minutes of the Second AGM of the Historic Houses Association, 4 Nov. 1975.

[34] Marcus Binney, 'The Future of Stonor', *Country Life*, 25 Dec. 1975, pp. 1794–1797.

Lord and Lady Camoys did not attend the auction, held on 28 and 29 January 1976. The lots included furniture and works of art, Lord Camoys' collection of natural history items (a stuffed crow was sold to the Natural History Museum for £28), as well as an assorted range of kitchen utensils. In total, the two days raised more than £110,000 for Lord and Lady Camoys, not least thanks to one antiques dealer from nearby Henley-on-Thames, Mrs Phyllis Mayo, who spent £30,000 acquiring items for her shop. Mrs Mayo also entertained hopes of making a parallel bid for the house itself, which she envisaged turning into a giant antiques store. But Mrs Mayo was not the only significant purchaser at what the newspapers called "Britain's most aristocratic jumble sale". George Levy, a Mayfair antiques dealer, bought several pieces of furniture including an important historic bed. He later revealed that he had, in fact, been acting on behalf of Lord and Lady Camoys' children.[35]

When, just a few weeks later in March 1976, the sixth lord died at the relatively youthful age of sixty-two, Julia's mother declined to speak to her daughter at the funeral. After her husband's body had been lowered into the grave outside the family chapel adjacent to the house, the dowager Lady Camoys reportedly "retreated into the shuttered, deserted house, slamming the door, bolting it fast".[36] Ownership of the house remained in limbo. Would it stay with the dowager, or would she sell it to Mrs Mayo while remaining in residence at the Dower House, possibly with her near-neighbour (and Agatha Christie's widower) Sir Max Malloran as her new husband? Sir Max declined, leaving the dowager to live on in isolation. The future of the house was eventually settled in 1978, two days before the deadline set by the tax authorities for resolving the CTT owed on the late Lord Camoys' estate.[37] Rather than accepting Mrs Mayo's offer to buy the property, it was sold instead to Lord Camoys' son, Thomas, now the seventh Lord Camoys. He consequently sold his Suffolk house and moved his family back in to Stonor. This period of troubled relationships at Stonor in the mid-1970s is not mentioned in the house's guidebook, which simply records that "by good fortune, we have been able to preserve the long traditions illustrated in our family history. We are doing everything possible to ensure that they are passed on to the next generation."[38] The return of Lord Camoys to the house at least meant that one important

---

[35] 'My Lady's Bed goes for £3,000', *Daily Mirror*, 30 Jan. 1976, p. 9.

[36] Camoys Stonor, *Sherman's Wife*, p. 320.

[37] Philip Howard, 'Stonor Family Return to Historic Home', *The Times*, 8 March 1978, p. 2.

[38] *Stonor* (2010), p. 31.

ambition could be fulfilled. After a year of repairs and restoration work, Stonor opened to the public on 1 April 1979. A report had been commissioned from Norman Hudson, then an adviser at Savills, on the feasibility of such a public opening. Other family members and local benefactors helped to furnish the house, which received seven hundred visitors on its first day of opening. It has been open for public visiting ever since.[39]

Browsholme, Sudeley, Knebworth, and Stonor are all examples of houses where a resident family's abiding passion has kept a home functioning even in the darkest of circumstances. The energy and determination that derives from such familial loyalty is not to be underestimated. The same point had been observed in the Gowers report, and it remains a truth today. Family life was the motor engine for the success of many privately owned homes, even as their owners experimented with different ways of making their houses pay for themselves.

[39] *Ibid.*, p. 5.

5

To be, or not to be?

When Biddy and Bill Cash saw a tumbledown, brick-built Jacobean manor house on a list of 'Threatened Houses of Architectural Interest' in June 1970, they couldn't resist the urge to investigate further. Bill was thirty-one and making his way in a career as a lawyer. Their son, William, had been born four years earlier, and Biddy and Bill liked the idea of establishing roots by means of a place in the country. On their first visit to Upton Cressett in Shropshire they found a completely derelict ruin. Pigs roamed freely around the wood-panelled rooms of the main house. The previous tenant, a farmer, had left behind the detritus of piles of grain and abandoned farm equipment. "It was a hot day," Bill later remembered, "the ground floor stank like a summer farmyard. There was chicken and pig manure everywhere." But there was to be no turning back. Biddy and Bill had fallen in love. William, their son, now explains that "my parents had become afflicted with that most British and expensive of diseases: the 'dream' of finding an old English manor house and restoring it, the more of an overgrown ruin beyond hope, the better."[1]

The family moved in and began the slow and painstaking task of restoring the property. None of it was easy. Bill decided that the best option, as a way of keeping control of budgets, was to renovate one room at a time, and never to spend more than a few hundred pounds per room. Plaster was repaired and painted white. Floors and roofs were made good. Biddy and Bill spent as much time as they could there, supervising builders when they weren't doing the work themselves. It was the saving of Upton Cressett. As William now says, "if a buyer or leaseholder hadn't been found, the house might have been yet another to fall victim to the wreckers' ball as a way of avoiding a costly Conservation Order."[2] Instead, Bill applied his detailed understanding of the law of listed properties to the business of his own restoration work. Bill shared his expertise by preparing a "Manual of Legislation Affecting Historic Buildings

---

[1] William Cash, *Restoration Heart: A Memoir* (London, 2019), p. 20.
[2] *Ibid.*, p. 19.

and the National Heritage" for the HHA in 1976.[3] Nearly forty years after his parents had first moved in, by which time Bill had established himself as one of the longest-serving members of parliament, William took over the reins at the property. William has since left his own legacy at the house, in the form of the colourful murals he commissioned from the artist Adam Dant in the 2010s. Upton Cressett is restored to full use as a family home and rural business centre, being home to several holiday cottages and William's wife's millinery workshop.

Upton Cressett is a living example of how a country house could be turned from a crumbling ruin to an asset able to pay its way. Another was Penhow Castle in Gwent, in south-east Wales. Film director Stephen Weeks, desperate to escape London and move to a place in the country, had stumbled across Penhow one weekend when he was out house hunting. Weeks made lists of mansions that had been requisitioned during the war and then subsequently abandoned by their owners. In the early 1970s Weeks was on one of his peregrinations and could not resist the temptation "of driving up a lane to a curious and attractive group of buildings that were sitting on a rocky knoll overlooking the old main road into Wales". They were the ruins of Penhow Castle, an early twelfth-century fortified site which had just recently been sold to a new owner. Weeks was devastated to hear this news, as the house fitted his requirements entirely. On being shown around he could not bring himself to look properly at the house that might have been his. "I looked through the chinks in my fingers at rooms which cried out to be loved again", he later explained. Weeks' luck was in, however. The sale fell through, so he was able to buy the place anyway. When he moved in, in 1973, he found he was living in what had become a fully functioning farm. The keep tower had had its windows, doors, and fireplaces blocked up to stop children or sheep wandering in. The great hall was being used as a granary, "to the delight of a growing population of rats". Below it, the lower hall was a log store, a cow shed, and a coal hole. The attics had been used as apple stores, until the floorboards had become too unsafe to use. That winter was harsh and freezing cold; the global energy crisis of those years delayed Weeks' plan to restore the castle. But his restoration project had begun in earnest by 1976, when he was able to reroof the great hall using oaks from an old Norfolk barn that he had bought and had transported to Penhow. Different parts of the largely abandoned castle became more and more inhabited. In 1978, a youth employment scheme gave Weeks a team of sixteen- to

---

[3] HHA Archive, Minutes of the First Meeting of the Council of the Historic Houses Association, 14 July 1976.

eighteen-year-olds, who set to work reconstructing a post-medieval kitchen. Archaeological investigations led to amazing finds from an abandoned moat: an old pair of spurs, an Elizabethan earring, a Nuremburg token, tons of pot-sherds. Weeks discovered the link between the castle and the Seymour family, and various American Seymours helped to fund the restoration work. In 1979 he held a Seymour festival at the castle, doubling as both a celebration of the eight-hundred-and-fifty-year-old link between the building and the family and an official opening event for the castle itself. Within just six years it had been rescued from being a wreck to being a visitor attraction, with a castle shop and a guidebook for children.[4]

Marcus Binney, the co-curator of the *Destruction* show at the V&A in 1974, had a nose for the most desperate examples of where a house's fate might be transformed in this way, provided there was sufficient will and determination. Binney made a habit of seeking out the most problematic cases to pursue, and in the 1970s and early 1980s there was no shortage of such properties. Riding on the success of the V&A show, Binney took the initiative in April 1975 to establish a campaigning group "dedicated to championing endangered historic buildings".[5] The work of SAVE Britain's Heritage was not confined to coun-try houses. It ranged far wider, across churches, factories, chapels, pubs, town houses. The formula for the group's work was established early on by one of its founder trustees, Simon Jenkins of the *Evening Standard* (and later *The Times*): "good punchy copy, statistics, and a juicy quote".[6] They were the same ingre-dients that had ensured the *Destruction* show had made such an impact, and they led, for example, to *Daily Mirror* headlines such as 'Spend a penny for ye olde loo' (in response to a press release about a threatened public convenience in Margate).[7] In many ways these 1970s campaigns, conducted with passion and zeal by Binney and his colleagues, were the start of what we now regard as the heritage movement in Britain.

Binney's 1984 memoir, *Our Vanishing Heritage*, recorded numerous instanc-es of houses on their metaphoric last legs. Finedon Hall in Northamptonshire and its collections were put on the market in 1972 after the death of the own-er, Colonel Baranger. No buyer was found, and within ten years it was in an

---

    [4] Stephen Weeks, 'Penhow Castle, Gwent', *Historic House* 4:1 (February 1980), 23–25.

    [5] Marcus Binney and John Harris, *The Destruction of the Country House: 40 Years On* (London, 2014), p. 5.

    [6] Marcus Binney, *SAVE Britain's Heritage 1975–2005: Thirty Years of Campaigning* (London, 2005), p. 15.

    [7] Binney and Harris, *40 Years On*, p. 5.

"advance state of collapse", although it was still not beyond salvation.[8] Ecton Hall in the same county had been empty for even longer, since 1952. Here the local authority could merely propose the same answer as at Finedon: the conversion of part of the estate at Ecton into a new housing development. That a scheme such as this could be considered for a house of such importance to the gothic revival movement confirmed in Binney's mind the "inadequacy and ineffectiveness of Britain's planning laws".[9] Things were little better at Buntingsdale House in Shropshire. Here, a modern housing estate once again intruded onto the historic estate, while the Smith of Warwick house had been inelegantly converted into apartments. At least a solution, of sorts, had been found. Such an outcome seemed impossible for Pell Wall Hall, also in Shropshire, one of the last country houses to be designed by Sir John Soane. Here, the estate was sold for development in the 1970s, which meant that on his arrival Binney was shocked to see the gate lodge dwarfed by a modern extension, "completely out of tune in scale, materials and colour". An even worse fate awaited the house. Although it had been in use as a boarding school run by the Brothers of Christian Instruction from the late 1920s, it had been left empty since 1965. After an initial plan to convert it to an entertainment venue fell through, its new owner applied for permission to demolish the house entirely. Permission was denied after the planning inspector found that insufficient care had been taken to find an alternative solution. When Binney visited a few years later, he found rainwater cascading through the central dome of the house. "Everywhere beautiful plasterwork was collapsing, or about to collapse. The timbers of the first-floor landing were sodden and rotten."[10]

Such scenes were matched by similarly grim sights at Belford in Northumberland, at Barlaston Hall in Staffordshire and at Dingley Hall in Northamptonshire. But although it was a depressing experience, Binney retained his profound and optimistic belief that solutions were always possible. The buildings themselves were not inherently problematic: it was the attitude of their owners. Solutions lay in the imaginative reinterpretation of houses, and their invigoration by a sympathetic scheme of development and refurbishment. In Kit Martin, Binney found a kindred spirit. Binney first met Martin in 1969 at Dingley Hall; by then, Martin had set up practice as an architect in Cambridge. Dingley was a perfect illustration of the Kit Martin method. The house was acquired by Martin not long after he first saw it in 1975. His first task was to

---

[8] Marcus Binney, *Our Vanishing Heritage* (London, 1984), p. 20.

[9] *Ibid.*, p. 26.

[10] *Ibid.*, p. 34.

convert the Elizabethan wing into a home for himself. He then divided the rest of the house into separate apartments – at first fourteen were planned, but this was subsequently reduced to ten. Each were sold in advance, with each of the sales funding the next phase of the work. The model worked and demonstrated that there was life yet in the country house. After Dingley, Kit Martin's next challenge was Gunton in Norfolk, which he was to make his own home. The entire purpose was to show how desperate-seeming cases of country houses apparently on their last legs could in fact be turned around and given renewed purpose by applying thought and care. Binney had drawn attention to the worst examples of mansions on their uppers in a series of SAVE Britain's Heritage reports, including *Tomorrow's Ruins* (1978) and *Silent Mansions* (1981). The Binney and Martin method was summarised in a SAVE publication in 1982 with the Shakespearean title *The Country House: To Be or Not to Be.*

By the early 1980s Binney and Martin reckoned there were, at a conservative estimate, around sixty or seventy country houses that could be rescued using their approach. The emphasis was on looking pragmatically at each situation, even for those houses where the rainwater was gushing down the cantilevered staircase. Two-thirds of the houses highlighted in *Tomorrow's Ruins* had been rescued five years later. The method was not without its detractors. Country house purists may have objected to the way houses were being divided up into separate apartments: a denial of their original design. It was a phenomenon that was evident to the authors of the Gowers' committee's report in 1950, who observed that although "not every house … lends itself to this treatment without loss of character", it could be a "good solution" where the character of a house was able to be preserved.[11] The judicious protection of character was central to Binney and Martin's approach. Sometimes it was necessary to divide houses into separate apartments simply to guarantee that such places remained lived in and loved. Other developers advertised in *Country Life* to find mansions that might similarly be suitable for conversion in this way, but few of them displayed the sensitivity and care shown by Binney and Martin. The key to their approach lay in respecting "the main structural divisions of the house" and retaining its principal features of interest and character.[12] Like a Red Book by Humphry Repton, the landscape format of *To Be or Not to Be* carried Kit Martin's drawings showing how country houses like Barlaston could be

---

[11] Ernest Gowers, *Report of the Committee on Houses of Outstanding Historic or Architectural Interest* (London, 1950), p. 47.

[12] Marcus Binney and Kit Martin, *The Country House: To Be or Not to Be* (London, 1982), p. 123.

11. Sophie Andreae at Barlaston c. 1982 (SAVE Britain's Heritage).

transformed and given new life. The cost, they argued, "need not be very much more than the cost of an equivalent floor area in new good quality housing", meaning that these schemes often did not require the historic buildings council to step in with a grant.[13]

By the early 1980s, therefore, writers such as Marcus Binney were openly recognising that tourism was not always the panacea that readers of Lord Montagu's *The Gilt and the Gingerbread* may have been led to believe. Unless a house also had a good collection, and a fine garden or parkland setting, it was unlikely to succeed on its own terms purely as a visitor attraction. The authors of the Gowers report had also observed that there were many other ways in which country houses could be reused, which went far beyond tourism. These included the use of houses as schools, colleges, seminaries, hospitals, arts centres, hotels, and nursing homes.[14] Some houses had been acquired by local authorities, either to be opened to the public as museums (as at Wollaton in Nottingham) or used as council offices. Companies sometimes bought up mansions for use as their corporate headquarters – after all, older buildings could at this time be purchased at a very inexpensive price compared to purpose-built or new buildings.[15] Binney and Martin did not object to country houses being refashioned for these new purposes, but clearly their preference was for houses to remain as domestic dwellings.

Nevertheless, general increases in car ownership, and in disposal incomes, also meant that the 1970s and 1980s were generally a period of growth for heritage tourism, even if it didn't always feel that way at times when the economy was heading into recession. Lord Montagu was adamant that being open to public access was essential to winning the support of government to the country house cause. "We must play the game", he counselled the attendees of the HHA's AGM in November 1975, by showing that owners "really welcome the public and … really know what public access means". No tax concessions would be possible without such a show of faith in the country house as a visitor destination. This did not mean that non-open houses were unable to join the association, but rather that the requirements of being able to influence government policy meant that the open houses tended to predominate when the association talked publicly of its work. After all, "the Treasury will be sympathetic" to owners if they were "genuinely welcoming people to visit".[16] Hence, when

---

[13]   *Ibid.*, p. 6.
[14]   Gowers, *Report*, pp. 42–48.
[15]   I am grateful to Norman Hudson for this observation.
[16]   HHA Archives, Minutes of the Second AGM, 4 November 1975.

Montagu addressed his fellow peers during the debate on the wealth tax in June 1974, he set out the economic facts. In 1967 there had been eighteen million visits to all heritage properties (ten million to state-owned heritage sites, five million to privately owned houses, and three million to National Trust places). By 1972 this number had almost doubled to thirty-four million. The growth had come mainly from the private sector, since visitor numbers to these places had tripled to fifteen million. Montagu was able to wave the provisional figures for 1973 in front of their lordships: by this time the total number of visits had risen to forty-four million, of which the private sector was responsible for twenty-three million, the National Trust for five and a half million, and state-owned sites for sixteen million. "As your Lordships will see," Montagu added, with some satisfaction, "the biggest growth has in fact been in the private sector, which has gone up 450 per cent, as compared with the others, which have gone up only 60 per cent."[17] The Countryside Commission had been equally enthusiastic in 1968 in endorsing visits to country houses as ways of "spending a day in the countryside". Such houses made excellent destinations not least because they combined indoor attractions – essential, given Britain's unpredictable summer weather – with outdoor attractions such as gardens and parks. Given that seventy per cent of tourists were estimated to use cars, country houses were increasingly accessible, and appealed to a wide range of age groups and demographics. The Commission's report into the tourism potential of country houses encouraged their owners to cultivate this domestic market by introducing a greater variety of facilities, "for example, wildlife, boating on the lakes, guided walks in the grounds and parkland, and riding stables".[18]

Such was the significance of tourism to the early HHA that the first edition of the association's journal carried the results of a survey of the state of country house tourism.[19] The largest of the HHA's member places ran a full six- or seven-day-a-week operation, opening for seven hours a day. Three-quarters of the two hundred or so houses that replied to the survey were not open anywhere near as much as this, advertising themselves as open for just one or two days of the week, typically for four hours. Hugh Tapper, the author of the survey and the HHA's first advisory officer, noted that a third of the houses had experienced difficulties in securing adequate road signage to direct potential

[17] HL Deb. 26 June 1974, vol. 352, col. 1536–1537.
[18] TNA, COU 3/676: Historic Houses Survey: a joint publication by the Countryside Commission and the British Tourist Authority.
[19] Hugh Tapper, 'Survey of Houses Open to the Public', *Historic House* 1:1 (Autumn, 1976), 15–16.

visitors to their front doors, a regular theme for discussion at the association's meetings. Tapper felt that houses needed to raise their game when it came to their spending on marketing, possibly by clubbing together with nearby houses in order "to achieve economy" rather than unnecessarily compete for visitor footfall. Tapper found that a quarter of the houses charged an entrance fee of thirty pence or less, and he was convinced that they were therefore selling themselves short, noting that "compared with other forms of amusement of personal expenditure a higher rate for admission could fairly be obtained even to small properties". This was particularly the case for the thirteen per cent of houses that were open only 'by appointment' for occasional group visits.[20]

A follow-up survey was undertaken later in 1976 by Professor C. W. N. Miles (of the University of Reading). Based again on a postal survey of houses, Miles approached his sample as a diverse group of businesses, all trying to pursue the same goal of keeping a house in a good state of repair, as a lived-in home, sometimes as an attraction for visitors, and always as an inheritance for the next generation. He observed the diversity among houses, dividing them into multiple categories depending on their visitor footfall. At the bottom of the list were the houses that might receive just a few hundred visitors a year. Such houses were likely to employ fewer people and were less likely to be assessed for tax under case 1 of schedule D.[21] At the top of the list were nine of the larger houses, which each received more than a hundred thousand visits every year. These were more likely to be part of larger estates (the median size was seven and a half thousand acres), were more likely to employ staff, and tended to fall under case 1 for tax purposes. All these houses stated that the purpose of opening to the public was to raise funds to contribute to the cost of maintenance. Miles noted that most of the sample were not profitable as

---

[20]   Norman Hudson notes: "Hugh Tapper, the retired Agent of Thoresby in Nottinghamshire, (then a private house and owned by Countess Manvers) was retained by the HHA in its earliest years as the very first Advisory Officer. He rushed round the country giving two-page concise reports summarising his advice as to what people should do. (I think they were charged at £25!) This is one of the first ways in which the HHA was effective in disseminating information, lessons learned from one house being able to be passed on to another." Personal correspondence to the author, 8 June 2023.

[21]   Income and corporation tax were charged according to definitions set out by law in various schedules. Schedule D applied to taxable income that didn't fall under another of the schedules, such as rent (schedule A) or profits from woodlands (schedule B). Case 1 of schedule D related to income from trades, and the significance of paying tax in this category was that it enabled legitimate business costs (such as on repairs) to be offset against income.

such – these businesses tended to make a loss – but that this loss would have been even greater if no public opening had been offered. Around a half of the sample had only opened within the previous eight years (since 1968). Public opening had meant that over a million pounds had been spent on repairs since 1970, an average of £2,905 per house (nearly £18,000 in today's prices). Nearly half of this money had come from reserves, but nearly a third had come from the sale of land. Nearly two-thirds of the sample, however, had received grants, while two-thirds of the staff employed in these businesses serviced catering concessions. There was no guarantee that a profit could be made here; rather this reflected "that visitors like (and probably now expect) to get a cup of tea and a bun". Miles ended his analysis by observing that the next generation of owners would be "influenced by more than sentiment". They would be making decisions about their houses in the context of the national debate about the future of such places, "and where the nation does not make a conscious decision that they should be preserved then they will crumble away".[22]

Surveys like this became increasingly available, enabling owners of historic properties to see what the market was doing, and just as importantly to see what their competitors were up to. In 1977 the English Tourist Board began a series of annual research reports called *Heritage Monitor*, researched and written by Max Hanna. The document sought to provide a helicopter perspective on the "conservation, preservation, and public use of England's architectural heritage". As such, it noted that thousands of buildings continued to be added to the official list: 14,450 in 1976, making 241,550 in total. Among these, there had been 377 applications for full demolition. None of them were for grade I-listed buildings, although the neglect of such important houses as Barlaston Hall, Dingley Hall, and Hylands House was noted. Of the historic buildings and monuments open to public access, the largest proportion (forty-four per cent) were in private hands. Nearly a quarter were held in guardianship by the department of the environment (the successor to the ministry of works), while thirteen per cent were owned by the National Trust (the rest were in local authority ownership). It remained a growth period for heritage tourism with sixteen properties opening regularly for the first time. The average price of admission across all these sites was just thirty-two pence, prompting Hanna to observe that heritage sites represented "bargains indeed in inflationary times". Privately owned houses had seen a seven per cent increase in visitor numbers in 1976, a time when the National Trust's visitor numbers had grown

[22] C. W. N. Miles, 'Historic Houses Survey 1976', *Historic House* 2:3 (Summer, 1978), 5–8.

by just one per cent. This, for Hanna, was entirely because privately owned sites were "usually more vigorously promoted than publicly owned ones". The most visited private sites could command the highest admission prices, with Beaulieu, Leeds Castle, and Woburn able to charge £1.20 per visitor. Overall, Hanna was impressed by the way that England's architectural heritage acted as a magnet for tourists from both home and abroad. "It is a powerful draw for the more educated high spending tourists", he noted, adding that few other factors gave England "such a comparative advantage over other countries".[23] The analysis was deemed sufficiently newsworthy to be covered by *The Daily Telegraph*, which noted the increase in visitors to privately owned houses while also highlighting the potential for tourists to visit churches and other historic properties.[24]

Tourism was therefore a significant issue for country house owners, albeit that it was also extremely hard work. At the annual general meeting of the HHA in November 1977, one disgruntled owner proposed an unusual item of 'any other business'. Mrs Oddie of Heath Hall was so thoroughly exhausted by the strain of keeping her house open to visitors that she suggested a form of country house general strike. All the association's properties, she proposed, should coordinate a nationwide closing of the doors over a bank holiday weekend. The purpose of this lockout would be to "demonstrate to the general public the problem of living and opening a house with unsocial hours and allied difficulties".[25] The proposal for industrial action fell on deaf ears. Indeed, the minutes recorded that Robert Cooke MP, owner of Athelhampton House in Dorset, "replied that he hoped Mrs. Oddie's proposal was a bad dream". Closing doors to commercial income was anathema to Cooke and most of the owners represented in the room. He counselled that it was far better "to continue to keep up the pressure in the way that the Association had in the past", and to show how houses could welcome paying visitors and be active in culture and the arts. Cooke had outlined this more positive perspective on the potential public role of country houses in a report that he prepared for the Conservative party in 1974, *Government and the Quality of Life*, in which he had asserted the role of historic houses as focal points for "the arts, craftsmanship, music and drama".[26]

---

[23] Max Hanna, *English Heritage Monitor* (English Tourist Board, 1977).

[24] 'Churches "A Tourism Asset"', *Daily Telegraph*, 26 May 1977, p. 16.

[25] HHA Archives, Minutes of the Fourth AGM of the Historic Houses Association, 1 Nov. 1977.

[26] Robert Cooke, *Government and the Quality of Life* (London, 1974), p. 8.

The topic of charging was one that Lord Montagu returned to in his vale-dictory address to the HHA's annual meeting in November 1978. Three years earlier he had predicted that houses would have an average admission price of £1 by 1980. This bold statement had been "greeted with disbelief" at the time. Yet he now observed that London Zoo was charging £1.75 for admission, and that admission to football terraces and cinemas typically already cost £1. "Some people say that we are not in the same business," he declaimed, "but I firmly believe we are. We are selling a good day out for the whole family." Families were making choices between sports fixtures, trips to the seaside, or heritage days out. "Those who grasp this message will, I am sure, succeed", he posited. "Those who won't have a grim future."[27] Nevertheless, for many houses tourism had become the saving grace, as British holidaymakers discovered the appeal of country house settings. Inevitably, it meant that houses changed as they extended their offer. William Cash likened the appeal of the 1970s and 1980s country house experience as equivalent to the appeal of the seaside to previous generations. The drives and avenues of Blenheim and Castle Howard in this way operated in much the same way that the esplanades, beaches, and piers of Brighton and Broadstairs did in the early twentieth century. What was now needed therefore was "a resort-like estate with ice-cream, tea rooms, avenues and car parks, a famous garden … or a safari park."[28]

The open embrace of tourism could also, however, have dramatic outcomes, as was seen at Warwick Castle. The Greville family had been granted the ruins of Warwick Castle by James I and had converted the medieval building into a substantial country home. Eighteenth- and nineteenth-century improvements saw Warwick Castle become the byword for luxury in aristocratic living. The castle had opened to public visiting through much of the nineteenth century, such that it had become a tourist attraction before the phrase was in circula-tion. Lord Brooke, the only son of the seventh earl of Warwick, had been one of the groups that Lord Montagu dubbed 'The Magnificent Seven' because of their dominance of country house tourism at the time. Along with Warwick Castle were Blenheim, Inveraray, Longleat, Woburn, Harewood House, and of course Beaulieu. At least a hundred thousand visitors a year was the requisite minimum number of visitors needed to join this exclusive club.[29] The group was made public in May 1975, when it was reported in *The Times* that they

[27] HHA Archives, Minutes of the Fifth AGM of the Historic Houses Association, 29 Nov. 1978.

[28] Cash, *Restoration Heart*, p. 39.

[29] Lord Montagu of Beaulieu, *Wheels Within Wheels*, p. 9.

had set up formally as a cooperative, to join forces to secure publicity for their houses and attract more foreign tourists. There was talk of special vouchers that would provide discounted admission to each of the properties. Lord Tavistock was quoted soberly as saying that cooperation would "bring considerable advantages in production costs and allow much wider distribution of our advertising material ... We are the spearhead of an attack to bring the historic houses of Britain to the attention of overseas visitors." Philip Howard in *The Times* cast more of a wry historical perspective on the issue:

> from these castellated or mullion-windowed strongholds in the Middle Ages some of their ancestors rode out to fight each other or the king and steal the neighbours' sheep. Today they compete for the number of visitors they can attract to their ancestral halls, made more popular with children's playgrounds, cafeterias, and safari parks, where herds of wild motor cars prowl with hungry cameras through the lines of neatly parked animals.[30]

This was a group of houses that were so important to country house tourism – attracting more than a third of all visits to privately owned houses – that they felt the need to form a grouping that stood apart from the Historic Houses Association. All seven were also HHA member properties and would remain so. But the early HHA did not consider itself a marketing organisation as such and did not undertake the sorts of activities carried out by the Magnificent Seven's cooperative.

Brooke was one of the ten founding members of the HHA's executive committee. In that first meeting in November 1973, Lord Brooke cited "the greatly increased cost of repair work because of inflation". He went on to bemoan the creep of modern regulations, such as in being obliged to provide rest rooms and accommodation space for staff and fireproof doors. He was not opposed to such measures but was mindful of the difficulties faced by owners of historic buildings in implementing them.[31] However, Lord Brooke's commitment to the stately home cause was called into question when he started selling parts of the Warwick Castle collection. He was denied an export licence for two views of Warwick Castle by Canaletto, and the local council threatened to deny listed

---

[30]   Philip Howard, 'Magnificent Seven form stately co-op', *The Times*, 2 May 1975, p. 5.

[31]   HHA Archive, Minutes of the Third AGM of the Standing Conference for Historic Houses, 8 Nov. 1973.

building consent for the removal of the Warwick Vase from the conservatory, a piece that originally came from Hadrian's villa at Tivoli.[32]

Then, in 1978, Lord Brooke took the final step. He sold the castle in its entirety and the remainder of its collections to the Tussauds group of family entertainments, which also owned the famous waxworks in London as well as Wookey Hole in Somerset and a tin mine in Cornwall. For £1.5 million Lord Brooke, by this time living in Paris, had divested himself of the family seat, along with all responsibility for its ongoing maintenance and repair. The price reflected the state of the property, which was in significant need of investment, particularly in the south wall. The sale drew much by way of response. A leader in the *Evening Mail* complained that "the money, it appears, means more to Lord Brooke than his heritage or his homeland."[33] Lord Brooke's cousin, Priscilla Greville, declared herself "absolutely horrified" by the sale, which she regarded as "a betrayal of all that the Greville family had stood for over the centuries". Meanwhile Lord Montagu sounded a cautionary note: "I think it is a very sad day when any great family is forced by circumstances to give up a great house like that."[34] Although he had written the textbook on how to monetise a stately home, he knew that "these houses are worth preserving for their own sake, not just to make money".[35] A leader in *The Times* did not hold back from expressing regret at what had happened, and in calling for an enquiry into the fate of the Warwick Vase. But it noted that cases such as this were fortunately rare: most owners devoted themselves to the ongoing care and protection of their houses, at considerable personal cost. The sale of Warwick Castle was therefore a warning sign of the potential dangers facing other houses. Penal rates of taxation could spell the sale of other such properties. "We can have 98 per cent taxes or great houses; in the end we shall not be able to have both."[36]

The Warwick Castle case highlighted the way that independently owned historic houses remained susceptible to decisions motivated more by private interest than the public benefit. Nevertheless, as HHA president, Lord Montagu remained keen to lay the emphasis on the many and varied public purposes that privately held houses served. For this reason, 1978 saw the introduction

[32] 'Export licences withheld from two Canalettos', *The Times*, 16 Nov. 1977, p. 8; 'Council ban on sale of Warwick Castle vase', *The Times*, 4 April 1978, p. 2.

[33] 'Selling a heritage into showbusiness', *Birmingham Evening Mail*, 4 Oct. 1978, p. 6.

[34] Martin Huckerby, 'Dismay and relief over sale of castle', *The Times*, 5 Oct. 1978, p. 6.

[35] Lord Montagu, *Wheels Within Wheels*, p. 10.

[36] 'The Sale of Warwick Castle', *The Times*, 5 Oct. 1978, p. 17.

of the first ever awards for heritage education, which over time would become known as the Sandford Awards. The concept of the awards emerged during the European Year of Architectural Heritage in 1975. Lord Montagu and Michael Saunders Watson of the HHA opened discussions with Lord Sandford, who that year was appointed the president of the Council for Environmental Education. Their aim was to find a way for the educational work underway in country house settings to be recognised. The format of the awards was simple: they were open to any heritage site where a concerted effort was being made to promote education. Owners and custodians were invited to submit details of their work to a panel of judges. The criteria for selection for an award included effective liaison with a local education authority and teachers, and the standards of the educational resources available. Although houses, such as Hagley Hall, were early recipients, the prize was shared among different types of heritage, many in public or charitable hands. Tatton Park, run by Cheshire County Council on behalf of the National Trust, won the award in 1980, having achieved a thirty per cent increase in the number of visits by schoolchildren. The next year Croxteth Country Park in Liverpool secured an award, as did Margram Park, owned and run by West Glamorgan County Council.[37]

Insofar as historic houses fulfilled an educational function, the case might have been strengthened for why their social purpose deserved better support from the state. But the argument was increasingly difficult to make at a time when social problems seemed so endemic. Riots broke out in July 1981 just five miles from Croxteth Park in Liverpool, in Toxteth, mirroring similar instances of unrest in other areas such as Brixton in London, Leeds, and Birmingham. Reviving the fortunes of the depressed inner cities became the special focus of the secretary of state for the environment, Michael Heseltine. It was not urban development, however, that Heseltine discussed when he addressed the HHA's annual general meeting in November 1981. Rather, he used his speech to propose a new approach to government heritage policy. The work of the historic buildings council for England, set up after the Gowers report of 1950, would now be taken over by a new quasi-autonomous public body, or 'quango', as they were known during Margaret Thatcher's first term of office. This body, a historic buildings and monuments commission, would make executive decisions at arm's length from government. It would comprise the operations of the historic buildings council, but also the work of civil servants in the department of the environment, whose removal from direct government employment would contribute to the general drive to reduce the size of the state – a key part of

---

[37] 'Margram Park wins Award', *Port Talbot Guardian*, 11 March 1982, p. 1.

Mrs Thatcher's political programme. In responding to the proposals, the HHA declined to offer a view on the politics of the situation, while naturally pointing out the importance of private owners to the ongoing maintenance of heritage assets. Although owners had been mentioned in the consultation paper, there was a danger that the term was being used to encompass other categories of owner, such as the National Trust or the Church of England. Owners such as these enjoyed tax benefits that were not available to the wholly private owners who formed the membership of the HHA. It was essential, therefore, that the new body should "recognise from the beginning the difficulties" faced by the private owner, who bore the full burden of taxation.[38]

The new-look commission was established under the terms of the 1983 National Heritage Act and began operating from 1984.[39] As a sign of the government's commitment to the cause of private ownership, Lord Montagu, the HHA's founding president, was appointed its first chairman. Montagu later recalled that he was selected for the role partly for his commercial experience, although it also helped that he did not have the personal conflicts of his rival candidates (in Jennifer Jenkins' case, being the spouse of an opposition politician; in the duke of Gloucester's case, being a working member of the royal family). Just as Montagu's flair for marketing and public relations had helped launch the HHA a decade earlier, so he could also take the credit for rebranding the 'Historic Buildings and Monuments Commission (England)' as English Heritage, and for commissioning its distinctive red-on-white crenelated logo, designed by Dick Negus.[40] English Heritage continued the work of grant-funding private owners; indeed the proportion of grants going to secular causes increased by a third in the first few years of English Heritage's operation, as its chief executive, Peter Rumble, reported to *Historic House* magazine in 1986.[41]

In the space of ten years, therefore, the fate of country houses had shifted radically. Its standard bearer, Lord Montagu, no longer had to worry about such places becoming 'roofless ruins' given how many of them had been rescued and restored back to use. Moreover, Montagu was now the single most important representative of the built heritage in the country, as the chair of the government's newest and most powerful heritage agency. After the dark

---

[38] 'Organisation of Ancient Monuments and Historic Buildings in England', *Historic House* 6:1 (Spring, 1982), 19–20.

[39] Simon Thurley, *Men from the Ministry: How Britain Saved its Heritage* (New Haven and London, 2013), pp. 250–251.

[40] Lord Montagu, *Wheels within Wheels*, pp. 228–231.

[41] Peter Rumble, 'Public Money for Private Houses', *Historic House* 10:1 (Spring, 1986), 13–15.

days of *Destruction*, the country house stood poised at the edge of a new era of recovery and revival. It is to this revival that the rest of this book will now turn, in a series of chapters that abandons a strictly chronological approach to consider instead some of the general themes of the revival of country houses over the last half century.

Part Two
Revival

6

In trust for the nation

One index of the revival in fortunes of privately owned country houses from the mid-1970s was the sharp fall after this point in the number of houses being offered to the National Trust. Those mansion properties that are nowadays held 'in trust for the nation' by either of the UK's National Trusts are mainly legacies of the post-war slump in country house fortunes in the 1940s and 1950s. Compared to this earlier phase of growth, relatively few mansion properties have been acquired by either of the Trusts since the conditions for country house owners improved so markedly after the finance acts of 1975 and 1976.

Perhaps we should not be so surprised by this. In many ways the high period of country house acquisition by the National Trust, from the 1940s to the early 1970s, was an aberration from its founding mission.[1] When the Trust was established in 1895, its focus was not so much on houses, or even on built heritage more generally, but on land and landscape. The social housing campaigner Octavia Hill is often presented as the Trust's founding spirit, given the missionary zeal with which she pursued her energetic campaigns to improve the lives of the poorest in society. Yet at the very heart of the National Trust was an idea about legal rights to property and ownership, which was wholly original, indeed radical, in its conception. For this, the Trust's founding chairman, the lawyer Robert Hunter, deserved full intellectual credit.

The ability to hold land in trust was not itself original. Such concepts dated back to the Middle Ages, developed, it was said, to ensure that the estates of crusading knights were protected during their long periods of absence. Houses and estates might be placed into trust in situations where an heir inherited before his majority, or where the owner was incapacitated because of illness or some other misfortune. Trustees for estates took responsibility for the property and sought to manage it not for personal gain but in the interests of beneficiaries. Landed estates could be further bound by the practice of entail, where an

---

[1] By the early 1970s, the Trust had already acquired three-quarters of the two hundred mansion properties that it owns today.

owner was cast as merely a temporary custodian, holding property on behalf of as-yet-unborn heirs. The arrangement meant that entailed estates could not be broken up by a single heir selling land to meet a short-term need. Such were the mechanisms by which landowners had kept their estates intact over many centuries and were the protections that the National Trust sought to imitate in the way it was established and given legal authority.

Hunter's particular innovation lay in his concept of land being held in trust not for the benefit of the members of a single family, but rather for the entire nation. Where Hill had initially suggested the name 'Commons and Gardens Trust' for this new entity, reflecting her campaigning preoccupations in the 1880s, Hunter operated on a bigger intellectual and conceptual canvas. In his mind there was no restriction on the type of asset that could be held in trust for the nation – the only criteria set out in the Trust's founding charter of 1895 were that the property had to be of natural beauty or historic interest. These assets were then effectively entailed to the nation by means of statute in 1907, which gave the Trust the legal power to hold its assets inalienably. After that date, the only way to break the inalienability of those assets that had been given this special status was to seek a separate countermanding act of parliament. Setting the bar so high in this way effectively locked assets in for all time, or 'forever, for everyone', as today's National Trust (in England, Wales, and Northern Ireland) summarises it.

Hunter had first conceived of the idea of such a property-holding entity when advising Hill on the possible options for saving a mansion property, Sayes Court in Deptford, London. But it wasn't primarily the fate of houses and estates that was foremost in Hill and Hunter's minds when they developed their early thinking about what would eventually become the National Trust. For Hill, the driving issue was the alleviation of poverty through access to green space and nature, and the spiritual needs of the poorest in society. Hunter's motivations were bound up with his earlier work for one of the country's first preservationist organisations, the Commons Preservation Society (CPS). Insofar as the CPS sought to 'save' portions of landed estates, this was principally to prevent common land from being developed. The movement to protect commons often pitched local agitators against the interests of landlords. The case that spurred the CPS into existence was that of Wimbledon Common, where earl Spencer threatened to carve the common into two – with one part as a public recreation ground but the rest developed as a private park and housing.

Although the Trust didn't set out to save country houses, nor were such properties completely off limits. However, the sheer expense of rescuing one house in 1907 – Barrington Court in Somerset – was sufficient to deter it from looking at mansion properties for the next three decades. If the early Trust took any interest in domestic architecture, it was on a smaller, more vernacular scale, such as at the Old Post Office at Tintagel, acquired in 1903. The Trust's early houses blended into the grain of the landscape. After all, the Trust's function, according to an early manifesto, was to preserve "natural features of animal and plant life" as well as to look after the ancient buildings and monuments that made up a treasured local scene. In so doing, the Trust had no interest in acquisition for its own sake, but rather as a "patriotic interest in those things, which in the crush of our commercial enterprise and in the poverty of landholders or in the lack of local care, run risk of passing away".[2]

By the early 1930s, the loss of so many mansion properties to decay or active demolition led to calls for the Trust to exercise its role as the saviour 'of last resort' of important heritage buildings. Leading the charge was Philip Kerr, marquess of Lothian, who made the case at the charity's annual general meeting in 1934 for the Trust to act as rescuer of country houses. The immediate barrier to this was the complex nature of estate ownership, in particular the terms of the strict settlements under which so many country houses existed. Changes to the National Trust's statutory powers in 1937 and 1939 cleared the way for the Trust to take on estate property, including vast swathes of farmland surrounding mansion properties. Lord Lothian left his own estate, Blickling in Norfolk, to the Trust in his will. When he died in New York in 1940, Blickling became one of the first mansion properties to be acquired under the Trust's new country houses scheme.

As houses were returned to their owners following military or educational occupation during the war, protection by the National Trust was increasingly seen as a way of preserving a family's association with a particular property. A run of important country house properties was acquired by the Trust during and after the second world war, among them Cliveden in Buckinghamshire (1942), Killerton in Devon (1944), Petworth in West Sussex (1947), and Attingham Park in Shropshire (1953). Sometimes these acquisitions were part of the settlement of tax liabilities following an estate duty charge. In these circumstances, National Land Fund resources were used to replenish treasury coffers with the value of the tax revenue forgone. Both Ickworth in Suffolk in 1956 and

---

[2] 'Its Aims and Works': early National Trust fundraising leaflet. Reprinted in Ben Cowell, *Robert Hunter: Co-Founder and 'Inventor' of the National Trust* (Stroud, 2013), p. 19. See also Ben Cowell, 'For the Benefit of the Nation: Politics and the Early National Trust', in Elizabeth Baigent and Ben Cowell (eds), *Octavia Hill, Social Activism and the Remaking of British Society* (London, 2016), pp. 295–316.

Hardwick Hall in Derbyshire in 1959 were acquired by the Trust through this route. The National Land Fund had been established by Hugh Dalton in 1946 as an endowment to buy land and property in memory of the war dead, or, in Dalton's words, a "thank-offering for victory, and a war memorial which many would think finer than any work of art in stone or bronze".[3] It was perhaps surprising that more houses were not saved in this way, although the slashing of the Land Fund's budget to just ten million pounds in 1957 was indicative of a preference within government for private-sector solutions to the country house problem.[4]

Nearly forty properties were given outright to the National Trust in the 1950s. The author of an article in the HHA's journal in spring 1977 wondered if readers would think of the Trust as a "monster with a cavernous mouth and an insatiable hunger", which "will not be satisfied until all the great country houses in England, Wales and Northern Ireland belong to it". The piece put forward an alternative perspective, pointing out that just eight country houses had been acquired by the Trust since 1972.[5] And it was true that from the mid-1960s the number of houses being offered to the Trust diminished markedly. Larger estates were still being offered and accepted. Knightshayes in Devon came to the Trust as a gift in 1973, as did the Welsh estate of Erddig. But estates on the scale of Wimpole (acquired 1976) or Kingston Lacy in Dorset (acquired 1982) were noticeable for being all the rarer compared to the situation twenty years earlier. True, Dunham Massey in Cheshire (1976), Plas Newydd in Anglesey (1976), and Cragside in Northumberland (1977) all came to the National Trust after 1975. But the number of properties received as a gift had practically halved compared to the 1950s, and it would fall to a trickle of fewer than a dozen by the 1980s and in subsequent years. The in-lieu route, which had been the method for how many houses had passed to the Trust in the years after the war, was increasingly used only sparingly, if at all. The article in the HHA's journal posited the view that it was in the Trust's interests, as well as in the interests of the nation, for country houses to remain in private hands. Readers were assured that the Trust would continue to make representations against developments such as the proposed wealth tax of the mid-1970s. Jack Boles, the Trust's director general, was quoted as saying that "the Trust wants owners of

---

[3]   Hugh Dalton, *High Tide and After: Memoirs 1945–1960* (London, 1962), p. 118.

[4]   Marcus Binney and Kit Martin, *The Country House: To Be or Not to Be* (London, 1982), p. 11.

[5]   'The National Trust', *Historic House* 1:3 (Spring, 1977), 24–25.

historic houses to win their battle". The Trust was there, he said, "as a possible solution to fall back on" if things did not work out.

The appearance of a Sotheby's auction marquee on the front lawn of Mentmore House in Buckinghamshire in May 1977 symbolised for many exactly the sort of crisis for which the National Trust was the potential solution. The Trust did not intervene here, however, and instead the Mentmore sale precipitated one of the most far-sighted policy responses by government to concerns at the loss of country house heritage. The creation of the National Heritage Memorial Fund (NHMF) in 1980 provided a solution for houses and collections like Mentmore that were under threat, albeit this sort of situation was by now becoming much rarer. The Mentmore case therefore highlighted the existence of another 'nuclear option' for country houses: the possibility of the government stepping in as rescuer at last resort.

Mentmore, with its fine collection, was the creation of Baron de Rothschild in the middle of the nineteenth century. A century later, the house had descended through marriage to the earl of Rosebery. The death of the sixth earl in May 1974 left the family with a hefty tax liability. The earl's successor opened talks with the government soon after with a view to the house and its contents being offered to the nation in lieu of tax. An idea emerged that Mentmore might become another outpost of the V&A museum, which had also been the solution for houses such as Ham House, Osterley, and Apsley House, all located in the greater London area. In February 1976, Mentmore was offered for sale to the government at the vastly discounted price of two million pounds. Government prevarication, prompted by fears of the ongoing costs involved in looking after a place such as this, led to a period in which private funds were sought to underwrite the arrangement with the V&A. But by early 1977 it was becoming clear that no straightforward source of funding was available. Lord Rosebery's tax deadline was fast looming, so on 19 January 1977 Sotheby's announced that the contents would be sold. The threats that now faced the house were significant enough for Marcus Binney's SAVE Britain's Heritage group to go to print with a pamphlet, *SAVE Mentmore for the Nation*, in February 1977. Binney also commissioned Norman Hudson to prepare a report on the feasibility of opening Mentmore to the public.[6] It was to no avail. The government's mind was settled, and in so doing it lost out on "one of the missed bargains of the century", as John Young described it in *The Times* on 19 May 1977.[7]

---

[6] Information from Norman Hudson, 8 June 2023.
[7] John Cornforth, *The Country Houses of England 1948–1998* (London, 1998), pp. 117–118; Arthur Jones, *Britain's Heritage: The Creation of the National Heritage*

The sale held by Sotheby's between 18 and 27 May 1977 raised six and a quarter million pounds – more than three times the amount that it had been offered to the government for a year earlier. The auction was a spectacular occasion. James Miller was part of the Sotheby's team that oversaw the sale and remembered the roads from London to Buckinghamshire being "clogged with traffic": "the press was camped out in the park, and the marquee for the first time equipped with telephones to allow worldwide buyers to participate in the bidding."[8] It was quite the most lucrative country house sale that had been seen in some time. The family retained some important pieces and returned them to Dalmeny House on their Scottish estate. Two significant pieces of furniture and a Gainsborough were acquired for the nation at the sale, at a price far higher than what they might have cost had the initial offer from Lord Rosebery been accepted. The National Gallery used its own resources to buy the important picture of Madame de Pompadour by Drouais.

The Mentmore sale led to a round of debate and commentary about the national attitude towards cultural heritage. By not accepting the house when it could have done, the government was judged to have been short-sighted in its approach. As *Historic House* magazine observed, the house and its collection could have been acquired at a bargain price, the cost of which could have been recovered by opening the house as a visitor attraction and then "selling off surplus pieces in rooms which would not be open to the public".[9] The treasury's approach to dealing with Mentmore was therefore directly criticised, and concerns were raised that the existing mechanisms were simply not strong enough to respond in cases when important heritage was under such direct threat as a result of tax liabilities. James Callaghan's government's response was a proposal for a National Heritage Fund which would be an emergency resource for situations like Mentmore, where a sudden rescue package needed to be found at short notice to ensure that a house and its collection could survive intact. The Fund was eventually founded under Mrs Thatcher's government in April 1980. The National Heritage Memorial Fund, as it was eventually titled, was an evolution of the National Land Fund, in that it was also conceived as an endowment to accumulate heritage assets for the benefit of the nation. The National

Memorial Fund (London, 1985), p. 40.

[8] James Miller, 'The rise and decline of the country house sale 1977–2020: from Mentmore to Chatsworth – a personal reflection', in Terence Dooley and Christopher Ridgway (eds), *Country House Collections: Their Lives and Afterlives* (Dublin, 2021), pp. 156–172, p. 158.

[9] 'Mentmore for the Nation?', *Historic House* 1:3 (Spring, 1977), 29–30.

Trust quickly proved to be a major beneficiary, with the memorial fund helping to transfer Canons Ashby in Northamptonshire into Trust ownership in
1981 and to provide an endowment for the National Trust for Scotland for Hill
House in Helensburgh in 1982.

Calke Abbey in Derbyshire was another house that only came to the Trust
after a last-minute intervention by the government. Marcus Binney noted that
this was "one of the very few major houses which had never been featured in
Country Life".[10] The house was unknown to Binney until he happened to spot
it on a map in November 1978 and went to look. "I walked slowly up over fields
until I reached the edge of the park, and there below, surrounded on all sides
by a vast park, was the house: beyond was a great lake, and to the right a little
estate church perched on a hill." But he got no further, deterred by a shoot,
the presence of which was heralded by a "tweedy figure with a shotgun under
this arm". It was some years before Binney was able to return to find out more
about this hidden gem of a house. Calke was built in the early years of the
eighteenth century but received a neoclassical makeover a century later with a
new front by William Wilkins. It was the interiors that so intrigued Binney and
other architectural historians including Gervase Jackson-Stops of the National
Trust. The house was a treasure trove. The drawing room had been largely
undisturbed since the Victorian era, with the furniture a riot of colour: "fresh
yellow and gold wallpaper, a warm pink carpet, a set of bright yellow dam-
ask sofas and chairs, and other chairs embroidered with pink and red flowers
on a pink background." Throughout the house, the collecting instincts of the
Harper-Crewe family meant a jumble of extraordinary artworks: paintings by
Landseer and Ruysdael, bronze age swords, Lamerie silver. Far from being the
mere "skiploads of junk", as Lord Vaizey witheringly dismissed it, the house was
a menagerie of miracles. For Jackson-Stops, even the timber stores recalled "a
scene from Diderot's *Encloypédie*", with a variety of tools hanging from every
hook, and drawers stuffed full of hinges and other assorted ephemera.[11]

Binney and his colleagues rushed to publish a sequence of *Country Life* articles on Calke, further raising its public profile. The house had been offered 'to
the nation' by the family to satisfy an eight-million-pound tax liability. This
had been accepted in principle, but the government was not prepared to provide the endowment that the National Trust also required. Howard Colvin said
that, unless the government relented and found the financial means to effect
a transition into National Trust ownership, the *Country Life* articles would be

[10] Marcus Binney, *Vanishing Heritage* (London, 1984), p. 74.
[11] *Ibid.*, p. 77.

Calke's obituary.[12] The pressure in the media mounted, stirred up by a campaign from Binney's SAVE that insisted *This Magical House Must Be Saved Intact*. In *The Times*, James Lees-Milne offered the thought that while Calke was not in the same league as Belton or Kedleston (which were both also in the process of being acquired by the Trust), the house was nonetheless likely to prove of enormous public interest, in the same way that Stubbs tended to attract more crowds than Rubens in the National Gallery. The relentless lobbying wore down a government not otherwise known for its generosity in releasing public funds. Nigel Lawson's first budget speech as chancellor of the exchequer in March 1983 contained a single commitment to increased public spending, which was funding for the rescue of Calke.

The saving of Calke Abbey by the National Trust was a victory for heritage campaigners. But the longer-term implications were less promising. Michael Saunders Watson, by now serving as president of the HHA, noted at its annual general meeting in 1984 that the saving of Calke alongside that of Belton House may have been a success story for the nation but did not bode well for private owners more generally, who would have preferred instead the right conditions in which they could "continue to live in and manage their properties".[13] The Trust said much the same thing when its Director General, Sir Angus Stirling, in its annual report for 1985, expressed the general preference for seeing historic houses "remain in the ownership of the families who cared for them in the past". The Trust therefore pledged to continue to support the sorts of legislative changes that might make that possible, principally meaning tax changes. Stirling acknowledged that fiscal conditions were better in 1985 than they had been ten years earlier, and therefore predicted (correctly, as it would turn out) that "the number of houses being offered to the Trust may reduce".[14]

The Trust would continue to take on country houses after Calke, but the number of such places being offered to the charity noticeably slowed from this point. Nevertheless, problems at houses such as Belton, Fyvie Castle, Canons Ashby, Weston Park, and Nostell Priory meant a great deal of pressure on the newly formed NHMF. In March 1985 the NHMF was granted an additional twenty-five million pounds to address some of these problems. Francis Curzon, the third viscount Scarsdale, was quoted in *The Field* in 1984 as being of the view that his family home, Kedleston in Derbyshire, was "ten times more

---

[12] *Ibid.*, p. 81.

[13] Minutes of the Eleventh AGM of the Historic Houses Association, 10 Nov. 1984.

[14] National Trust Annual Report for 1985, quoted in Robert Hewison, *The Heritage Industry* (London, 1987), p. 71.

important than Calke". When he succeeded to the property in 1977, he was determined that it would not go the same way as Mentmore had in the same year. Nine years of negotiation followed, until the house and park were saved in August 1986 through the intercession of the NHMF and the National Trust. Lord Scarsdale agreed to gift the house and park to the Trust, along with a million-pounds-worth of art and cash. The NHMF stepped in with an offer of £13.5 million towards the purchase of furniture and art, while the Trust promised to put a million pounds from its reserves towards the acquisition as well as to raise another two million pounds in contribution.[15]

Another trend that emerged was for the Trust to take on the grounds of country house properties, without assuming responsibility for the building. Sheringham in Norfolk was acquired by the Trust in 1987 with help from the NHMF, the Countryside Commission and Norfolk County Council. The house was immediately leased to a private occupant, while the Trust took control of the publicly accessible parkland, a rare survival of a landscape based on an original Red Book design by Humphry Repton in 1812. The mid-nineteenth-century gardens of Biddulph Grange were acquired in 1988, again with the assistance of the NHMF. The internationally important gardens of Stowe House in Buckinghamshire were acquired in 1990 with the help of an anonymous benefactor, as well as an NHMF grant and a public appeal. The house at Stowe remained in use as a school, as it had since the early 1920s. Meanwhile, the landscape at Croome, Lancelot Brown's first major commission, was acquired by the Trust in 1996 by means of a grant from the newly created Heritage Lottery Fund.

Houses acquired by the Trust since the 1990s have tended to be smaller and quirkier than those acquired in previous decades. The social history of such places has sometimes been more important than their architectural merit. The unique sixteen-sided house A La Ronde in Devon was purchased in 1991 through an NHMF grant. Greenway, also in Devon, was a villa-type mansion acquired mainly for its association with the crime novelist Agatha Christie. Red House in Bexleyheath, south London, was acquired for its close association with William Morris. Three historic houses that had been turned into luxury hotels (Bodysgallen near Llandudno, Middlethorpe Hall near York, and Hartwell House in Buckinghamshire) were given to the Trust by a private benefactor in the early 2000s. The only major country houses of any size and significance acquired by the Trust in the last thirty years have been Tyntesfield in Somerset in 2002, and Vanbrugh's Seaton Delaval in Northumberland in 2009.

[15] 'Kedleston: Secured for the Nation', *Historic House* 10:2 (Summer, 1986), 24–27.

A significant factor in whether houses remained in private hands was the capital taxation framework. As noted previously, the position changed dramatically in 1975 when the old estate duty, a tax on death, was replaced by capital transfer tax (CTT), a charge on any gift whether made in the lifetime of the donor or at the point of inheritance. The full impact of CTT on historic houses was ameliorated by the concessions granted in 1975 and 1976: the ability to seek a conditional waiver of the CTT charge by opening to the public, or the ability to create a maintenance fund, free of a tax charge, that could generate the income needed to pay repair bills into the longer term. Where the establishment of a maintenance fund was at first a one-way street, improvements to their functioning followed in 1981 when taking capital out of a fund became possible.

Few imagined that the CTT system would change any time soon – after all, the old estate duty had lasted for eighty years. But in his budget of 1986 the Conservative chancellor of the exchequer, Nigel Lawson, replaced CTT with inheritance tax (IHT). IHT in many ways mirrored the former estate duty, except that the duty to pay the tax now fell on the beneficiary rather than the deceased's estate. A tax-free arrangement was now available in the form of a potentially exempt transfer (PET). A PET made it possible for property to be passed to an heir free of inheritance tax provided that the donor continued to live for the next seven years.

While there remained the risk that the donor could die within the seven-year period, the new system placed the onus onto owners to plan for their succession. An owner who encouraged their heir to take an active interest in the house, perhaps by joining the HHA's successors' group, could hand the property over in good time. The smart policy for historic properties now became to live at the house for no more than around three decades. This was enough time for heirs to appear; by passing their property on before they were too long in the tooth, owners could effectively 'retire', knowing that the family home was in good hands. Any attempt by the donors to continue to live at the property would be regarded as a 'gift with reservation' and could nullify the tax advantages if adequate rent was not paid for those reserved benefits. The HHA began running seminars on the theme of succession, the first being at Eastnor Castle in 1986, called 'Our Heritage and the Next Generation'. James Hervey-Bathurst, the heir to Eastnor, summarised his advice to others in his position by explaining that,

> running a stately home and estate today can be a career. It is full time, demanding and, in my view, should have an age limit imposed. We, the heirs

promise that we will hand over when our turn comes, but please, parents, make sure that we get something worth keeping.[16]

The alternative to a direct handover of property from parent to child in this way was to find an alternative ownership structure for the longer term. Here, one option was to establish family property within a trust. A trust was simply a situation where one or more trustees stood as proxies to represent the owner's interests, in situations where that owner might not necessarily be best placed to make their own decisions. The legal changes of the mid-1970s made it possible for houses, their contents, and their surrounding lands to be established in the form of charitable trusts. So-called gifts of public benefit would see ownership pass from individual owners into the hands of a group of charitable trustees. CTT would be waived on this transfer, provided that the Charity Commission was satisfied that a minimum level of public access was offered. Such an arrangement was generally a one-way ticket: once property had been transferred into the hands of trustees, it was unlikely to unwind and revert to being in private freehold ownership again.[17]

Levels of capital taxation in the mid-1970s were such that the charity route proved viable for some major houses. This was helped by the generous attitude of the Charity Commissioners, who chose not to object to arrangements where a family might continue living in a house long after it had been transferred into a charitable trust (provided, of course, that the family paid a market rent for the accommodation). Nor did the commissioners take issue with instances where boards of trustees of charitable houses included representatives of the families whose property had been divested in the creation of the trust. As Marcus Binney and Kit Martin observed, such concessions on the part of the commissioners were "worthwhile to produce so great a public gain".[18] The charitable trust route sometimes resulted from a refusal of the National Trust to take on a property. Burghley in Lincolnshire was one such house. When it became clear that the National Trust was not going to take on the house and its collection, the family set themselves up as an independent charitable trust. Under this arrangement, the family could continue to live at the property. Arundel, too, became a charitable trust in 1975, after the National Trust insisted on an endowment that was five times more than the Charity Commission had recommended.[19]

[16] 'The Next Generation', *Historic House* 10:3 (Autumn, 1986), 30–33.

[17] Binney and Martin, *The Country House*, p. 19.

[18] *Ibid.*

[19] David Littlejohn, *The Fate of the English Country House* (Oxford, 1997), p. 125.

The need for an endowment was well understood by the Trust. By now, the Trust had codified its endowment requirements into a formula for calculating the minimum amount that would be needed before the charity could even begin to contemplate taking on freehold possession of a mansion property. The so-called 'Chorley Formula', named after Roger Chorley, Trust chairman from 1991, looked at the typical annual outgoings of a property, built in a margin for the likelihood of substantial repairs once every thirty or forty years, and then added some more for contingencies.[20] Very roughly, it often meant that the Trust required income-producing assets equivalent to the market value of a property before it was willing to take on its custodianship. This prudent and conservative financial approach was essential to ensuring that the Trust did not overreach itself or take on too many properties that it then was required to maintain in perpetuity. Private charitable trusts had the same need for long-term financial endowments. Leeds Castle had a £1.4 million kitty after its charitable trust was established in 1974. When the Chatsworth charity trust was established in 1981, a Poussin was sold to put £1.65 million into the reserves for the ongoing care of the house. The NHMF provided endowments that helped to establish some important charitable foundations set up for houses in the 1970s and 80s, among them Weston Park in Shropshire, Burton Constable in East Yorkshire, and Hopetoun House near Edinburgh.

One advantage of houses striking out on their own as independent charities was that the house could continue to benefit from farming incomes, where the surrounding estate remained in private hands. The National Trust was a significant owner of farmland but tended to derive its income from rents rather than in-hand farming (although Wimpole in Cambridgeshire was one place where the Trust continued to farm the estate directly after taking it on in the mid-1970s). The benefits of the charitable trust model were actively debated at the HHA's first seminar, organised for the day before its first AGM in October 1974.[21] The major disadvantage of the charitable trust route was the loss of control. As the chairman of the HHA's taxation and political committee, Anthony Furse, remarked in *Historic House* magazine in 1985, the creation of a charitable trust invariably meant a house and its collection falling "absolutely

---

[20]   The formula is reproduced in Francis Fulford, *Bearing Up: The Remarkable Survival of the Landed Estate* (London, 1998), p. 54. Fulford explained that he included it to "amuse readers, with houses big or small, who, on a wet afternoon, wished to while away the time working out how big an endowment the National Trust would require to take over their property".

[21]   Minutes of the First AGM of the Historic Houses Association, 23 Oct. 1974.

out of the family's control; preservation of the asset has been given priority at the expense of family interests". Families could retain an interest in the house, but on a non-profit, arms' length basis only. Furse outlined the different forms of charitable trust mechanism that could be deployed: if not wholesale transfer, then it was possible to lease property to a charity for a time-limited period (as at Knebworth), or to create a term charity lasting only for a limited period. There was also the partial option, such as where a charitable trust was created for a single asset, whether this was a bridge in the park, a small folly, or a set of objects in the collection.[22]

Furse cited the example of Thirlestane. Here, Gerald Maitland-Carew had inherited the castle in 1970, along with "an estate of approximately 1,500 acres, the contents of the house, plus a tax bill for full death duties". He also inherited a building that was in an advanced state of decrepitude. One night in the winter of 1972, not long after Maitland-Carew had left his career in the army to live full-time at Thirlestane, a grand piano had fallen through the floor of the morning room owing to the extent of the dry rot in the beams. The National Trust for Scotland declined to take the house unless everything else – land and collections – was given alongside it. Maitland-Carew sought help with the urgent repair bills and was at first turned down before being given five thousand pounds as a contribution to a feasibility study. It led to a "horrifying report" that pulled no punches in relation to the work that was needed. Having funded the feasibility study, the historic buildings council then generously found fifty thousand pounds towards the first phase of the work. When it was then discovered that the principal tower of the building was moving and threatened to topple backwards into the main part of the castle, the historic buildings council found spare funds for the emergency remediation work. By 1982 the house was in the best shape that it had been for a decade, and redecoration work had begun to the interiors. A kitchen was converted to a tearoom, and public conveniences were installed for the first time. Budgeting for twenty thousand visitors in his first year, Gerald Maitland-Carew was shocked to receive just a quarter of this amount. With the recessionary winds of 1983 blowing, he cast around for a solution to the problem that the upkeep of Thirlestane was simply beyond his means. Thanks to the lawyer Douglas Connell, a bespoke charitable trust was created, formed of three-quarters of the castle, its entire contents, and thirty-eight acres of land. Gerald retained a wing of the house and a large lawn. Of the seven trustees, Gerald would nominate one to be chairman while the remainder would be appointed by government. The model worked, so that

[22]   Anthony Furse, 'Charitable Intention', *Historic House* 9:2 (Summer, 1985), 17–19.

by the end of its first year Gerald wrote: "By some miracle a great national treasure has been saved for the nation through good advice, help and hard work, so that future generations of visitors can enjoy this wonderful family home."[23]

For Anthony Furse, however, there remained a sadness when a house fell out of family ownership in this way:

> above all, the continuing involvement of the family using and living in a house is a great attraction to the non-specialist visitor who does not always appreciate the orderly perfection of impeccable interiors in quite the same way as the connoisseur. Well-arranged flowers, logfires, a sleeping dog, random cushions, current newspapers and books, evidence of children, leave a pleasing personal impression.

This remained the prevailing view among many heritage professionals. Even the secretary to the NHMF, Brian Lang, would concede that moving a house into a trust, or gifting it to the National Trust, was never the optimal outcome, and was, in some ways, an admission of failure. Far better for the house to remain in private hands. "The heart of an historic house", wrote Lang, "is its family; it is the family which gives the house its meaning ... The goal for important houses must be to retain the house, contents and family together, as an entity."[24] One way in which this could be guaranteed was by earning revenues from commercial activities such as film and television work. Another was by selling the family silver – the collections that adorned the walls of country houses. The next two chapters examine these two phenomena, which have been central themes of the revitalisation of many country houses in the last fifty years.

---

[23] Gerald Maitland-Carew, 'A Secure Future for Thirlestane', *Historic House* 8:4 (Winter, 1984), 21–23.

[24] Brian Lang, 'Kedleston: Secured for the Nation', *Historic House* 10:2 (Summer, 1986), 24–27, at 25.

7

To the manor reborn

The plot of one of the most popular BBC television comedies of the late 1970s and early 1980s hinged upon the fate of a minor country house and estate. *To the Manor Born* was first broadcast on 30 September 1979 and from the beginning the show received consistently high viewing figures.[1] The narrative arc of the series would have been familiar to anyone who had taken an interest in what had happened to country houses over the course of the previous century. In the opening episode, recently widowed Audrey fforbes-Hamilton took control of Grantleigh Manor, the ancestral home with which her family had been associated for four hundred years. She discovered that her late husband's debts had put the house at risk. She subsequently lost the house at auction to Richard DeVere, whose personal fortune derived from the company he founded, Cavendish Foods. Despite the pedigree implied by these names, DeVere in fact represented new money, having risen from roots in the East End of London. Audrey resented his ascendancy as lord of the manor and looked on, with disapproval, from her new home – a cottage on the estate.

The final episode of the first series of *To the Manor Born* was watched by nearly twenty-four million people, making it the fourth most popular television event of the decade.[2] The show was recommissioned for a further two series, before it finally ended in 1981. The success of the situation comedy showed, perhaps, that the UK television-viewing public intuitively understood distinctions between old and new money, and the humorous potential in the reversal of traditional class roles. The series appealed to the same underlying consciousness of British class culture that had driven the success of films such as Joseph Losey's 1971 adaptation of L. P. Hartley's *The Go-Between*, or the television drama *Upstairs, Downstairs*, first broadcast in the same year. *The Go-Between*, filmed at Melton Constable Hall in Norfolk, used the *mise-en-scène* of

---

[1] Although this may also have had something to do with the fact that the BBC's main competitor, ITV, was off air at the time of the transmission of the first episode, due to prolonged industrial action.

[2] See <https://www.comedy.co.uk/tv/to_the_manor_born/trivia/> [accessed 9 Sept. 2023].

an Edwardian country house to tell the story of a love affair that crossed class lines. The film was a critical and box office success: Harold Pinter's screenplay won a British Academy Film Award, while Margaret Leighton was nominated for an Oscar for her role as the matriarch of the house. Meanwhile, the co-creators of *Upstairs, Downstairs*, Jean Marsh and Eileen Atkins, had originally conceived of it as a drama set in an English country house and called *Behind the Green Baize Door*. The idea was that the show would be as interested in the goings-on in the servants' hall as it was in the conversations taking place in the saloon or drawing room. By the time *Upstairs, Downstairs* had made it to television screens the action had been relocated to a townhouse in Belgravia, with Marsh herself taking a role as the housemaid Rose Buck.

The Go-Between and *Upstairs, Downstairs* both demonstrated the popularity of film and television adaptations that dwelled on class and class differences. A further illustration of this would be provided by the 1981 Granada Television adaptation of Evelyn Waugh's *Brideshead Revisited*. Jeremy Irons and Anthony Andrews were in the leading roles as Charles Ryder and Sebastian Flyte. They were joined by a cast drawn from British acting aristocracy, among them Laurence Olivier, John Gielgud, Claire Bloom, and John Le Mesurier. Filming in 1979 and 1980 had been interrupted, first by an ITV technicians' strike and then by Jeremy Irons' casting in Karel Reisz's film of *The French Lieutenant's Woman* (1981), in which he starred alongside Meryl Streep. So pivotal was Irons and his character to the entire series, which was narrated in Charles Ryder's voice, that the filming schedule was held up to accommodate him. *Brideshead Revisited* was another drama based on class distinctions, with much of the tension arising from Ryder's fascination with the world of the aristocratic Marchmains. The novel was originally published in 1944, and when it was reissued in 1959 the preface carried a comment by Waugh on the despoliation of "our chief national artistic achievement" by the hand of tourism and leisure: "Brideshead today would be open to trippers, its treasures rearranged by expert hands and the fabric better maintained than it was by Lord Marchmain." The saving of the country house through tourism and leisure left Waugh presenting the novel to a post-war generation as a "panegyric preached over an empty coffin".[3]

It was a further irony, therefore, that the filming of the novel provided such a significant boost to the revenues of the house that would become forever synonymous with Brideshead. Castle Howard in North Yorkshire was the home of the HHA's second president, George Howard. Not long after filming

---

[3] Evelyn Waugh, *Brideshead Revisited: The Sacred and Profane Memories of Captain Charles Ryder* (London, 2000 edn), p. ix.

had begun, Howard also became the chairman of the BBC, having previously served on its governing board. Howard was hence an influential media figure in his own right. It was in part due to Howard's influence and enthusiasm that the use of houses, parks, and gardens by film and television companies would become such a recurring topic at early meetings of the HHA. It was one of the "fields of possible co-operative action by owners" that was discussed at the second annual meeting of the original standing conference of historic house owners in November 1972. On this occasion, the assembled owners deliberated on the merits of having "an agreed scale of facility fees for TV and film-making at historic properties" as well as a similarly agreed scale of charges for conferences and receptions held at their properties. The previous year, the director general of the National Trust, Jack Boles, had told the meeting that agents working for the Trust had already been sent guidance on these lines. Howard gave the meeting the benefit of his own experience of dealing with film and television companies. Of "paramount importance", he said, was "a proper contract between owner and film-maker", and he had already provided the British Tourist Authority with a copy of the standard contract that his own legal advisers had devised so that other owners could consult the model.[4] With George Howard in control at the BBC, Norman Hudson of the HHA negotiated the first standard filming contract with BBC productions, for filming at privately owned properties.[5]

Howard later remembered that the contract to film *Brideshead* at Castle Howard had come at exactly the right moment, bringing much-needed income at a time when the terrible weather and even worse economic conditions had led to a forty per cent drop in visitor numbers. Aside from declaring that 1981 was, for these reasons, "a year to forget", Howard devoted his editorial in the spring 1982 edition of *Historic House* magazine to the virtues of film and television work for historic properties. He did add a note of caution, however. First, he reiterated the importance of owners signing clear contracts with production companies. Second, he recommended that someone from the family remained on or around the set for the duration of the filming, not only to prevent damage but also to authorise any movement of furniture or other alterations that the film crew might need.[6]

---

[4] HHA Archive, Minutes of the Inaugural Meeting of the Standing Conference of Historic Houses, 2 Feb. 1971; Minutes of the Second AGM of the Standing Conference of Historic Houses, 9 Nov. 1972.

[5] Information from Norman Hudson, 8 June 2023.

[6] 'President's Review', *Historic House* 6:1 (Spring, 1982), 5.

True to form, Howard took a characteristically hands-on approach to over-seeing the work on the set of *Brideshead*. Derek Granger, the producer of the series, recalled that Howard "became a sort of property master extraordinary". On one occasion, Howard was horrified that the set designers had put tinsel on a Christmas tree ("Good God! Tinsel! Never", he had cried). Another time, a hatbox was urgently needed for a shot, so Howard "went flying off to some cobwebbed attic and managed to find the Dowager Duchess of Grafton's which she'd taken to Cannes in 1923". Howard's son Simon, who was later to assume overall management of Castle Howard, found the *Brideshead* filming experi-ence thoroughly enjoyable. He mixed with the actors and technical crew while queuing for bacon sandwiches at the mobile catering unit, describing it all as "a bit like a benevolent invasion. It's all rather fun."[7]

It didn't really matter that Waugh may have had an entirely different house in mind as the setting for his novel. He was great friends with the Lygon fam-ily who owned Madresfield in Worcestershire, a somewhat less ostentatious house, albeit one also full of treasures and delights.[8] Where Castle Howard announced its presence in the landscape through its sheer scale and baroque splendour, Madresfield blended in much more naturally: a red-brick Elizabe-than manor house that was approached on the level and was surrounded by a moat. Nevertheless, Castle Howard's distinctive roofline was a ready match for Brideshead's "high and insolent dome", and there was something very familiar about the way that Brideshead was referred to by the Marchmain family as a castle even though, like Castle Howard, it was nothing of the kind. ("We had a castle a mile away," Sebastian explains to Charles in the novel, "... then we took a fancy to the valley and pulled the castle down, carted the stones up here, and built a new house. I'm glad they did, aren't you?")

Film was not the only means by which the doors to country houses were being opened in the late 1970s, whether literally, visually, or figuratively. A whole generation's earliest cultural engagement with country houses occurred with the publication of Mark Girouard's illustrated volume *Life in the English Country House*, published by Yale University Press in 1978.[9] Girouard's book broke new ground by talking about architectural heritage in mainly social terms. The book's starting point was that the country house was a manifestation

[7]   Michael Watkins, 'Castle Brideshead', *Illustrated London News*, 1 Oct. 1981, p. 67.

[8]   Pauline Byrne, *Mad World: Evelyn Waugh and the Secrets of Brideshead* (Lon-don, 2010).

[9]   Mark Girouard, *Life in the English Country House: A Social and Architectural History* (New Haven and London, 1978).

of social, economic, and political power relations. The architecture, layout and landscapes of country houses were conceived by Girouard as being the way in which power relations in English society were made and sustained. Like film and television dramas of the time (and since), Girouard's study was as interested in the below-stairs aspects of country house life as it was in what happened in the enfilades of grander rooms. Girouard knew intimately of what he wrote. A relative of the duke of Devonshire, his youth had been spent shuttling between Hardwick, Chatsworth, and other Devonshire properties.[10] Responses to the book were hugely positive: it proved a surprise publishing hit. Peter Thornton, one of the curators of the V&A's *Destruction* exhibition, was convinced that the book had transformed the way country houses were seen and understood: "No single action, no piece of legislation or fiscal legerdemain, nor even a massive transfusion of cash, could possibly be as effective as the publication of this work in the fight to preserve our country houses in a sensible and telling manner."[11] The book won the Duff Cooper Memorial Prize in 1978, and the W. H. Smith Literary Award in 1979. It reached a sizable audience, and has hardly been out of print since, having been republished in multiple editions, most popularly as a soft-backed full-colour edition.

Girouard's book could be said to have provided the set text for a whole generation of film and television producers who deployed country house settings. Technological enhancements by the late 1970s had made in situ filming a much more affordable and higher quality proposition and meant that all manner of film and television work could now be done away from the studios and on location. As George Howard noted in 1982: "The introduction of lightweight video cameras, the huge increase in the cost of set construction in studios, the flexibility gained by emancipation from the shackles of the studios, the increase in reality – all these and many more reasons lie behind the trend." He was convinced therefore "that these developments will be of great benefit to historic houses".[12]

So important was filming as a source of revenue for country houses that the HHA published a dedicated advice manual for house owners. This was first

---

[10] The present author remembers seeing Girouard's signature in the guest book for Hardwick Hall for the early 1950s, before the time when the house was taken over by the National Trust. Girouard later wrote the National Trust's first guidebook for Hardwick.

[11] Peter Thornton, 'Review of *Life in the English Country House*', *Burlington Magazine* 120:909 (1978), 855, quoted in Oliver Cox, 'From Power to Enslavement: Recent Perspectives on the Politics of Art Patronage and Display in the Country House', *Art and the Country House*, <https://doi.org/10.17658/ACH/TE581> [accessed 9 Sept. 2023].

[12] 'President's Review', *Historic House* 6:1 (Spring, 1982), 5.

developed during George Howard's time as president and was written and pre-pared by the association's retained technical adviser Norman Hudson.[13] The manual set out the clear advantages to film productions being made at historic sites, where a greater level of authenticity could be achieved than on studio sets. Moreover, by their nature historic house settings meant that cast and crew could work together in a secluded space for a designated length of time, without distraction. It meant that the actors could "imbibe the atmosphere of a place", enhancing their performances.[14] However, the manual noted that the arrival of a film crew was also "demanding and disruptive", akin to that of "a circus coming to town". Plenty of space would be needed to allow for mobile catering crews, hair and make-up facilities, actors' trailers and rest rooms, pro-duction offices, prop studios, and power generators. Special care was need-ed to ensure that historic fabric, whether outside or inside, was not damaged by the machinery that film crews brought with them, or by the unthinking actions of cast and crew while on site. The solution was always in the contrac-tual arrangements reached between the house and the film production com-pany. As HHA president, Howard repeatedly encouraged owners to get proper contracts in place with film and television production companies. A template contract was circulated from the association's small offices, by then located on Charles II Street before they moved to Ebury Street in Belgravia.[15] The HHA manual advised strongly that owners should not sign contracts until they were content that every aspect of concern had been addressed – including the finan-cial return. Clauses in contracts would address the consequences of significant damage being caused and enshrine the liability of the film production company to cover the cost of any restoration or redecoration that would be needed at the conclusion of the shoot. Contracts would also need to offer guarantees that sufficient insurance cover was in place for all eventualities.

During the 1980s and 90s, the UK became an increasingly attractive choice for production studios for location work. In part, this was a result of the direct encouragement of government. A British Film Commission was established in

[13] The manual went through several editions, with Sarah Greenwood as co-author.

[14] Norman Hudson and Sarah Greenwood, *Film and Photography in Historic Houses and Gardens* (London, 1983), pp. 6–7.

[15] The HHA's offices have always been in this part of London. Starting by sharing premises with the BTA on St James Street, the offices moved first to Charles II Street, and then to Ebury Street, before moving (for the next thirty years) to Chester Street, also in Belgravia. The offices are now barely five minutes' walk away from Chester Street, on Buckingham Palace Road. Proximity to Whitehall and Westminster was one of the motivations for this location.

1991, sitting above fourteen separate regional film commissions. The number of overseas productions being made in the UK grew accordingly, for example from thirty-six in 1993 to fifty in 1994.[16] The HHA laid on a special training event for its owner members in 1995, to give them the latest advice on dealing with film and TV companies and guidance on the tax consequences of leasing historic property for a period of filming. The success of *Brideshead*, after all, had helped to cultivate a new genre: the country house period drama. Productions such as *The Shooting Party* (1984), filmed at Knebworth and starring James Mason and Edward Fox, catered to the growing taste for costumed dramas in historic settings.[17] The producers Ismail Merchant and James Ivory became internationally known for their blockbuster British film productions, with the English scenes in films such as *A Room with a View* (1985) shot at locations that included the National Trust's Emmett's Garden in Kent. Another Merchant-Ivory production to star Helena Bonham Carter was *Howard's End* (1992), shot partly at Brampton Bryan in Herefordshire. Multiple country houses were used to film the next Merchant-Ivory production in 1995, a version of novelist Kazuo Ishiguro's 1988 novel *The Remains of the Day*. Dyrham Park and Badminton House (Gloucestershire), Powderham Castle (Devon), and Corsham Court (Wiltshire) were all used to represent the fictional Darlington Hall.

The global success of the Merchant-Ivory partnership meant that other period dramas soon went into production. Arundel Castle (West Sussex), Broughton Castle (Oxfordshire), Wilton House (Wiltshire), and Syon House (London) were all used as locations in *The Madness of King George* (1994), an adaptation for film of Alan Bennett's drama about George III, starring Nigel Hawthorne. Visitor numbers to Lyme Park in Cheshire, a National Trust property, grew because of the starring role it played in a 1995 BBC adaptation of *Pride and Prejudice*, in which Colin Firth's Mr Darcy was filmed emerging from a swim in the lake in wettened shirt and breeches. The film's success increased the interest in adaptations of Jane Austen's novels. Montacute House (Somerset) and Saltram (Devon), both National Trust properties, were used as locations for Ang Lee's *Sense and Sensibility* (1995), while the London-based ballroom scenes were filmed at Wilton House. A BBC production of *Little*

---

[16] 'Filming at Historic Houses', *Historic House* 19:2 (Summer, 1995), 31–34.
[17] *The Shooting Party* featured, as production runner, Henry Lytton Cobbold, son of David Lytton Cobbold. He recounts the experience in chapter 12 ('The Shooting Year') of his memoir *Great Great Great: Lines, Tracks and Happy Highways to Knebworth House* (Knebworth, 2022).

Dorrit (2008) included scenes filmed in the parterre at Chenies Manor House (Buckinghamshire).

By the turn of the new millennium, film and TV work had become a staple income for many historic house properties. Most of the larger houses and estates were able to make significant amounts of money in this way. Blenheim (Oxfordshire) played host to such films as *Indiana Jones and the Last Crusade* (1998), starring Harrison Ford in the title role and Sean Connery (in real life, just twelve years older than Ford) as the archaeologist's father. Luton Hoo was a setting for the James Bond film *The World is Not Enough*, as well as for Richard Curtis' hit of 1994, *Four Weddings and a Funeral*. Knebworth House became almost as famous for its film and television work as it had been for its music concerts, being the setting for, variously, *Batman* (1989), Stanley Kubrick's *Eyes Wide Shut* (1999), and, later, *Paddington 2* (2017). The *Harry Potter* franchise made use of country houses and estates, most notably Alnwick in Northumberland (which doubled for Hogwarts, the fictional wizarding school), but also Blenheim.

An example of the steps that needed to be taken when production companies came knocking was provided by Neston Park in Wiltshire. Neston already had twenty-five years' experience of film and TV work by the time that a BBC production company contacted them looking for a venue for an adaptation of *Lark Rise to Candleford*. As the agent later explained, the estate's first move was to require a three-year contract to be signed before any filming began. A timetable was compiled, so that the filming was not interrupted by the milk lorries that arrived daily to transport the outputs of the dairy farm. A detailed contract was also drawn up to ensure that the rights of the tenant farmer were protected. Planning consents were secured, both for the temporary installation of filming facilities and for some minor adjustments to the listed buildings used in the filming. Despite the effort involved, it still made business sense for the estate to sign the contract.[18] There was a lot to consider. However, as Sir James Scott of Rotherfield Park in Surrey said, although leasing your home to a film company was a somewhat masochistic act, the income it generated helped to offset the adverse tax movements that had been experienced by country house owners.[19]

The experience might be regarded as masochistic in other ways too. When in 1991 the twenty-first Baron Saye and Sele received a request from the BBC for some aerial filming of his family's home at Broughton Castle in Oxfordshire, he

---

[18]   'Location, Location, Location', *Historic House* 34:4 (Winter, 2010), 40.

[19]   James Scott, 'Tax Update', *Historic House* 34:4 (Winter, 2010), 11.

12. Documentary filming at Layer Marney Tower, Essex with Elizabeth I on the film set (Nicholas Charrington, photo courtesy of Layer Marney Tower).

saw little reason to refuse. Film contracts had previously made useful contributions towards the repair of Broughton, a fortified manor house dating from the early fourteenth century. Being in demand as a film setting was a boon for Lord Saye and Sele. Broughton was an expensive property to maintain. Every time a film crew arrived for an extended period of filming – perhaps a few days, perhaps longer – he knew that more repairs would be possible on the house. And the money was certainly needed, as keeping Broughton wind- and water-tight was a never-ending task. It helped that Broughton was so accessible, being just ninety minutes' drive from the centre of the film and TV industry in London. As well as *The Madness of King George*, Broughton was the setting for several other historical dramas from *Joseph Andrews* (1977) to 1982's *The Scarlet Pimpernel*, and would go on to be the setting for *Shakespeare in Love* (1998) starring a fourth cousin of Lord Saye and Sele, Joseph Fiennes. Broughton was also used for the 1984 Rob Lowe vehicle *Oxford Blues* and the Tom Selleck, Steve Gutenberg, and Ted Danson comedy *Three Men and a Little Lady* (1990), as well as episodes of the BBC's *Agatha Christie's Miss Marple* (starring Joan Hickman as the eponymous amateur sleuth) and Patricia Routledge's situation comedy of manners *Keeping Up Appearances*.[20] A contract for aerial filming, of course, was much easier to arrange. There was no film crew to accommodate on site, with their endless demands and the ever-present danger of damage to the physical fabric of the house. No, what could be better than to allow the BBC to fly a light aircraft over the house, permitting it to be filmed in the golden glow of a summer's evening? Lord Saye and Sele therefore agreed to the request, in return for a comparatively modest fee.

It turned out to be something of an expensive mistake. The aerial footage became the signature opening sequence in a new BBC One television series, *Noel's House Party*, which would appear in a prime-time Saturday evening slot from its inception in November 1991 and for the next eight years. Broughton doubled as the incarnation of Crinkley Bottom, the fictional house inhabited by Noel Edmonds and a cast of familiars including the effervescent Mr Blobby, a fictional children's television character who would go on to become a celebrity in his own, pink-polka-dotted right. As the aerial footage lingered over Broughton, in all its golden glory, the camera angle switched to Noel Edmonds, the genial bearded host of the show. *Noel's House Party* was one of the unquestioned television hits of the 1990s, meaning that Broughton Castle became a familiar sight in living rooms right up until the sixth series when the title credits were at last changed. During all this time, and for some time after, several film producers reportedly avoided using Broughton Castle, out of fear that it would be far too readily identifiable as the home of Mr Blobby.

The curse of *Noel's House Party* would affect another country house that had become a familiar sight to television viewers. The grounds of Cricket House, which had been the location for *To the Manor Born*, were refashioned in 1994 as Crinkley Bottom, or Blobbyland, a theme park based on the Mr Blobby character. The theme park was extensive, covering many acres of the former landscaped grounds with attractions such as the Crinkley Bottom Roundabout and Fun Village and the steam railway line with its Gunge Mines. At its heart was Mr Blobby's own house, Dunblobbin', but also included were various other commercial concessions: the Noddy in Toyland rides, and the Animals of Farthing Woods experience, adjacent to Crinkley Bottom High Street. Plans to develop a replica of Noel's own house – a facsimile of Broughton Castle in other words – were dropped due to objections from planners. The theme park opened in July 1994 and proved immediately popular. Hundreds of thousands of visitors came, encouraged by a constant stream of newspaper stories.

[20] Broughton featured as Carldon Hall in an episode from the first series of *Keeping Up Appearances* in 1990 called, appropriately, 'Stately Home'.

A couple decided to get married at the site, with Mr Blobby acting as their best man. Other stories, however, were less positive. There were reports of the elephants in the adjoining wildlife park being affected by the noise and excitement coming from the park. The local planning authority was unhappy with the road signage erected to direct visitors, as well as with the general visual intrusions of the theme park. No action was taken, however, and Crinkley Bottom faded away almost as quickly as it had appeared. In 1997 Edmonds parted company with the family that owned Cricket House, and the park was repurposed back to the wildlife park that had been established there thirty years earlier. All mention of Mr Blobby and his entourage was expunged. For years the memory of Blobbyland lived on only as a half-life: the ghosts of faded funfair rides amid the wooded parkland landscape, the shell of Mr Blobby's house decaying amidst the undergrowth. It became a popular haunt for ruin-hunters and psycho-geographers looking to excavate ignoble relics of the recent past. In 2008 the family sold Cricket House entirely. It is now a fashionable hotel and resort.

Over-association with a particular television show or personality was just one of the risks associated with inviting production companies into country house locations. But this was less of a problem for Wrotham Park in Hertfordshire, which played host to several bestselling British films of the 1990s and early 2000s. These included contemporary dramas such as Stephen Fry's *Peter's Friends* (1992), in which a group of university friends are reunited at the family estate of the eponymous character, played by Fry himself. A few years later Wrotham would be the location for a different sort of country house drama. *Gosford Park* (2001) by Julian Fellowes was a reinvention of an Agatha Christie murder mystery, set in the early 1930s. Its impressive cast of British actors included Maggie Smith, playing the part of the countess of Trentham. The success of *Gosford Park* revealed that the public appetite for aristocratic drama had not diminished in the early years of the new millennium. The fact that the plots of these dramas had barely changed – they were essentially variations on Isobel Colegate's novel *The Shooting Party* (1980), or even Jean Renoir's *La Règle du Jeu* (1939) – did not seem to matter much at all.

Fellowes was encouraged to write a follow-up to *Gosford Park*, this time as an episodic TV drama. The countess of Trentham made a reappearance, albeit now retitled as the countess of Grantham, in a drama first broadcast on ITV in 2015. Fellowes records that he was initially hesitant that *Downton Abbey* would repeat *Gosford Park*'s success, thinking that "it would be like trying to make lightning strike in the same place twice". The managing director of Carnival Films had no such reservations: "I knew it would play to the strengths of television and had a hunch it would be very popular."[21] *Downton* would become a worldwide phenomenon, running to six series and two feature film adaptations. The silhouette of its location in the opening credits – Highclere Castle in Berkshire – would bring that house a new level of international fame. Nobody seemed to mind that the fictional *Downton* was set hundreds of miles away, in North Yorkshire, where the earl of Grantham's house sat amid coal mines and shooting moors.[22] Highclere had originally been Fellowes' suggestion for *Gosford Park*, although it was turned down by director Robert Altman for being too far from London's hotels. It worked well for *Downton*, since it signalled that the series was at some remove from the world of Jane Austen adaptations, where the mansion settings were frequently selected for their stucco and Palladianism. Moreover, Highclere had the other benefit of being the home of a longstanding aristocratic family, the earls of Carnarvon. This meant that remarkably little needed to be provided by way of props, aside from the introduction of a few strategically placed potted palms. The absence of original servants' quarters, however, meant that the 'below stairs' scenes needed to be filmed on a purpose-built set at Ealing Studios, sixty miles away.[23]

In *Gosford Park*, Fellowes' aim had been to convey the sense that the country house world of the 1930s was soon to come to an end. For the first series of *Downton*, Fellowes chose to set the action twenty years earlier, somewhere between the end of the Victorian period and the first world war. The appeal of 1912 was that the stratified social order remained in place (the show was nothing if not an *Upstairs, Downstairs* for the twenty-first century). But strains were clearly appearing: "Trades unions, women's rights, Marxism, were all waiting in the wings and it would only take a couple of years of war before they started to stride centre stage." England was "teetering on the brink" of rapid transformation, but cars, electricity, and telephones made the scenario even more relatable for viewers. Fellowes noted that after the second world war, the social world depicted in *Downton Abbey* had vanished. But, he added, a revival would come three decades later. By that time, owners were living in their country houses differently – in ways that were profitable, rather than a drain on resources. In this way, "Britain's old families have written and continue to write another chapter in their long history."[24]

21 Jessica Fellowes, *The World of Downton Abbey* (London, 2011), p. 177.
22 Newby Hall here was indeed the home of Lord Grantham.
23 Jessica Fellowes, *The World of Downton Abbey*, p. 182.
24 Julian Fellowes quoted in Fellowes, *ibid.*, pp. 7, 179.

8

Treasure houses

Nothing symbolised the revival in the fortunes of British country houses so much as the *Treasure Houses of Britain* exhibition that opened in Washington DC in November 1985. Ten years on from the V&A's *Destruction of the Country House* exhibition, the *Treasure Houses* show saw more than seven hundred works of art from over two hundred of the largest and most prestigious of British country houses assembled at the National Gallery of Art. Arranged in the east wing of the gallery in a sequence of interiors conceived by curator Gervase Jackson-Stops, the exhibition brought together portraits of British royalty, furniture, tapestries, and works by Constable, Canaletto, and Velasquez.

The show had been a long time in the making. The minutes of the HHA's first annual general meeting in October 1974 recorded that a feasibility study had been commissioned into the possibility of a "Treasures of Britain exhibition" being toured in America in the winter of 1976.[1] The original idea was for a show that would travel around the United States for six months – the condition being that it would need to be entirely "self-supporting".[2] The enthusiasm for the idea from the HHA's executive committee followed on from research trips that a number of them had made across the Atlantic (Lord Brooke had been unable to attend the 1974 AGM because he was on one of these trips). The *Destruction* show had been a direct inspiration. The director of the National Gallery, J. Carter Brown, had visited the V&A in 1974 to witness *Destruction*, and recalled the "sickening" sense of loss that the show had inspired. This sense of loss had stayed with him in the intervening period, providing some of the "driving spirit" behind the Washington exhibition.[3] *Treasure Houses* was just as much a political statement as the *Destruction* exhibition had been, but now aimed to imprint on visitors another set of messages: that British artistic

[1] HHA Archive, Minutes of the First AGM of the Historic Houses Association, 23 Oct. 1974.

[2] HHA Archive, Minutes of the Fifth Executive Committee Meeting, 18 Sept. 1974, 74/41 (v).

[3] 'Best of British Treasure', *The Times*, 16 Oct. 1985, p. 14.

culture was alive and well, and continued to be looked after on the walls of its country mansions, which in turn were the powerhouses of the tourism and leisure industry.

By the summer of 1982, the preparations for the *Treasure Houses* show were well advanced. George Howard, writing in the HHA's house magazine, anticipated that it would be "a major exhibition and celebration" amounting to "the greatest single promotion of the British historic house that has ever been held in the United States". Indeed, he went on, it would be "one of the greatest exhibitions ever mounted anywhere". Howard was speaking as chairman of the British organising committee and sought to rally interest and support from among historic house owners. His two UK-based organisers were John Harris, the co-curator of the *Destruction* show, and the National Trust's Jackson-Stops. Howard gave notice to owners to expect word from Harris and Jackson-Stops, who would need to visit hundreds of houses to make their selection for the show. Howard provided some reassurance ahead of these visits: "all they will need to do is to have a look around, take some measurements, and perhaps a polaroid photograph ... If they get in touch with you, please be as welcoming and co-operative as you can. They will be working under great pressure of time and if they visit you may have to arrive just after breakfast and depart not much later." It was axiomatic to Howard that Harris and Jackson-Stops would not be interested "only or even primarily in your Rubens or your Chippendale". Howard envisaged an exhibition that would show "life below stairs as well as upstairs", and a series of rooms that would not just be great showrooms but workaday rooms, "for example, the gun room, the estate office, the carpenter's shop, the billiard room and the conservatory". In fact, when the exhibition eventually appeared three years later, its focus was firmly centred on the grandest state rooms and the priceless objects they contained, rather than the more multi-layered, upstairs-downstairs vision that Howard had initially sketched.[4]

Howard had set out his views on country houses' collections a year earlier in an article for *Historic House* magazine.[5] Where public museums tended to put equal emphasis on conservation, research, storage, and display of historic objects, Howard averred that the private owner tended to put "display and enjoyment of a work of art" before all else. This did not mean that conservation was not important, just that it was not a private owner's primary duty, in the way that it was for a museum. This could have unexpected benefits for the

---

[4] 'President's Review', *Historic House* 6:1 (Spring, 1982), 5.

[5] George Howard, 'Conserving Art in Houses', *Historic House* 5:1 (Summer, 1981), 18–19.

artwork. A picture "darkened by years of dirt and successive layers of varnish" may in fact be in a better conserved condition than a picture that had been "scrubbed rather too violently while in a public collection". Similarly, historic textiles and fabrics, kept in drawers for generations and rarely exposed to sunlight, might be in a better state than those fabrics held in museum collections and put on permanent display. Thick castle walls and well-built mansions might provide better and more consistent environmental settings in which to store items than galleries with their surging crowds of visitors. Howard added that the mania for temporary exhibitions, for which works of art were jetted around the globe to be shown in unfamiliar gallery conditions, presented a particular threat to their conservation.

The latter point was somewhat ironic given Howard's own enthusiasm for exhibitions. He participated in a previous HHA exhibition that had marked the nine hundredth anniversary of the building of the Tower of London, and which was hosted on the top floor of Selfridges department store. This show, called *Noble Heritage*, was held between May and September 1978. It brought together objects from nineteen different houses, including Charles I's despatch box and waistcoat on loan from Sudeley Castle, a medieval two-handed sword from Warwick Castle, and a Bible from Inveraray Castle that had belonged to the ninth earl of Argyll, executed in 1685 for leading a rebellion against the accession of James II. Howard loaned some porcelain to the exhibition, for which Selfridges covered all transport and insurance costs.[6] Another precursor to the Washington show was an exhibition called *Treasured Possessions*, mounted at the London showrooms of Sotheby's in December 1983 and January 1984. Like the Washington exhibition, this show was based on loans from British country houses – in this case, seventy-five HHA member properties – with the express intention of providing a shop window onto the collections held privately but open to public viewing. The president of the HHA, Michael Saunders Watson, made clear the political intent, describing the show's aim as being to demonstrate "that private ownership and public enjoyment are essential partners in maintaining the richness of this important part of our cultural inheritance, both for present and future generations". For Saunders Watson, the sense of partnership – between the private and the public, as well as between the present and the future – was itself as much of a 'treasured possession' as the artworks on display. Those artworks included a Constable from Mirehouse in Cumbria, a Flemish tapestry loaned by Robert Cooke MP from Athelhampton in Dorset, and Repton's Red Book for Sufton Court in Herefordshire. Alan

---

[6] Information taken from an interview with Dorothy Abel Smith.

Clark MP loaned a Henry Moore sketch from Saltwood Castle, while Saunders Watson loaned the Zoffany portrait of the Watson brothers from Rockingham.[7]

The *Treasure Houses* exhibition in Washington in 1985 was an even bolder statement of the importance of country houses within British cultural and artistic life. It used the same basic model of the *Treasured Possessions* show – the loan of paintings and artworks from country houses – but vastly expanded the range of objects shown while transposing them across the Atlantic. Carter Brown linked the show to the five hundredth anniversary of the Tudor succession in 1485, "the moment at which the defensive, inward-looking castle began for the first time to become the domestic, outward-looking country house." The aim was that everything in the exhibition would come from country houses, ideally those that remained extant and with their collections intact.[8] The duchess of Devonshire later claimed that Carter Brown had conceived of the idea of the exhibition while staying at Chatsworth in the summer of 1981. She saw the show on four occasions but said that she would have liked to have seen it forty times more. It was the "best exhibition I have ever seen, really faultless", she said. Much of this was due to the design, with each of the rooms recreating the tableau of a period or era, from a late medieval hall house to a Renaissance long gallery, to rooms devoted to Lord Burlington and the Palladian revival and Robert Adam.[9]

While the national museums and galleries in London were a permanent showcase for cultural treasures, even they might have struggled to create an exhibition of this scale and depth. British art at the Washington show was represented by the Gainsboroughs on loan from Bowhill, Bowood, and Houghton. There were works by Reynolds from Castle Howard, Chatsworth, and Woburn. Weston Park loaned a Van Dyck, along with others from Broadlands and Corsham Court. From Longleat came a Tintoretto, from Wilton a Raphael. The sheer number of objects loaned was a demonstration of what could be done when private owners agreed to combine their efforts in a cooperative way. The National Trust played its part too, loaning pictures from Petworth and Ickworth, embroidery from Hardwick, candlestands from Knole, and a John Linnell sofa from Kedleston. As Jackson-Stops told David Littlejohn, "It was trying to put the English country house on the map as an international tourist attraction. And on the whole, I think it did get the message across – that it isn't

---

[7] *Treasured Possessions* – Sotheby's exhibition catalogue (London, 1983).
[8] *Treasure Houses* (New Haven and London, 1985), p. 11.
[9] Deborah Devonshire, *All in One Basket* (London, 2012), pp. 275–284.

The Treasure Houses of Britain
Five Hundred Years of Private Patronage and Art Collecting

13. *Treasure Houses* exhibition catalogue, 1985.

our museums, it's our country houses that are the great asset of the country."[10] For Deborah Devonshire, all that was missing was a representation of the reality of the British country house, such as "a couple of toys (one broken), a sofa covered in newspapers, stray novels, an old dog flopped down by the fireplace and the smell of wet macs".[11]

The exhibition was a masterpiece of project management, partnership working between the public and the private sector, and public relations management. The British Council invested seven thousand pounds in an IBM

[10]   David Littlejohn, *The Fate of the English Country House* (Oxford, 1997), p. 129.
[11]   Devonshire, *All in One Basket*, p. 280.

computer to work out the most cost-effective routes for lorries to travel the country collecting paintings, sculpture, and furniture from two hundred and twenty castles and manor houses. The British and American governments covered the indemnity policies needed to insure the operation. British Airways offered a fifty per cent reduction in its freighting costs. Sponsorship came from the Ford Motor Company, while the National Trust and HHA both made financial contributions. The British Tourist Authority received some criticism for coming relatively late to the party, announcing that it would set up an information desk at some distance from the gallery itself. Much of the publicity therefore had to be generated by the owners themselves. The HHA encouraged some owners to give talks about "what living in a stately home is really like" – executive secretary Terry Empson, a former civil servant who had joined the association in this role in 1981, explaining his concern that "the silver wine coolers and humidors, the full-blown ermine hung family portraits and the gilded furniture may give the impression that the owners are rich". Lady Victoria Leatham of Burghley House was duly dispatched to provide the alternative perspective and explain how her house now needed re-roofing and involved an eighty-yard walk between the living room and the kitchen.[12]

The biggest public relations coup of all for the show came from the visit made in its opening week by the exhibition's patrons, the Prince and Princess of Wales. The British royal couple had been on an extended overseas trip, travelling first to Australia and then on to Hawaii, where they were festooned with garlands of flowers. They then flew to Andrews Air Force base in Maryland and were taken from there to the White House to meet the President and First Lady, Ronald and Nancy Reagan. They returned to the White House the following evening for a gala dinner, at which the President, in his after-dinner speech, welcomed "Princess David ... Princess Diane ..." on her first trip to the USA. This inadvertent *faux pas* aside, the princess created a stir of her own when she took to the dancefloor that evening with *Saturday Night Fever* actor John Travolta. The royal couple visited the *Treasure Houses* exhibition the next day, but the questions at the press conference inevitably turned to Diana's choice of dance partner the previous evening. "I think you enjoyed it, didn't you darling?", her husband interjected when a journalist asked Diana if she had enjoyed the dinner reception. After all, the prince

---

[12]   Leslie Geddes-Brown, 'How our Treasure Houses went West', *The Sunday Times*, 8 Sept. 1985, p. 43.

reportedly added, "she would be an idiot if she did not enjoy dancing with John Travolta, wouldn't she?"[13]

Celebrity gossip aside, most reviews of the show declared it to be an outstanding success. Not all commentary on the exhibition was wholly adulatory, however. George Plumptre in *The Daily Telegraph* acknowledged the "monumental achievement" of the exhibition but was melancholic at the thought that sponsorship was unlikely ever to be offered to recreate the show in Britain. He also noted the elitist flavour of the show, which featured works loaned by fourteen of the country's twenty-six dukes. In Plumptre's view, the exhibition did little to show support for the struggling smaller houses, which continued to face an uncertain future.[14] Historians Linda Colley and David Cannadine provided even more acerbic lines of commentary. Colley remarked that "like the landed classes it commemorates this exhibition is gorgeous in its accumulated wealth full of the pride and dignity of hereditary power and elitist and ultimately mischievous in its rationale". Colley felt that there was nothing intrinsically cultured about the investment choices of landowners: they regarded their art collections as being of secondary importance compared to their houses and grounds, and artworks were quickly jettisoned when the going got tough. Although the exhibition had been an occasion for signifying the importance of art remaining in situ on the walls of British country houses, Colley felt the exhibition's greatest achievement was in showing how much better those artworks looked when hung from the walls of a public gallery, accessible and well-lit.[15] David Cannadine, writing in the *New York Review of Books*, also regarded the exhibition as propaganda, conceived and executed on a grand scale, for the British aristocratic way of life. He took issue with the largely unchallenged assumptions that lay behind the show, which uncritically celebrated "the rise and efflorescence of superior secular patronage in the aftermath of the dissolution of the monasteries". Cannadine felt the exhibition gave a misleading impression of British country houses, since there were "no stuffed birds, no stags' heads, no elephants' feet" as might normally be seen in such houses. The exhibition gave "only the cosiest view of the landed classes' world", with no reference to industry, poverty, or the sources of wealth of country house owners.

[13] Christopher Thomas, 'Reagan pays tribute to "Princess David"', *The Times*, 11 Nov. 1985, p. 1.

[14] George Plumptre, 'Open House to Show off a Few Family Knick-knacks', *Daily Telegraph*, 2 Nov. 1985, p. 14.

[15] Linda Colley, 'The Cult of the Country House', *Times Literary Supplement*, 15 Nov. 1985, p. 17.

If the same essay was being written today, Cannadine would no doubt have also noted the lack of any reference to colonialism and the slave trade.

In any case, Cannadine argued, Americans already had access to a great many artworks from British country houses. Many USA galleries had bought paintings and objects from British country house collections at the end of the nineteenth century, when owners experienced the first of the economic downturns to which their estates were periodically prone. If the aim of the exhibition had been propaganda, he continued, it could possibly backfire. Much of the exhibition was "a rhetorical exercise, displaying works of art, tugging at the heartstrings, appealing to snobbery and nostalgia, all in support of an idealised view of the country house and its owners". Yet by assembling so many objects in one place, and displaying them with such bravura confidence, the owners had fatally undermined the image that they so desperately wanted to convey: that only they had the expertise and understanding to display Gainsboroughs, or Titians, or Mortlake tapestries. On the contrary, here was a modern-day museum, open to all, showing works of art "in near-perfect conditions of display and access". It was only the indifference of Margaret Thatcher, Britain's prime minister, to both museums and country houses that meant the owners were saved from the logical consequences of their own exhibition: the breakup of their collections and their reversion to public museums and galleries.[16]

The tone of Cannadine's criticisms foreshadowed those of other 1980s commentators on heritage such as Robert Hewison. Hewison's *The Heritage Industry* in 1987, subtitled *Britain in a Climate of Decline*, carried a chapter title that was borrowed directly from Cannadine's essay: 'Brideshead Re-Revisited'. Like Cannadine, Hewison's invective sought metaphorically to pull back the arras and undermine the mythmaking at stake when country houses were on show. Drawing too on the title of Colley's essay, Hewison evoked Waugh's reference in his preface to the revised version of *Brideshead* in 1959 to the "cult of the English country house", and to the national love affair with such buildings. "By a mystical process of identification," Hewison posited, "the country house becomes the nation, and love of one's country makes obligatory a love of the country house."[17] Hewison did, at least, have an instinctive understanding of the role that collections had historically played as sacrificial offerings for the main house.

[16]   David Cannadine, 'Brideshead Re-Revisited', *New York Review of Books*, 19 Dec. 1985.

[17]   Robert Hewison, *The Heritage Industry: Britain in a Climate of Decline* (London, 1987), p. 53.

These more critical perspectives on the country house tended to dampen the public outrage at the loss or destruction of houses and their collections that had been prompted by the V&A's *Destruction* exhibition. Nevertheless, the HHA continued to highlight the threats that country house heritage faced. In the early 1990s, Michael Sayer and Hugh Massingberd were commissioned by the HHA to undertake a major survey of what had happened to country houses in the period from 1979 to 1992. The study was conceived as a sequel to the *Destruction* exhibition, which had taken the story to the mid-1970s. The intention was to ratchet up the pressure on government, which had proved seemingly deaf to entreaties about the pressures that private owners were under. Without more support from government, suggested William Proby, the chair of the HHA's taxation and political committee, "the inexorable decline of the privately owned historic house will continue and may well increase."[18] The study was comprehensive, taking three years to complete. Its conclusions, according to HHA president the earl of Shelburne, were "deeply disturbing". Houses were expensive to maintain, and for Shelburne the sale of artworks to pay for their upkeep was akin to "losing a cherished relation". Having to sell the entire estate was even worse, like "losing a child". And yet, according to Shelburne's assessment of Sayer's study, it was happening at "an unprecedented rate".[19] Sayer's study stood as a thorough and detailed riposte to Cannadine's and Colley's debunking of the aristocratic idolatry on show in the *Treasure Houses* exhibition. Sayer focused primarily on estates rather than houses: the traditional form in which much land in England had been organised. These estates might be one or two thousand acres in extent, with some a great deal larger than this. Intrinsic to Sayer's argument was the unity that country houses and their estates formed. The separation of a country house from its estate was often the beginning of the end: without its wider landholdings, a house might all-too-easily be converted to a leisure centre, a hotel, or a conference venue. With regret, Sayer noted that the sale of traditional estates appeared to be on the increase. Families who had held the same estate for two or more generations were increasingly choosing to sell up. In fact, in the preceding two decades more than four hundred and fifty seats had been sold in this way. The pace appeared to have quickened with the change of government in 1979. Since then, more than two hundred and fifty family estates had been sold, an average

[18] HHA, *Annual Report 1989/90*, p. 13.
[19] Earl of Shelburne, 'Foreword', in Michael Sayer with Hugh Massingberd (eds), *The Disintegration of a Heritage: Country Houses and their Collections 1979–1992* (Norwich, 1993), pp. vii–viii.

of twenty or so a year. Moreover, nearly a quarter of the estates that had come to market had already been resold, suggesting a more transient breed of owners was on the rise.[20]

The study therefore drew attention to the slipping away, almost without notice, of an entire social order. A recent example was Brympton d'Evercy in Somerset. The house had been highlighted in the Gowers report as an exemplar of the English manor house, and the property had been a stalwart member of the HHA since the association's foundation. The family had reclaimed the house after it had been leased as a school. It had been a Herculean task, in which Charles and Judy Clive-Ponsonby-Fane had taken a personal, hands-on interest. The couple started to open the house to public viewing, and in 1990 the property won the HHA's Garden of the Year Award.[21] But in the summer of 1992, it was put onto the market: the family simply were not able to continue in residence. The rising costs of repairs (including VAT at seventeen and a half per cent), the falling level of English Heritage grants, and punitive rates of taxation were all cited by Sayer as the underlying factors for such sales. At the heart of Sayer's book was a profound melancholy at the ending of a traditional way of life: that of the so-called "vanishing squirearchy". As if it was a world about to be lost, Sayer quoted W. G. Hoskins' romantic evocation of a Devon manor with its "wind-flung rooks on December afternoons, branch-strewn parks emerging from the curtains of fine rain, rambling, stone-flagged houses set all alone at the end of muddy lanes, darkened by beeches and sycamores". Massingberd meanwhile cited Tennyson's words about his own family's house, Gunby Hall in Lincolnshire, "a haunt of ancient peace". The traditional form and structure of the British countryside was giving way, it seemed, to a dry, transactional modern world, where houses would become no more than "soulless, antiseptic museums", if they survived at all.[22]

After *Treasure Houses* there was some discussion as to whether a version of the show should be transferred to or somehow recreated in Britain. The view at the time was that this was too difficult to achieve, since "the scale and magnificence of the Washington exhibition could not be duplicated". If another exhibition was to be held, and this time in the UK, it would have to be "done in

---

[20]   *Ibid.*, pp. 2, 8.

[21]   Jane Fearnley-Whittingstall, *Historic Gardens: A Guide to 160 British Gardens of Interest* (Harmondsworth, 1990), p. 61.

[22]   Sayer, *The Disintegration of a Heritage*, pp. 5, 14, 20.

a more distant future".[23] More than a decade later, however, the critical voices of Cannadine, Colley, and Hewison did not deter the HHA from undertaking another exhibition, to mark the association's quarter century in 1998. The venue this time was the Tate Gallery, and the curators were Karen Hearn, Robert Upstone, and Giles Waterfield. Perhaps the experience helped to fuel the novel that Waterfield would publish a few years later, a scathing (and very funny) satire of the world of museums and exhibitions.[24] *In Celebration: The Art of the Country House* followed much the same model as *Treasure Houses*, in that it assembled items from over fifty houses. For Sir William Proby, the HHA president at the time, the exhibition was an exercise in the celebration of "the survival of the privately owned house". It was the first time that such an exhibition had been mounted in a major British museum, and the selection of objects was designed to show the diversity of the "architecture, the visual arts, garden and park" located within HHA properties.[25] In *Country Life*, Hearn and Upstone celebrated the way in which owners continued to collect contemporary art pieces alongside their historic family portrait collections, such as the Lucian Freud from Chatsworth and the Graham Sutherland from Saltwood Castle.[26]

In Celebration appeared alongside the publication of John Cornforth's state-of-the-nation report on *The Country Houses of England 1948–1998*. This was produced as an update of the report Cornforth had written for the HHA and British Tourist Authority in 1974. Twenty-five years on, Cornforth highlighted that many of the same threats continued to prevail: the lack of money for essential repairs, the constant pressure to sell land or artworks to meet financial black holes, and the shortsightedness of sudden changes in government policy that turned out to have damaging impacts on country house properties. Nevertheless, his conclusion was to a degree more optimistic than it perhaps had been in 1974. At that time, the imminent disappearance of country house heritage had seemed a very real prospect. Now, with various enlightened changes to government fiscal policy in the intervening years, things were perhaps on a more even keel. Cornforth anticipated that not all the places he had highlighted in his overview would necessarily still be there in twenty-five or fifty years' time. And yet he was convinced that "houses will continue to

[23]   HHA Archive, Minutes of the Thirteenth AGM of the Historic Houses Association, 19 Nov. 1986.

[24]   Giles Waterfield, *The Hound in the Left-Hand Corner* (London, 2002).

[25]   Karen Hearn, Robert Upstone, Giles Waterfield, *In Celebration: The Art of the Country House* (London, 1998).

[26]   Karen Hearn and Robert Upstone, '25 Years of Historic Houses: A Renaissance to Revel In', *Country Life*, 12 Nov. 1998, pp. 46–49.

challenge their occupants not to fail them" and, moreover, that "families will find new ways of carrying out that challenge".[27]

One of the trends that Cornforth anticipated would continue was the role of the country house as a repository for collections of art and artworks. Collecting in practice often relied on luck, intuition, and canny deal-making. Michael Saunders Watson gave an example of this when he recounted how he had spotted a portrait of one of his ancestors, by Lely, coming up at auction. He already possessed a copy of the portrait at Rockingham, albeit of slightly inferior quality. With trepidation, he put in an offer above the asking price, and it was with some relief that he discovered that he had been outbid. The new owner, a dealer, cleaned the portrait and put a new price on it which was five times the amount Saunders Watson had originally proposed. Saunders Watson reckoned that his chances of acquiring the portrait had now entirely disappeared. But the dealer sensed that an arrangement might be possible and visited Rockingham to discuss possible options. While there, he showed interest in some watercolours and a stable scene by Seymour. Saunders Watson soon found himself the owner of the original Lely in return for the combination of these artworks and a cash payment, which he used as his acquisition fund for Rockingham Castle. Although Saunders Watson was at pains to point out that he was not advocating a general policy of owners selling off their collections, he observed that this might be necessary from time to time. And if it meant the creation of a cash surplus that could be invested in new art, so much the better.[28]

Plenty of works of art have been sold from country houses. It was the rush of so many owners to dispose of their artworks in this way in the early twentieth century, to keep their house afloat, that led to the introduction of a system of export controls, the Waverley Criteria, in 1953.[29] The sale of artworks was also explored in detail by Sayer's book, which trawled auction house catalogues and yearbooks to construct an appendix listing all the significant art sales made between 1979 and 1992. There was nothing new here: the 1950s and 60s had seen Harewood sell its Titian, Longford Castle its Velasquez, and Coughton Court its Largillière portrait.[30] The National Heritage Memorial Fund had noted in

[27] John Cornforth, *The Country Houses of England 1948–1998* (London, 1998), p. 323.

[28] 'President's Review', *Historic House* 11:3 (Autumn, 1987), 5.

[29] See Ben Cowell, 'Saving Country Houses and their Collections in the Twentieth and Twenty-First Centuries', *Art and the Country House* (2020) <https://doi.org/10.17658/ACH/TE580> [accessed 9 Sept. 2023].

[30] See Oliver Miller, 'The Picture Collection', in Roy Strong, Marcus Binney, John Harris, *The Destruction of the Country House* (London, 1974), pp. 103–106.

its first annual report in 1981 "the continuing pressures on owners of important heritage items to dispose of them to meet tax demands or, quite simply, to cope with recession and provide for the future".[31] However, a new wave of the country house sales had now begun. The example of Mentmore in 1977 was followed by similar (if less famous) sales at North Mymms in Hertfordshire, Ellel Grange in Lancashire, and Shotesham in Norfolk. The prices reached at Tyninghame in East Lothian in 1983 proved to James Miller, who had worked on the Mentmore sale for Sotheby's, that Mentmore was "no fluke".[32] Other such sales took place at Belton in Lincolnshire in 1984 (of the items not being transferred to the National Trust), Hilborough in 1985, and Sheringham, also in Norfolk, in 1986. Miller notes that there were eighteen such country house sales in the years 1977 to 1997, compared to just four in the preceding two decades. Such sales sometimes represented the offloading of surplus 'kit' from overfilled attics or storage rooms, as was the case with the attic sale at Castle Howard in 1991. But they could also mark the end of an era, as a family gave up its connection with a particular property, as manifested in the artworks and treasures it had accumulated there. Crossrigg Hall in Cumbria and Benacre Hall in Suffolk were examples from the 1990s and early 2000s.[33]

James Miller noted that the popularity of country house sales after Mentmore was another aspect of the cultural impetus still enjoyed by the major mansion properties. It was "the magic of buying direct from a great stately pile" that turned events like these into pure "theatre". As Miller noted, "a powerful mixture of a family and its history, a house and its setting, a catalogue that beautifully promoted the objects in that context and with luck, long warm summer days in the British countryside, all of which created an insatiable allure for collectors, dealers and the public."[34] The Castle Howard attic sale of 1991 had 1,636 lots and raised more than two million pounds. This was in addition to the sale of paintings such as Reynolds' portrait of *Mai*, which also left Castle Howard at around this time.[35] A sale at Syon House in 1997 included objects from other Northumberland houses such as Alnwick Castle and Albury Park,

---

[31] Quoted in Cornforth, *Country Houses of England*, p. 179.

[32] James Miller, 'The Rise and Decline of the Country House Sale 1977–2020: From Mentmore to Chatsworth – A Personal Reflection', in Terence Dooley and Christopher Ridgway (eds), *Country House Collections: Their Lives and Afterlives* (Dublin, 2021), pp. 156–172, p. 160.

[33] *Ibid.*, p. 166.

[34] *Ibid.*, pp. 161, 170.

[35] In 2023 *Mai* was sold again and acquired jointly 'for the nation' by the National Portrait Gallery in London and the Getty Museum in Los Angeles.

in addition to some from Warwick Castle and from Corsham Court. A similar event was held at West Wycombe Park, now owned by the National Trust. The ultimate attic sale took place at Chatsworth in 2010, which featured items from that house as well as from across the Cavendish properties, including Chiswick, Hardwick, and Lismore Castle in Ireland. The sale proved enormously successful as, in Miller's words, "helicopters flew in, and prices flew up".[36]

For many, the sale of artworks from country houses has been a cause of sadness and melancholy. For Tim Knox, the steady drip-drip of house sales from Warwick Castle, Luton Hoo, and Castle Howard represented "a considerable loss to cultural provision outside London". What he feared most was British houses following the pattern of their equivalents over the Channel. France's legal framework meant that collections were frequently divided between family members on death, rather than inherited by a single named heir. Was Britain ending up on the same trajectory, with owners forced to sell items because of the lack of funds for renovations to their mansion properties? "It would indeed be a sad thing if British country houses became like those beautiful, sad, empty, châteaux of the Loire", Knox noted.[37]

On the other hand, as Giles Worsley posited, although arts sales from country houses were often regarded as tragedies, they could just as easily be interpreted as the precise opposite: a key part of the "survival strategy of the country house in the twentieth century".[38] Moreover, as James Miller has observed, art sales were evidence of owners' astute awareness of market trends. When the market was buoyant, many more pieces came forward for sale. But if suddenly the market moved to putting more value on land (such as for development), the art sales might dry up. As Miller put it, owners were "quick to react to changes in the market. That is why they survive."[39] It is noticeable that there have been far fewer country house auctions in the last decade or so, which perhaps also has something to do with the growth in internet auction sales.

The complete loss of artworks was not always the outcome in situations where houses had to capitalise an asset to meet a repair bill or a tax demand. The option to offer artwork in lieu of a tax payment had been available since 1896 and continued in the eras of capital transfer tax and then inheritance

[36] Miller, 'Rise and Decline', p. 172.

[37] Tim Knox, 'The Stripping of the Country House: The Gomes Lecture, 2016', *Emmanuel College Magazine* XCVII (2015–2016), 32–45, 45.

[38] Giles Worsley, 'Beyond the Powerhouse: Understanding the Country House in the Twenty-first Century', *Historical Research* 78:201 (August 2005), 423–435, 425.

[39] Miller, 'Rise and Decline', p. 172.

tax. To be considered for exemption, artworks had to be of "national historic, scientific or artistic interest", whether this was judged on their own terms or by virtue of being "historically associated" with a particular house. Under the terms of conditional exemption, the status was only made possible for art that could be seen by the public, whether for a designated number of days or on application. The details of what could be seen, where, and how were kept on an inland revenue list that was held at the V&A museum and, before the era of the internet, not especially well publicised.[40]

Changes in the tax code in 1980, although drafted a year earlier under the previous Labour administration, made it easier for artworks to be accepted in lieu of capital tax but to remain in situ in the house in which they hung. This 'in situ' option had been orchestrated by John Cornforth, who was able to persuade officials of the need to reconsider which artworks counted as 'pre-eminent', as well as encourage a clause that considered the setting of an artwork. An early case was Joshua Reynolds' portrait of Lady Mexborough, which hangs in the long gallery at Doddington in Lincolnshire. The portrait had hung here since the 1760s, when Doddington was getting its Georgian makeover courtesy of owner John Delaval, brother of the aristocratic subject of the portrait. Having the painting accepted in lieu made it possible for the Jarvis family to reduce the tax that was required following the death of Ralph Jarvis in 1973. In 1983 ownership of the Mexborough painting formally passed over to Leeds City Council (owners of Temple Newsam), though it never left its location and has remained there ever since.[41]

The acceptance-in-lieu-in-situ option made surprisingly good sense, if one could get over the seeming contradiction of an object being given to the nation while also remaining in the same place. It at least meant that a collection's association with a house was not severed, while guaranteeing an object's long-term stewardship by a public body. As Cornforth noted in 1998, it was perhaps surprising that it had not been used more often, albeit that, clearly, the option could be presented in an altogether less charitable light by those without as much sympathy for the careful balances intrinsic within the UK tax

[40] In 1993 the 'V&A List' was renamed as 'The Register of Conditionally Exempt Works of Art', and it was made clear that copies were also held at the National Library for Scotland in Edinburgh, the National Museum of Wales (Cardiff), and the Ulster Museum (Belfast). HHA, *Annual Report for 1993/94*, p. 17. When the list was finally digitised and made available on the internet, the HHA sought the views of officials as to whether access obligations applied to enquiries that might now come from non-British residents. See HHA, *Annual Report for 1995/96*, p. 21.

[41] 'Lady Mexborough at Home', *Historic House* 11:3 (Autumn, 1987), 24–27.

system.[42] These arguments rose to prominence thanks to the comedian Mark Thomas and his Channel 4 series in 1996. Thomas sought to catch out owners who might not respond to requests to see artworks for which the tax had been waived, or to point out the limited number of days that might be available to see a particular artwork. But although new attempts emerged from time to time to 'expose' the reality of this tax arrangement, it seemed to have general support among the taxpaying public. After all, the acceptance-in-lieu-in-situ arrangement meant that many more objects were on show to the public than would otherwise be the case if they had been sold to a wholly private buyer or even offered outright to a public museum or gallery. (The storerooms of most national museums and galleries are already over-full, with four-fifths or more of their collections typically held away from regular public access.) The acceptance-in-lieu-in-situ option meant that the sculpture gallery at Newby remained intact and a key part of the visitor experience there. The transfer of Roman sculptures from Castle Howard to the National Museum of Liverpool in 2015 meant that the displays in the antique passage and great hall laid out in the 1730s and 1740s could remain exactly as they were.[43] In situ arrangements have also been used at Corsham Court, Hagley, Sledmere, Mellerstain, Cawdor, Paxton, Highclere, and Sudeley. While not an acceptance-in-lieu example, the bookcases at Powderham Castle in Devon designed by John Channon of Exeter were purchased by the V&A in 1985–6 and immediately loaned back to the house (the National Heritage Memorial Fund contributed nearly half a million pounds to the transaction).

The sale of works of art could sometimes lead to their purchase by a public institution, an outcome made easier by the Ridley Rules in 1990. These rules meant that the government could take into consideration an offer to purchase, whether from a private or public source, when deciding whether to grant an export licence.[44] This was the route that meant the Bassano of *Christ on the Way to Calvary* from Weston Park and Frans Hal's *Young Man with a Skull* from Elton Hall both ended up in the National Gallery collection. Artworks sold by the marquess of Bristol in 1996 were purchased by the National Trust (with help from lottery funds) and returned to public display at Ickworth.[45] Mean-

---

[42] Cornforth, *Country Houses of England*, p. 177.

[43] Wendy Philips, 'Checks and balances: respecting private owners and protecting the national heritage', in Dooley and Ridgway (eds), *Country House Collections*, pp. 173–185, p. 183.

[44] Frances Wilson, 'UK Export Controls and National Treasures', *Santander Art and Culture Law Review* 5:2 (2019), 193–208, at 203.

[45] Cornforth, *Country Houses of England*, p. 161.

while, a pair of pietra dura mounted, inlaid ebony cabinets from Castle Howard were acquired by the Fitzwilliam Museum in 2016 as a result of being export stopped and then offered for sale to a public institution.[46] Sometimes outright sale was unavoidable, given the financial pressures on properties. Hence, sales of crucial pieces by Constable (from Sudeley) and by Holbein (from Houghton) were prompted by the need to provide resources for ongoing maintenance of those two houses. Sayer calculated that art sales raised over two hundred million pounds between 1979 and 1992.

The fact that some of the items on show in the *Treasure Houses* exhibition were subsequently sold by their owners need not detract from the significance that collections and their care play in the management of country houses. Art sales from houses continue today: a survey of owners in 2017 showed that an astonishing one in six admitted to having sold an artwork in the previous five years to pay a repair bill or similar.[47] However, owners now have different options, including that of commissioning exact replicas while sending the original into secure storage (or to the auction house).

[46]   Philips, 'Checks and balances', p. 181.
[47]   Historic Houses Policy Survey (2017). See also Cowell, 'Saving Country Houses'.

9

Living above the shop

In his valedictory address as inaugural president of the Historic Houses Association, Lord Montagu gave a bravura account of his five years in the role. Over the course of those years, he said, a mixed economy approach to country houses had been adopted. No longer was the government at odds with owners. A true partnership was now in place, involving the triangulation of the state with, on the one side, an emboldened and growing National Trust, and on the other the private sector. The formation of the association was essential to the working of this heritage triumvirate; it was, after all, "a coherent and effective lobby to represent private owners ... a body representing the private sector which the State could itself consult." It was in the best interests of private owners to keep their houses and to pass them on to their successors. It was equally in the government's interests for this situation to prevail. Therefore, the government needed to avoid constantly changing the rules relating to taxation: the "altar of fiscal egalitarianism" that dictated draconian new capital tax policies needed to be shunned if heritage was to survive intact. It was hard enough living in one of these houses, Montagu argued, let alone being bled dry by the tax authorities for the privilege. The government needed to make concessions, or else owners would simply give up the ghost. After all, Montagu went on, "we know the hardships of living above the shop – how much more comfortable we would be in a smaller, warmer house."[1]

With these words Lord Montagu effectively summarised the existential dilemma faced by those responsible for privately owned country houses. These places were lived-in family homes. Yet their ongoing survival was also dependent on those houses being active places of business, whether as tourist attractions or as hospitality venues. Living above the shop was a practical necessity for anyone born into the life of a country house owner. Owners wanted both to maximise their business revenues and minimise the impact that business activity had on the day-to-day lives of them and their families. They could not depend on direct help from the government: which government, after all, would see their mission as being to enable the owners of stately homes to maintain

---

[1] Minutes of the Fifth AGM of the Historic Houses Association, 29 Nov. 1978.

their lifestyles? Rather, the government needed to encourage the conditions in which country house businesses could flourish. This chapter therefore considers the role that country houses have played in being simultaneously family homes and commercial business premises.

Alan Clark, the Conservative MP and owner of Saltwood Castle in Kent, recalled in his diaries a visit that he and his wife Jane had made in the early 1980s to Lord Montagu's home at Beaulieu in Hampshire. The visit gave Clark a perspective on the realities faced by country houses that had been transformed into tourist venues. As soon as the couple had ventured into the walled garden, they were spotted by Montagu and invited in for tea. Clark described how Montagu, "in the time-honoured role of stately home proprietor", had been "peeping from behind the curtains in his first floor flat, counting the visitors". Although the couple had not been angling for the invitation, being that day merely "spontaneous nosey-parkers", the politician could empathise with Montagu's beady-eyed and somewhat obsessive behaviour. "It's a kind of sample polling technique", Clark reasoned. "A given number at a particular locality at a given time will allow one to predict, fairly accurately, what the daily total is going to be." Returning to Beaulieu a few years later in September 1984 for the annual Autojumble meeting (a sort of car-boot sale devoted to motoring items), the Clarks were once again invited in by the proprietor. Montagu lived in an apartment in Palace House at Beaulieu, where Clark described him as "a prisoner in his own surroundings". It was an unfair account by someone Montagu clearly regarded as a friend. Clark portrayed Montagu as being surrounded by staff who appeared not to know too much about their employer.[2] When Montagu went to get the Clarks a pair of tickets for the attraction, he queued up with the rest of the visitors at the ticket booth. "No one seemed to bother much", Clark recorded. He simply could not understand why Montagu would put up with living in such a public environment: "The pressures at Palace House must, during the summer 'Season', be intolerable." As an example, Clark described seeing "three very obvious burglars" trampling over Montagu's private lawns, "laughing and sneering". It was, for Clark, "the sort of thing that, at Saltwood, would have made me dash back indoors and fetch the 12-bore". But no one seemed too interested. Montagu was busy doing the rounds of his

---

[2] The attendant at the motor museum, where the Clarks had first presented themselves, had put the radio call out for "Mister Montagu", which had gone uncorrected by "Control", "who clearly didn't, himself, know any better".

attraction, while the "gormless and pasty" guards appeared indifferent, if they appeared at all.[3]

Perhaps the best-known flagbearer for the cause of country house business in these years was Deborah Cavendish, wife of the eleventh duke of Devonshire. Debo, as she was familiarly known, acquired celebrity status as the archetypal stately home chatelaine. She regularly contrived photo opportunities in which she was shown scattering seed for the hens in the home farm or wrote magazine and newspaper articles about domestic realities at Derbyshire's most popular heritage attraction. Fundamentally, Debo knew that the house and estate needed to wash its face financially. She was certainly not averse to finding ways of making money, using the methodologies that Montagu had set out in his 1967 book, *The Gilt and the Gingerbread* – albeit that Montagu had been largely dismissive of the efforts made by Chatsworth before Debo. With a touch of aristocratic false modesty, the duchess gave the credit for some of Chatsworth's commercial innovations to Dorothy Dean, her housemaid from 1968 to 1981. Dean had been the first to realise that "people wanted to take something home from Chatsworth, a souvenir to remind them of their visit". At first this consisted of a rudimentary range of items set out on trestle tables in the orangery at the end of the visitor route: "guidebooks, postcards, playing cards, matches and bonbons".[4] Dean would spend the morning in cleaning overalls, and then change into shopkeeper's clothes for the afternoon shift behind the table. By 1978 the table, and the proceeds of a kiosk in the garden selling ice creams and plants, were turning over more than £75,000 a season. Debo, personally, was hooked: "I loved the shop and often served behind the counter. I was so interested in what people wanted and why … We printed better guidebooks, improved our range of postcards, laid in stocks of the ubiquitous tea towels, and out they all flew." By this time, she had already opened the Chatsworth farm as part of the visitor experience. In 1978 this was followed by a farm shop – now a ubiquitous enough feature of many publicly open country houses, but back then still something of a novelty. The farm shop proved a success, and over time more and more commercial features were added to Chatsworth: a restaurant in the carriage house, a permanent shop in the orangery designed by Philip Jebb. The house at Chatsworth was vested in a charitable trust in 1980, which depended for its income on commercial receipts from these ventures. It hardly mattered that one or two ventures would prove unsuccessful – such as a brand of Chatsworth-made jams and chutneys, and a Belgravia branch of the

---

3   Alan Clark, *Diaries* (London, 1993) pp. 92–93.

4   Deborah Devonshire, *Wait for Me!* (London, 2010), p. 267.

14 . Deborah Cavendish, duchess of Devonshire, 21 May 1985 (Trinity Mirror / Mirrorpix / Alamy Stock Photo).

Chatsworth farm shop. The duchess' personal drive and enterprise helped to push Chatsworth into the super-league of visitor attractions. By 1991, the year the eleventh duke died, it was making an annual turnover of nearly five million pounds and employed more than a hundred people.[5]

5 *Ibid.*, p. 273.

Lord Montagu's testimonial speech in November 1978, quoted above, took place against the backdrop of a shifting political landscape in the UK. The years that followed would see some radical changes to the country's economy, not all of them favourable to the owners of country houses. The Conservative administration that came to power under Margaret Thatcher in May 1979 sought a transformation in societal attitudes. Any innate deference to landed interests tended to shrivel away in the embrace of free-market capitalism. Mrs Thatcher was more interested in the creation of new wealth, rather than the preservation of existing agglomerations of the stuff. She therefore sought out those who knew how to create wealth rather than those who blocked its creation, whether those blockers were trade unionists or old-fashioned aristocrats. The Historic Houses Association, being a combination of both these things, might have considered itself likely to be out of favour in such a climate.

A decade on from Montagu's farewell speech, in November 1988, the normally sedate atmosphere of the HHA's annual general meeting, held at the Kensington Exhibition Centre, was shaken to its core by the invited guest speaker. This was no firebrand revolutionary, seeking wilfully to undermine the credentials of the nation's landowners. On the contrary, this was a man at the very heart of the establishment of the day: a high-profile member of Mrs Thatcher's cabinet. Nicholas Ridley had been invited to address the meeting in his role as secretary of state for the environment. He did not pull his punches. Although historic houses had been under threat for much of Ridley's lifetime, he could see all too clearly that "things had changed". Incomes were up, new-made millionaires abounded, and tax rates had fallen from ninety-eight per cent at the margin to a more reasonable forty per cent. For Ridley, it all meant that historic house owners needed to sharpen their list of demands from government.

No longer could owners come to government to plead that their family inheritance was about to disintegrate. Rather, it was for the owners themselves to ensure that this did not happen. Ridley admitted that the government wished "to see great houses maintained, lived in and loved". But it was axiomatic to him that the state "cannot provide a permanent guarantee to a particular family". After all, it was all too often the case that families might have married into a property, might have bought it, or might be "robber barons" or "property speculators". "I am not impressed by the case of the *anciens pauvres*" said Ridley, boldly, to an audience of *anciens pauvres*. There had to be room for today's *nouveaux riches* to join the club. The state was not going to intervene to retain a situation that was inherently unfair to new money. If owners could not stand the heat, they should get out of the Tudor kitchen. Or, as Ridley more bluntly put it, "if present owners cannot keep up their commitments, the solution is to sell, as it always has been." State ownership was not an option. Nevertheless, Ridley was optimistic that country houses would survive. They tended to do just that. Owners just needed to disabuse themselves of the idea that the state would bail them out. And there needed to be opportunities – both for new purchasers of old buildings, and for new builders of new buildings, able to hold their own with the best of the past.[6]

The HHA responded by refuting large parts of Ridley's argument. The earl of Shelburne, as president, pointed out the sheer number of losses, a direct result of less propitious economic circumstances. It was, he felt, an unacceptable level of change, implying the loss of an entire way of life. Government could still tip the balance in favour of saving heritage by choosing to reduce tax rates and making other easements to make life easier for owners. Nevertheless, Ridley's words were not wholly disregarded. Many of the members present that day would have agreed with much of what he said. Owners knew that the future of their houses sat necessarily with them. Government handouts had never really been the issue. Far from it, house owners were used to standing on their own feet and finding their own routes to survival. The impetus to diversify was already well-established among owners: arguably, it is what they had been doing for more than a century. During his time as HHA president, Michael Saunders Watson had made it clear that the association's mission was "to encourage and develop alternative means of public access to historic houses such as conferences, concerts, etc., rather than simply relying on the casual day visitor".[7]

An example was provided by Castle Ashby in Northamptonshire. In 1979 the marquess of Northampton left Castle Ashby and moved his family to their other home at Compton Wynyates. A future purpose for Castle Ashby was suddenly needed, to avoid it sitting as an empty house and to cover the cost of its upkeep. The family had retained a small flat there, and entertained hopes that one day it might return to use as a family home. For this reason, they did not want to make too many drastic alterations to the house, which might prohibit

---

[6] Nicholas Ridley, 'The November Speech', *Historic House* 13:1 (Spring, 1989), 25–26. Derek Sherborn recalled attending a drinks party at Nicholas Ridley's house in November 1987, and being appalled at Ridley's view that the state should not intervene to save whole collections of art. Instead, in Ridley's view, the artworks should be sold on the open market to private owners who could afford to have them on their walls. "I began to realise what an absolute fraud he was", Sherborn concluded. See Sherborn, *An Inspector Recalls*, pp. 255–256.

[7] Minutes of the Tenth AGM of the Historic Houses Association, 22 Nov. 1983.

that future scenario. Yet it still needed to be "kept alive". Various options were considered: turning it to a hotel or health farm; transforming it to a theme park along the lines of Alton Towers; letting it become a residential centre; or turning it into a permanent visitor attraction. The latter option was rejected due to the saturation of the historic house tourist market in that part of the country. The other options were ruled out because of the requirement for extensive alterations to the fabric of the property. In the end, the option with the most appeal was that of Castle Ashby reopening as a conference centre and events venue. It was felt that this option might cater not just for conferences but also for "social functions; product launches; exhibitions; external events; filming facilities; medieval banquets and any other event that required the use of space, inside or out, with full licensed catering facilities". Enough work had been done to bring the centre into use by December 1980, and it was launched publicly at a press day in May 1981.[8]

What diversification meant was spelled out by viscountess Cobham, who lived at Hagley Hall in Worcestershire and was shortly to become an adviser to the UK government. For Lady Cobham, diversification meant using ingenuity to spot opportunities. If the estate had a forestry enterprise that it was keen to continue, despite the increasing costs involved in this line of business, then it was incumbent on owners to think of new ways of making money from it: either by planting Christmas trees or by hosting war games "run in a discreet corner" of the estate. Uninhabited cottages could be let as holiday homes. The park could play host to horse trials or fireworks displays, or other more adventurous activities, from "buggy-driven treasure hunts to hovercraft races on a lake". The house meanwhile might be perfect for corporate "think tanks" or for product launches.[9] Indeed, the house was available for functions throughout the year and, according to an English Tourist Board guide, "virtually all activities" were considered, "from conferences to medieval jousting".[10]

Another flagbearer for diversification was Roger Tempest at Broughton in Yorkshire. Broughton was an archetypal HHA property: thirty generations of the Tempest family had lived at the hall, which stood at the heart of a three-thousand-acre estate. The difference lay in the change of attitude that its latest owner represented. Roger Tempest, who had worked for the media businessman Eddie Shah, brought new ideas when he returned to the property.

---

[8]   Peter Chubb, 'From Stately Home to Conference Centre for All Occasions', *Historic House* 5:2 (Autumn, 1981), 20–23.

[9]   Penny Cobham, 'Diversify or Bust?', *Historic House* 13:3 (Autumn, 1989), 18–20.

[10]   English Tourist Board, *Putting on the Style* (London, 1981), p. 34.

Traditional forms of income such as from shooting and fishing continued to be important. But Tempest chose to lease these out rather than manage them in-house, settling for a reduced level of income but with far fewer costs (and risks) to bear. Cottages were let on market rents, collected quarterly by standing order rather than monthly. The events in the park were entirely contracted out to third party event organisers. But the most striking thing about Broughton was the conversion of redundant estate buildings to active business use. This had been started by Tempest's father in the early 1980s, when the first unit had been leased to a designer of Norwegian oil platforms. Soon, Roger had converted so many other buildings that Broughton was home to thirty-five companies employing three hundred and fifty people.[11]

One changing aspect of the country house business at this time was the widening of what was considered the 'season'. Traditionally, houses had opened their doors for the extended Easter weekend, remained open for the two May bank holidays, attained their highest visitor numbers in July and August, and then closed in September or October. Many owners who opened their houses for a minimum twenty-eight days a year, for tax reasons, kept to exactly this pattern.[12] The quiet months could therefore be used for vital conservation work, and for keeping the house and grounds free from excessive trampling in wintry weather. But the larger houses increasingly found that there was good business to be had by opening in the so-called shoulder months. This might be in February for the snowdrop season (as at Hodsock Priory in Nottinghamshire), or it could involve increasingly elaborate December openings, at first through Christmas fairs and Santa's grottoes, and then through outdoor light shows that took full advantage of the long dark nights. Michael Saunders Watson, in an editorial for *Historic House* in 1988, foresaw exactly this when he posited that a successful winter market was there for the taking if only owners were brave enough to be in the vanguard.[13]

Saunders Watson argued that the country house had the advantage of being "the genuine article" in an era increasingly dominated by theme parks such as Alton Towers in Staffordshire. The Corkscrew ride was installed at Alton Towers in 1980; by 1990 the park had been acquired by the Tussaud's Group and entered a further phase of expansion. For Saunders Watson, a lived-in country

---

[11] 'Securing the Future', *Historic House* 19:3 (Autumn, 1995), 20–24.

[12] Many still do, in fact, not least because revenue rules dictate that the twenty-eight days of opening must include the bank holidays in May and August.

[13] Michael Saunders Watson, 'President's Review', *Historic House* 12:1 (Spring, 1988), 5.

house could be simultaneously a tourist attraction and a slice of domestic authenticity, as well as fulfilling a social purpose to its local community. Country houses could offer reality, as a counterpoint to the sometimes-crass commercialism of the UK tourist sector. Places like Kentwell Hall in Suffolk developed reputations for historical re-enactments: here, the hundreds of volunteer participants who would spend their summer holidays camping in the grounds and living as Tudors or as civil war-era soldiers.[14] At Goodwood in West Sussex, another sort of diversification was on offer. Here, the emphasis was on different varieties of sport, perhaps understandable for an estate that could lay claim to being the place where the rules of cricket were first laid down (in 1727). The future duke of Richmond had been a boy of eleven in 1966 when the motor racing circuit that his father had laid out in the grounds was closed. Once in a position to do so, in June 1993, the duke introduced a Festival of Speed in the grounds, as a reminder of the motor sports that took place at the house in the years after the second world war. Expecting an audience of three thousand, the duke and his team found they were dealing instead with a crowd of nearly ten times that number. The motor circuit itself was reopened in September 1998 and race events laid on under the theme of the Goodwood Revival. One hundred and forty-five thousand spectators were soon descending annually on Goodwood, requiring a team of more than seven hundred staff to be employed in and around the estate.[15]

Over time, new attention was paid by historic house owners to the interpretation and presentation of their properties. This often involved borrowing techniques developed in the USA. Where the UK was considered to have a competitive advantage in the practice of conservation, as well as a rich and diverse inheritance of actual heritage assets, North America was considered to lead the field in communicating the meaning and significance of places. The US National Parks Service was held up by Neil Cossons, the director of Ironbridge Gorge Museum and future chair of English Heritage, as the exemplar when it came to understanding and responding to audiences' needs. It was a new approach, as it started from the assumption that, far from being palaces of 'treasures' to which people would dutifully flock regardless of the quality of the experience, country houses needed to earn the attention of their visitors. Cossons led the way in introducing this way of thinking, declaring that

[14] Noël Riley, 'History According to Kentwell', *Historic House* 17:1 (Spring, 1993), 23–25.

[15] James Peill, *Glorious Goodwood: A Biography of England's Greatest Sporting Estate* (London, 2019), pp. 266–268.

"interpretation is essential if, as a society, we are to develop a wider appreciation for our heritage".[16] A similar theme was followed by Merlin Waterson, whose reinterpretation of Erddig for the National Trust had been one of the first to present the house from the perspective of the domestic servants who lived there.[17]

Historically, country houses were places where hospitality was a principal function: welcoming guests from near or far, throwing open the doors for parties and festivities, and entertaining visitors to overnight stays. It might be not so surprising, therefore, that many country houses have chosen hospitality and accommodation as a means of staying afloat. The conversion of country houses to hotels was a phenomenon noted in the Gowers report in 1950. Invariably, it meant a huge change to the character and make-up of a house. Down Hall in Essex, which initially converted to a school in the early twentieth century, became an antiques business and conference centre from 1967. From 1986 it operated as a luxury hotel. It retained many of the physical characteristics of a country house, but perhaps what was lost was the emotional resonance of being a home. One example of where such hotel conversions have been carried out successfully was the Historic House Hotels group. This chain of hotels was founded in 1979 with the direct intention of bringing abandoned country houses back to life. Each of the three houses in the group had superb heritage credentials. Hartwell House in Berkshire dated from the seventeenth century, and hosted King Louis XVIII during his exile from France. Bodysgallen Hall in Snowdonia was another seventeenth-century survival, while Middlethorpe Hall near York was rescued from being used as a nightclub. Each of these houses was accurately restored, losing nothing of their historic character. Indeed, the whole point was to recreate in these houses "the atmosphere of a well-run and comfortable country house in its hey-day". The only difference now that they were commercial concerns was that "so many more people are able to enjoy them".[18] They were perhaps the most successful of all historic house hotel conversions and started out as HHA member properties. In 2008 the three houses were given to the National Trust, to guarantee their long-term protection.

[16] Neil Cossons, 'What *is* interpretation?', *Historic House* 11:2 (Summer, 1987), 16–18.

[17] Merlin Waterson, 'Diversity and Dimension: Interpretation of Historic Houses', *Historic House* 11:2 (Summer, 1987), 20–22. For Erddig, see Merlin Waterson, *The Servants' Hall* (London, 1980).

[18] 'How Bodysgallen Hall was Restored as a Country House Hotel', *Historic House* 6:2 (Summer, 1982), 17–19.

Some houses also found it possible to integrate hospitality businesses into a domestic setting. At its simplest, this could be an extension of the existing social life of houses. After all, as was pointed out by one entrepreneur, "if you can easily entertain twelve friends for dinner or several acquaintances for a shooting weekend, is it not a tempting option to think of providing the same service commercially?" All that was needed was "five or ten reasonably appointed bedrooms" and a large house's commercial potential could be fully realised. The idea was explained by Jan Curd, whose company Heritage Placements was set up to broker exactly this sort of business.[19] Heritage Circle was another organisation that provided a similar service. Run by Elizabeth and John Denning from Burghope Manor in Bradford-upon-Avon, Heritage Circle was aimed primarily at wealthy Americans. It had the feel of an exclusive club, allowing travellers the chance to stay in well-preserved castles and manor houses. Upton Cressett in Shropshire was a member, and William Cash, son of Bill and Biddy, recalled his early experience of the hospitality profession:

> The whole point was for your owner-host to mix your gin and tonic before a black-tie dinner with the family … As a young teenager, I would wear a blue velvet jacket from C&A, with a clip-on bow-tie, and pass around prawn crackers and crisps. It was my first introduction to country-house stage-set acting.[20]

Integrating commercial hospitality into a private residence in this way had its downsides. Viscount and viscountess Brentford of Newick Park in East Sussex opted to lease out their thirteen bedrooms to up to twenty-five guests at a time at weekends and sometimes during the week. At first, they saw this as an extension of the occasional social events that they ran for charities or the local church. But soon they found they had taken on a business that involved not a small amount of risk. Although some evenings involved a full house of twenty-five guests, at other times they might be joined by just two paying residents. Given that the costs involved in employing a chef and service team were similar whether the catering was for twenty-five or two, they soon learned that maximising occupancy was key to the business. More marketing staff were taken on, and over time the couple found they had to step away from being personally involved in the business.

[19] 'Hospitality – Country House Party Style', *Historic House* 10:2 (Summer, 1986), 14–17.

[20] William Cash, *Restoration Heart: A Memoir* (London, 2019), p. 42.

A little commercial hospitality could indeed end up destroying a house's atmosphere as a private, domestic residence. Weston Park in Staffordshire evolved from being a private house offering occasional gourmet dinner events to being a full-blown events and conference venue after the house was given 'to the nation' in 1986. Newick Park eventually became a permanent country house hotel, although it has now once again reverted to being a family home.[21] According to Michael Sayer, more than a hundred of the four hundred and sixty houses sold from the 1970s to the 1990s became hotels, leisure centres with golf courses, or commercial, educational, and other institutions.[22] Nor were these conversions necessarily cheap or easy to achieve. S. J. Packe-Drury spent the best part of a hundred thousand pounds to bring Prestwold Hall near Loughborough in Leicestershire up to the sort of standards that were required from conference and events venues. Attending to the requirements of the Food Safety Act (1990) meant installing new dishwashers and refrigerators. The requirements of the alcohol licensing regime and electricity regulations all meant additional costs on top of the money that had to be spent expanding the car parks, installing new fire alarms, and increasing the provision of extra toilets to accommodate events for up to two hundred people. The business proved a success, but the family were forced to move out of the main house and into a self-contained flat, sufficiently soundproofed to keep out the noise of the discotheque. (Even here, new building regulations carried minimum standards for acoustic insulation.)[23]

Owners had their work cut out dealing with endless regulations that required full compliance, whether these applied to buildings, health and safety, employment, or food and drink. It was one of the reasons why not everyone would be enthusiasts for the diversification cause. Francis Fulford was just one owner who cast a sceptical view in his book *Bearing Up*, which placed more emphasis on the risks and problems involved in diversifying an estate. While it was perfectly possible to make decent profits, such ventures could also mean "losing buckets of money", leading to the inevitable sales notice in *Country Life*.[24] The Prince of Wales, addressing the twentieth anniversary AGM of the HHA in 1993, also referred to the difficulties attendant on business diversification in country house settings. He explained that the 1960s and 1970s had seen

[21] 'Hospitality – Country House Party Style', p. 15.

[22] Michael Sayer, *The Disintegration of a Heritage: Country Houses and their Collections, 1979–1992* (Norwich, 1993), p. 8.

[23] 'Food for Thought', *Historic House* 16:4 (Winter, 1992), 20–22.

[24] Fulford, *Bearing Up*, p. 151.

endless new features installed: safari parks, adventure playgrounds, and other measures that "only added to the complexity" of the burdens that such houses faced. But not every house was suitable for initiatives like these. What each house needed, the prince argued, was "a John Harvey-Jones of its own", referring to the most famous business troubleshooter of the day. "In many cases," the prince continued, "his advice would be blunt and painful."[25]

When regulations were occasionally eased, new opportunities for enterprise often emerged. One such business opportunity embraced by historic house owners from the mid-1990s was the new freedom to host wedding events on their premises. Wedding law in England and Wales was formulated in the eighteenth and nineteenth centuries, with the twentieth-century system based largely on principles established in the Marriage Act of 1836. This created the civil wedding option as an alternative to the Anglican wedding, with civil weddings in registry offices gaining more credence as a secular alternative to religious ceremonies from 1857.[26] The Marriage Act of 1949 codified the basic distinction between religious ceremonies and civil weddings, with religious wedding events taking place according to different religious traditions, whether Anglican, Jewish, or Quaker. The distinctions were stark: civil weddings were not to have any religious content or overtones, while Anglican weddings took place according to their own rules and regulations, as determined by the Church of England or Church of Wales.[27] The situation changed with the Marriage Act of 1994. For the first time, a civil wedding could take place in a setting other than a registry office. Premises could apply to become venues licensed to host wedding ceremonies led by a civil registrant.

The 1994 act opened a whole new area of business opportunities for country houses in England, which after all often had the ideal set of conditions for wedding events. Couples could now pledge their vows in grand rooms beneath ornate plaster ceilings or surrounded by ancient wood paneling and ancestral

---

[25]   HHA Archive, 'HRH Addresses the Annual General Meeting of the Historic Houses Association at the Queen Elizabeth II Conference Centre, SW1. Tuesday 16th November 1993'. Earlier that year (on 2 July 1993), the Prince of Wales had convened a seminar on the built heritage, attended by prime minister John Major, the heads of the National Trust, English Heritage, and the HHA, and those heritage crusaders Marcus Binney and Simon Jenkins.

[26]   Law Commission, *Celebrating Marriage: A New Weddings Law* (London, 2022), p. 6.

[27]   See also Rebecca Probert, *Tying the Knot: The Formation of Marriage, 1836–2000* (Cambridge, 2021). Marriage law was always markedly less restrictive in Scotland compared to England, as residents of Gretna Green can testify.

portraits. There were orangeries or glasshouses where drinks could be taken, spilling out onto summer lawns edged by abundant flower beds. And those same lawns could accommodate marquees suitable for vast wedding breakfasts, with those tents then repurposed as evening dancefloors until streams of taxis came to take guests away in the small hours. The fact that bridal couples, and other members of the wedding party, could sometimes take overnight accommodation in the house or in estate cottages was another reason why country houses were particularly well placed to take advantage of the easing of wedding regulations. There remained restrictions. Rooms could only be licensed if they were devoid of any religious symbolism or iconography: a civil wedding was not permitted to have any religious content. It made for moments of farce, as owners subtly drew registrants' gaze away from any cruciform shapes that might have been incorporated into plasterwork or portraiture. The regulations also dictated levels of public access and could involve significant additional costs for owners. But by and large, country house owners found that their properties made exceptionally good wedding venues and increasing numbers of owners paid significant amounts of money to become licensed premises for hire. Around a third of all Historic Houses properties today advertise themselves as wedding venues, demonstrating how a change in the law can generate significant amounts of business activity.

Browsholme and Combermere Abbey, houses that featured earlier in this book, have both benefited from relaxation in wedding regulations. Having survived the threat of demolition in the mid-1970s, Combermere's future looked anything but certain. Sarah Callander Beckett, great granddaughter of Sir Kenneth Crossley, was faced with an unenviable choice in her mid-thirties. Having made a career in public relations, Sarah was living in the USA and working for the British company Laura Ashley. The eldest of three girls, Sarah had first refusal on whether to take on the challenge of Combermere Abbey. Her time in the USA was a formative influence, investing her with a 'can-do' attitude. Being at that time unmarried meant a degree of freedom of choice that others might not have. Resolving that the family home "definitely needed a fresh pair of eyes and the benefit of younger energies", Sarah moved back in and began the job of restoring Combermere.[28]

As she saw it, the challenges were multiple. The house remained an ongoing problem, requiring significant amounts of investment. But the means to provide this investment was being frittered away through the ongoing sale of land from the estate. Since agriculture was the sole source of income, Sarah

[28] Callander Beckett, 'An Inheritance Restored', p. 71.

15. Hayley and Umesh's wedding at Combermere Abbey, Cheshire (Liam and Bee Crawley, photo courtesy of Combermere Abbey).

could see the problem all too clearly. Meanwhile, the barns and farm buildings across the estate remained dilapidated and unused. Sarah's mother continued to live on the estate, and Sarah was mindful of the need to avoid being overly drastic in her management choices. At the same time, change was needed. Sarah decided therefore to appoint her mother as farm manager, while at the same time she drew a halt to the continued sale of land. This left Sarah with the time to focus on the house itself and its immediate surroundings. A block of Victorian stables was converted in the early 1990s to a range of holiday cottages. For Sarah this was the gateway "to a new world of tourism and hospitality and the stepping-stone to all the other subsequent enterprises we now have".[29] Another change happened when two friends asked Sarah if they could get married at Combermere, following the legal changes of 1994. The acquisition of a wedding licence changed everything for Combermere. The house now hosts sixty weddings a year, with guests accommodated in the estate's thirty-four holiday cottages.

Combermere continued to have problems. In 1996 an English Heritage grant was secured for emergency repairs to the roof above the library which was in danger of imminent collapse. Once that problem had been addressed,

[29] *Ibid.*, p. 72.

the restoration of the house continued apace; in 2016 the business won the Historic Houses' Restoration Award for the singular achievement of rescuing Combermere from the brink of destruction. Today, Combermere is a successful small business, with a hard-working staff team. Its success has been due to business diversification. Estate buildings have been converted to offices and light industrial units and tenanted by local businesses. A twenty-five-year lease of land for use as a solar park provides a steady stream of income. A proposal for new housing on estate property secured planning permission as an enabling development, meaning that it would not normally have been given the go-ahead but for the demonstrable benefits it brings to Combermere Abbey itself.

Browsholme Hall in Lancashire continues today as a successful historic house business and is another exemplar of business diversification. Robert Parker, who is employed as the technical adviser to Historic Houses, also owns and runs an auction market on the outskirts of nearby Clitheroe. Income from Browsholme derives partly from agriculture but also from hospitality and events. A tithe barn near the main house was refurbished with a European Union grant as well as support from the Country Houses Foundation (now the Historic Houses Foundation). The investment means that the barn now serves as a modern events facility. Weddings and other celebrations can be hosted here, at sufficient remove from the house to avoid any collateral damage from the excesses of late-night revelries. The solid stone walls provide excellent soundproofing, while the money is made from the drinks sold at the in-situ bar. The newest addition, a pizza oven in the courtyard beyond, offers another form of added value income generation. The installation of a dozen accommodation pods in the woods beyond the tithe barn means that guests can now also be offered overnight accommodation for their event. The diversification of Browsholme epitomises the way that houses have been made to work for themselves in the early twenty-first century.

10

A design for life

A mostly instrumental long-player record that took its inspiration from the English landscape dominated the album charts in October 1974, and in the week of the opening of the V&A's *Destruction of the Country House* exhibition. *Hergest Ridge* was Mike Oldfield's follow-up to the phenomenally successful *Tubular Bells*, his bestselling debut of 1973.[1] The sleeve of *Hergest Ridge* featured an aerial shot of the titular landscape feature: a distinctively shaped hill outside Kington in Herefordshire, close to the Welsh border. Oldfield had retreated here, to a house called The Beacon, as a way of coping with his sudden fame and public profile as well as to draw inspiration for his music.

A mile or two from Hergest Ridge, and therefore just off the edge of the aerial photograph on the sleeve of the record, was an equally distinctive country house and garden. Hergest Croft had suffered the depredations of wartime requisition after it was converted to a boarding school for girls. Nevertheless, it had narrowly escaped a listing in the catalogue for the *Destruction* show, and the family had resumed residence in 1953. In a clear case of nominative determinism, the Banks family made their money in banking (as well as in industry and the law). But successive generations of the family were also keen on banking of a more physical kind: building up the embanked surroundings of their house through plantings of trees and shrubs. William Hartland Banks married Dorothy Alford, daughter of the dean of Canterbury and, like her husband, a talented natural scientist. Together they first laid out the gardens at Hergest Croft in 1895, around the time that the house had been built to a fashionable arts and crafts design. The gardens became known for their exotics and other distinctive plantings: azaleas, cedars, rhododendrons, maples, and birches. The trees planted after the war by William and Dorothy's son Dick Banks, an industrialist and director of ICI, now have national collection status.

Dick's eldest son, Lawrence, made a career in banking, but also had a passionate interest in gardening. The two sides of his life were combined when

---

[1] In fact, in the weeks before the exhibition opened, *Hergest Ridge* had been knocked off the top spot by its predecessor, *Tubular Bells*: one of the few times a recording artist has ever been supplanted by one of their own records.

he became treasurer of the Royal Horticultural Society. His wife Elizabeth, a landscape architect, also served as chair of the HHA's gardens committee, and became president of the Royal Horticultural Society in 2010. Lawrence Banks was the inaugural chair of the HHA's gardens committee, which met for the first time in November 1976.[2] The creation of such a committee, so soon after the formation of the association, reflected widespread concern over the future of country house gardens. John Cornforth's 1974 study drew attention to the collapse in the number of people employed to manage gardens compared to the situation just a generation earlier. Cornforth found that the vast teams of gardeners, divided into separate departments according to whether they tended the glasshouses or managed the flower beds, had by now "quite disappeared". One head gardener Cornforth spoke to had begun his working career as one of twenty-five gardeners and was now just one of a team of three. For many places, a team of three would have been a luxury. Cornforth did not pick up on any noticeable decline in the quality of gardens but did notice the change in gardening styles that this reduction in labour foretold. Bedding plants which needed to be laboriously planted out each year were increasingly replaced by perennials. "Obviously, this cannot or should not be done in certain historic gardens," noted Cornforth, "but then Britain is not overburdened with *gardens a la française*."[3]

Many of the problems had set in during the second world war, when ornamental gardens had been ploughed up for food production. The war meant that the nation's historic gardens suffered "involuntary neglect for a period of five years", as the garden historian Jane Fearnley-Whittingstall put it in a survey of the HHA's gardens in 1990.[4] When he addressed the HHA's annual general meeting in 1977, Banks spoke of how gardens had always felt like the "junior partner" to houses. Consequently, they remained "under great threat". A Country Land and Business Association (CLA) survey had revealed that four-fifths of garden owners were worried about the future of their landscapes and could not see any possibility of passing gardens on to heirs or successors who would have the same degree of interest or care for them. The inaugural edition of the HHA's magazine stressed that the problem facing gardens was essentially one of money. The socially progressive ambitions of the government to increase the wages of the lowest-paid workers spelled trouble for the employers of gardeners, who were among the least-paid workers of all. "Garden owners are

---

[2] *Historic House* 1:2 (Winter, 1976), 11.
[3] Cornforth, *Country Houses in Britain*, p. 18.
[4] Fearnley-Whittingstall, *Historic Gardens*, p. 23.

threatened with being crushed between the upper millstone of frozen pay and higher taxes and the nether millstone of higher wages", claimed the journal: "Morton's fork has become the Treasury's pitchfork."[5]

Banks thought that the garden members of the association tended to take less interest in the mundane details of how the tax code might affect significant landscapes, nor take as strong an interest in the importance of tourism for garden properties. To rectify this, Banks' committee included representatives from the Royal Horticultural Society, the National Trust and the National Trust for Scotland, and the National Gardens Scheme. Banks had struck up a dialogue with the International Committee on Monuments and Sites (ICO-MOS) to explore whether an equivalent to listing could be introduced for gardens as it had for buildings and had persuaded Michael Saunders Watson that gardens would feature in the next round of talks with the chancellor of the exchequer, Denis Healey. Sure enough, by 1980 the HHA had secured the valuable concession that gardens, as well as buildings and collections, were eligible for exemption from capital transfer tax.[6]

Gardens and designed landscapes have always been integral to the life of mansion properties, and so deserve a chapter of their own. The historic house itself was only ever one part of an ensemble that included its wider garden and parkland setting. This has been true ever since large mansion houses started to be built in countryside locations, usually at the heart of large, landed estates.[7] Medieval deer parks that might have surrounded castles or manorial halls gave way to designed landscapes that, with the growing influence of classical forms of architecture, might feature axial avenues of trees and strategically placed terraces and viewing platforms. Later, the more naturalistic styles associated with Georgian designers such as Lancelot 'Capability' Brown saw more emphasis on the replacement of geometric lines in the landscape with sweeping grassland and informal 'clumps' of tree plantations, which were useful not only as sources of timber but also for game management. The hold that Brown had over the English landscape tradition was never so great as to lead to the eradication of flower beds and other ornamental features, and the fashion for these

[5] *Historic House* 1:2 (Winter, 1976), 11.

[6] HHA Archive, Minutes of the Seventh AGM of the Historic Houses Association, 26 Nov. 1980.

[7] Histories of the British landscape garden tradition are legion, and include for example Tim Mowl, *Gentlemen and Players: Gardeners of the English Landscape* (Stroud, 2000), and Tom Williamson, *Polite Landscapes: Gardens and Society in Eighteenth Century England* (Stroud, 1995). The economics of country house gardens are explored in Roderick Floud, *An Economic History of the English Garden* (London, 2019).

returned more emphatically in the nineteenth century. By the early twentieth century, the services of gardeners such as Gertrude Jekyll and Harold Peto were in demand from country house owners. Peto's design for his own house at Iford in Wiltshire can still be seen, laid out across a series of terraces on a sharp incline of land. As landscape architect Michael Balston pointed out to readers of the HHA magazine in 1982, a house and its wider landscape were "an indivisible whole, which cannot be treated as two separate entities". However financially desirable it may be to separate them, Balston argued that a house and its garden "can never really be divorced".[8]

Nevertheless, gardens often did not get the same attention as houses and collections. If the V&A exhibition in 1974 had highlighted over a thousand houses as having been demolished or lost, Balston estimated that the number of gardens similarly lost was five or ten times greater. The HHA was alert to the possibility of gardens being sidelined and made great efforts to push gardens to the foreground where possible. An international gardens year was mooted for 1977.[9] Yet an unhelpful perception lingered that gardens played second fiddle to the houses, despite the evidence of visitor numbers which showed just how popular gardens tended to be. The loss of garden teams was highlighted by one garden owner, Mrs Boscowen of High Beeches, when she addressed a regional meeting of the HHA in 1980. Given levels of taxation, even one gardener was beyond the means of many owners, Mrs Boscowen explained. The consequence, however, was the rapid disintegration of a garden. "The most satisfying pictorial landscape can be lost in three or four years," she continued, "and a formal garden quicker than that." Given that wages made up seventy per cent of the cost of running a garden, a regular and inflation-proofed income was necessary. Mrs Boscowen saw tourist visitors as the answer, provided the admission fee was set at the right level. This ought to be above one pound, as was the case in France. At this level, Mrs Boscowen needed ten thousand visitors a year, although she felt that her garden was unlikely to sustain this level of footfall. Nevertheless, the appreciative comments that visitors to High Beeches had made had proved to be an "unexpected pleasure" to Mrs Boscowen and her husband.[10] Garden historian David Jacques offered his own advice to historic

---

[8] Michael Balston, 'The House and its Landscape', *Historic House* 6:2 (Summer, 1982), 14–16.

[9] HHA Archive, Minutes of the Fourth AGM of the Historic Houses Association, 1 Nov. 1977.

[10] 'Problems and Pleasures of running a heritage garden', *Historic House* 4:1 (Spring, 1980), 25–26.

garden owners in the 1978 edition of the HHA's magazine. A national list of important gardens was still not yet in existence, and this made it all the harder for a garden to apply for one of the grants that were in scant supply. Jacques recommended that owners devised management plans that would make clear how a garden could be sustained once restored, whether through tourism or country sports such as fishing and shooting. Much could be done to create efficiencies, so that everyone played their part in maintaining a garden. Naturally too, Jacques put an emphasis on recording of garden features.[11]

At the HHA's AGM in 1983 the condition of the country's historic gardens "remained a worry"; moreover, public funds in the form of grant aid were not available to gardens in the way that they were to houses or parklands. It was not long, however, before gardens started to receive official attention. In Scotland, Elizbeth Banks produced the first register of significant landscapes for the Scottish Countryside Commission. The newly created English Heritage followed the example and began officially to register landscapes from 1983. The HHA was instinctively opposed to gardens being listed in the same way as buildings, for fear of the regulatory burdens that this could imply. This perhaps helped to keep the register a somewhat lighter-touch form of designation compared to listing, though the presence of a garden on the register had some weight in planning terms.

Meanwhile, as a gesture of its support for the horticultural endeavours of its member houses, the HHA established an annual garden of the year competition, sponsored by Christie's, and first awarded in 1984. The idea for such an award emerged from a chance remark made by Charles Clive-Ponsonby-Fane, chairman of the HHA's gardens committee, when he observed that gardens "were increasingly the key to attracting visitors to country houses".[12] The award sought to focus attention on the settings of great houses, as a boost to their visitor numbers, and was awarded by a simple ballot of HHA members and friends. The first winner of the award was Heale House in Wiltshire, where gardens on the banks of the river Avon had been laid out by Harold Peto in the early twentieth century. Sure enough, the numbers of visitors coming to see the gardens at Heale, with its Japanese tea house, quickly shot up. Subsequent winners of the award experienced a similar boost to their visitor numbers, as well as to the morale and confidence of their gardening teams. These included some of the most striking of the gardens that remained in private hands: Newby Hall

---

[11]   David Jacques, 'Restoring Historic Gardens and Parks', *Historic House* 2:3 (Summer, 1978), 13–15.

[12]   'Garden of the Year Award', *Historic House* 28:3 (Autumn, 2004), 26.

in North Yorkshire (1986 winner), Arley Hall in Cheshire (1987), Forde Abbey in Somerset (1992), and Athelhampton in Dorset (1997).

The award often highlighted gardens with particularly rare or impressive selections of plantings. Borde Hill in West Sussex was one such garden. Stephenson Robert Clarke purchased the house in 1893. The garden surrounding it was filled with species of plants brought back from plant-hunting expeditions in the early years of the twentieth century, to places as far apart as Burma, China, Tasmania, and the Andes. The result was a garden filled with exotic species of trees, shrubs, and plants. A rhododendron garden, an azalea ring, and a rose garden made Borde Hill a regular destination for gardening aficionados. A Chinese tulip tree (*Liriodendron chinense*) was planted in 1913 with seed brought back from China by the plant collector Ernest Henry Wilson (also known as 'Chinese' Wilson). A camelia hybrid, *Camellia x williamsii* 'Donation', won a prestigious Award of Garden Merit in 1941. In the round dell, banana, palm, and bamboo trees were clumped alongside a giant gunnera (a rhubarb). Amid a group of old potting sheds, a microclimate existed that allowed for the growth of species of plant usually found only in the southern hemisphere: Clianthus 'Flamingo', Sollya heterophylla, and hardy nerines. Borde Hill was in this way a paradise of global plantings, taken root in the southern English countryside. The place had gained charitable status in 1965, which meant that decisions about its management and conservation rested with independent trustees and not solely with the Stephenson Clarke family. It also enabled them in 1997 to secure lottery funding for the restoration of Victorian greenhouses and further rounds of planting, as well as improvements to pathways to enhance disability access.[13]

The garden of the year award celebrated the variety of garden styles and designs on show at HHA member places. The joint winners in 1998 were Iford Manor in Wiltshire, which continued Harold Peto's terrace gardening of the early twentieth century, and Mellerstain in Berwickshire. At Athelhampton in Dorset, winner in 1997, the award recognised the effect of the topiary in defining the spaces and rooms of the garden nearest to the manor house. Kiftsgate, winner in 2003, was a different place altogether: an extravagant display of planting that tumbled artfully down a Cotswold hillside. Here too there was space for the modern: a still, rectangular pool of inky black water. The garden of the year award recognised the freedom enjoyed by private owners to be creative and innovative in transforming the spaces around their houses.

---

[13] 'Borde Hill', *Historic House* 29:2 (Summer, 2005), 24–26.

16. Kiftsgate Court Gardens, Gloucestershire, winner of the Garden of the Year Award 2003 (photo courtesy of Kiftsgate Court Gardens).

Gardens in institutional ownership could show similar levels of creativity. It was as though the act of gardening could unleash a creative interest in the 'shock of the new' that exceeded anything ever shown by interventions in built architecture. Some National Trust gardens developed reputations for horticultural excellence, often surpassing the achievements of those properties' original owners. The gardens of Sissinghurst Castle in Kent, for example, were famous as the creation of Vita Sackville-West and her husband Harold Nicolson. They have been maintained by the National Trust since 1967, and the Trust's gardeners have arguably been just as influential in continuing to develop the gardens as Sackville-West and Nicolson were. Pamela Schwerdt and Sibylle Kreutzberger were joint head gardeners here until 1990 and received the Royal Horticultural Society's Victoria Medal of Honour for their achievements in 2006. Since then, other gardeners have earned minor celebrity status in the horticulture world by occupying the same position, including Alexis Data and, most recently, Troy Scott Smith. At Anglesey Abbey in Cambridgeshire, the father and son combination of Noel and Richard Ayres did as much to extend and enliven the gardens as head gardeners for the National Trust as the property's owner Lord Fairhaven had before his death in 1966. Meanwhile, at

Packwood House in Warwickshire, Tim Richardson has commended the way that head gardener Mick Evans has been given the freedom to "experiment horticulturally in the most high-profile parts of this garden".[14]

Privately owned houses remained the places where perhaps the highest levels of innovation were possible in relation to gardens and settings. Conditions of private ownership gave gardeners a freedom and creative licence that might be denied to them under more institutional ownership arrangements. For Tim Richardson, this freedom initially meant a focus on developing the interest in colour and form that was first manifested in the arts and crafts movement.[15] In a garden setting, attention was paid to building up the patterning and complexity of herbaceous borders, such as those at Newby Hall in North Yorkshire or Arley Hall in Cheshire. For Richardson, this fashion had reached its apotheosis by the early 1990s, which was "the end of a floriferous road which had been developing since the late Victorian period".[16] Perhaps the enthusiasm for such high-maintenance planting schemes had been knocked by the great storm of 1987, which did so much damage to gardens and parklands across the UK. In its wake came more naturalistic planting schemes and more minimalist approaches to garden design.[17] The so-called New Perennial movement involved many more grasses and perennials and an approach that was more in harmony with wild nature. It was influenced by designs from Europe, from the Low Countries and Germany, but also had British proponents such as garden designer Beth Chatto, whose garden near Chelmsford in Essex featured plants that could be sustained in dry or shady positions. This more relaxed approach to horticulture was also seen in other places where owners were inspired to experiment with wildlife-friendly gardening methods. Great Dixter in East Sussex, the home of the gardener Christopher Lloyd, exemplified the method, where a partnership with Fergus Garrett created one of the most visited and loved of all gardens in contemporary Britain. Highgrove, the Gloucestershire home of the Prince of Wales, the future King Charles III, proliferated with the influence of countless leading lights from the world of horticulture. At Deans Court in Dorset, the kitchen garden was cultivated from the 1960s according to 'no dig', organic methods, which kept its soils intact.

[14] Tim Richardson, *The New English Garden* (London, 2015), p. 36.
[15] Tim Richardson, *English Gardens in the Twentieth Century* (London, 2005).
[16] Richardson, *New English Garden*, p. 8.
[17] The HHA was involved in giving out grants to its member properties to help with the recovery from this event.

The work of the Dutch plantsman Piet Oudolf at Bury Court announced the arrival of the New Perennial style in Britain. It was noticed by Sir Charles Legard, who invited Oudolf to advise on the walled garden at Scampston Hall in North Yorkshire. At the time the walled garden was devoted to the growing of Christmas trees. In the hope that the garden might become part of the visitor experience at Scampston, Oudolf was minded to remodel it entirely as a series of interlocking rooms comprised of meadows, box, and drifts of grass. Tim Richardson has called it "one of the most interesting and ambitious gardens of the first decade of the twenty-first century".[18] The garden featured signature motifs of Oudolf's style, such as the plantsman's walk and a perennial meadow.[19] Oudolf also worked at Trentham in Staffordshire, where the house had been abandoned by its owners, the dukes of Sutherland, in the early twentieth century. Although the mansion was taken down, the bones of the extensive Victorian gardens remained, and Charles Barry's lower parterre was replanted by British gardener Tom Stuart-Smith, who also laid out the extensive gardens at Mount St John in North Yorkshire. At Trentham, Oudolf added two flanking borders in a naturalistic style, as well as a meadow area, a 'River of Grass', nearby. Richardson has suggested that Trentham, despite its depressed and blighted history since the late nineteenth century, "is now the best place in Britain to get an idea of cutting-edge plantsmanship, since two of the world's leading protagonists have been given their head to design spaces of imagination and verve".[20] Oudolf would be appointed to design the memorial garden for the victims of the World Trade Centre attack of 2001. Other examples of New Perennial planting can be found at Waltham Place in Berkshire, where Henk Gerritsen laid out a naturalistic garden for the Oppenheimer family from 1999. Here, herbaceous plantings were eschewed in favour of strategic placements of grasses such as *Stipa arundinacea*.

British garden designers have continued to flourish in recent decades. Dan Pearson, influenced by Beth Chatto, laid out an influential garden around the Jacobean house at Armscote Manor in Warwickshire, featuring wildflowers, plantings of native British trees, and sculpted areas of lawn. The ruins of Lowther Castle in Cumbria were augmented in the 2010s with Pearson's Garden in the Ruin. The planting of roses, geraniums, and narcissi brought colour and life to a place that stood as a monument to aristocratic excess. Other designers such as George Carter, James Alexander-Sinclair, and Arabella

[18] Richardson, *New English Garden*, p. 51.
[19] 'Walled Garden at Scampston', *Historic House* 29:2 (Summer, 2005), 32.
[20] Richardson, *New English Garden*, p. 81.

Lennox-Boyd have made gardens of international significance in recent years. Lennox-Boyd's extensively planted hillside garden at Gresgarth in Lancashire won the Judges' Choice prize in the Garden of the Year competition in 2020. Roy Strong, who followed the 1974 *Destruction* exhibition at the V&A with a show on garden history, made his own garden with his wife Julia Trevelyan Oman at The Laskett in Herefordshire. After the National Trust declined to take on his creation, Strong gave the garden to a charity that now opens it to public access. Garden creations like that of Columbine Hall in Suffolk, home of Leslie Geddes-Brown and Hew Stevenson from 1993, have also proved popular destinations for garden-loving visitors, keen to see how private owners have responded creatively and personally to the settings of their homes.[21]

Even the bravest or most confident of National Trust head gardeners may have stopped short of introducing the kinds of radical interventions into garden landscapes seen at Boughton or Heveningham. At Boughton in Northamptonshire, the duke of Buccleuch commissioned landscape designer Kim Wilkie to create a garden feature to occupy space next to the historic garden mound. Wilkie proposed Orpheus, a breathtakingly original landscape feature that entirely met the objectives of the commission to create a beautiful new form of design for the twenty-first century. Drawing inspiration from the formal gardens of the late-seventeenth and early-eighteenth centuries, Orpheus performs a clever landscape trick, by inverting a pyramid that descends seven metres below the level of the historic garden terraces. At the base of the inverted pyramid, a pool of still water reflects the sky above. Wilkie's designs represented a modern, twenty-first-century equivalent of eighteenth-century landscape gardeners such as Charles Bridgeman (who had worked at Boughton) and Lancelot 'Capability' Brown. At Rotherfield, a wholly private house in Hampshire, Wilkie inserted a grass-covered amphitheatre. Heveningham in Suffolk was one of Capability Brown's last designs. Where eighteenth-century designers at times chose to demonstrate their mastery over nature, here Wilkie's designs sought to restore equilibrium. Wilkie produced a masterplan that proposed restoration of the original meanders of the river Blyth, the planting of new areas of broadleaf woodland, and the wetting of meadows. A Victorian garden behind the house was replaced with Wilkie's trademark grass terraces, arranged in a Fibonacci series. Charles Jencks' Garden of Cosmic Speculation in Dumfries has also proved inspirational, with similar designs appearing at

---

[21] Hew Stevenson and Leslie Geddes-Brown, *Columbine Hall: The Story of a House and Its Transformation* (2018).

places like Easton Walled Gardens in Lincolnshire and Througham Court in Gloucestershire.

One especially dramatic landscape intervention of recent years has involved the absence of any intervention. This more passive attitude was a response to the over-exploitation of modern agriculture and the accompanying decline in biodiversity of species. The concept of 'rewilding' was first developed by conservationist Frans Vera, who observed that, if left alone, natural landscapes in temperate areas tended to revert to steppe-like conditions where animal, plant, and insect life found their natural balance. The challenge was to resist the temptation to intervene to correct perceived problems, such as the sudden outbreak of a virulent plant disease. Vera advocated here that diseases should be left to run their natural course, just as the trunks of fallen trees or the carcasses of dead mammals should be left in situ rather than tidied up and disposed of. Although such an approach might offend conventional ideas of landscape maintenance, it did so in the interests of allowing nature to flourish. Insect life would feed and proliferate on dead timber and rotting flesh, which in turn provided new sources of food for birds and other animals which might return after having been obliterated by the monoculture of industrial farming.

Isabella Tree and Charlie Burrell visited Vera's experiment with rewilding at Oostvaardersplassen in the Netherlands around the same time that Vera's book, *Grazing Ecology and Forest History*, was translated into English. Tree and Burrell's own estate, Knepp in West Sussex, had become a monster that required constant feeding. Incomes were dependent on sales of the estate's ice cream range, and profits were marginal. Inspired by Vera's innovation, Tree and Burrell set about recreating the Serengeti in West Sussex. Except they didn't. They simply stopped farming and let nature do the work. The three-and-a-half-thousand acres of the estate were given a strong perimeter fence, but otherwise all internal divisions were abandoned. In place of the dairy herd came an altogether different assortment of animals: Tamworth pigs, English longhorn cattle, Exmoor ponies. All were left to roam, forage, and generally disturb the landscape as best they could. Into nature's interstices – the scarring of the ground by the rooting of the pigs, the rotting hollows of fallen timbers – returned insect life not seen for centuries, including a colony of Purple Emperor butterflies.

The experiment was not without its controversies, such as when applying the principle of non-intervention to the rapid spread of ragwort across the estate. But the scrub-like landscape that now surrounds Knepp Castle is testament to a wholly new concept of landscape, supplanting centuries of interventionist thinking. The Knepp estate today generates income from the sale of organic free-range meat, as well as from the idiosyncratic tourist experience of going on a 'Knepp safari'. Isabella Tree's bestselling memoir of the experiment, *Wilding*, has helped to encourage similar experiments on other estates.[22] Land in Lincolnshire is being rewetted as part of the Wilder Doddington project on the Doddington estate. The Wild East project aims to return twenty per cent of land to nature and involves part of the Somerleyton estate in Suffolk reverting to grazed wood pasture. The speed with which such projects have been introduced reflects the advantages of estates that remain in private ownership. Few public or charitably owned places would have had the brazen confidence to make such dramatic changes to land management practices: the enthusiasm of individual proselytisers of the cause would soon have been smothered by endless bureaucratic committees, risk assessment exercises, and the careful weighing up of pros and cons. Individual owners like Charlie Burrell and Isabella Tree have shown that they can simply put a plan into action, just as landowners have been doing on estates for centuries. Such developments demonstrated that eighteenth-century traditions of landscape improvement by private owners very much remained evident in the twenty-first century, as landowners reimagined their role in facing modern-day challenges such as climate change and biodiversity loss.

22 Isabella Tree, *Wilding* (London, 2018).

11

Country house rescue

By the early 1990s, country houses were in a better position than they had been a decade or so previously, but their future remained far from secure. This chapter returns to the pivotal question of how houses have been rescued and restored over the last half century, and the changing contexts within which this has happened, particularly in the last few decades.

The fate of Pitchford Hall in Shropshire, a half-timbered house held by the Colthurst family for nearly five hundred years, was a reminder of how wider political and economic events could have implications for heritage. The family was hugely invested in Lloyds of London, which suffered catastrophic losses in the aftermath of the Piper Alpha oil rig disaster of 1988. The losses forced the family to sell Pitchford and its contents, but not before they offered it and seventy-six acres of grounds 'to the nation' for just under two million

17. Pitchford Hall, Shropshire (photo courtesy of Pitchford Estate).

pounds. The house was arguably of some significance: it had been selected as one of the residences to which the royal family might be taken in the event of evacuation during the war. The National Trust expressed an interest, but that year had already offered to take on Chastleton in Oxfordshire with support from the National Heritage Memorial Fund. The Conservative heritage minister, David Mellor, rejected the idea that Pitchford might be saved by direct government intervention, which led to the arrival of Christie's auctioneers in September 1992.

As with Mentmore fifteen years earlier, the government had passed up on a bargain. Those who came to watch the auction get underway in the marquee could see the quality and significance of the collection. The sales catalogue featured paintings by Hoppner, Reynolds, and Cornelius Jonson, as well as furniture, silver, ceramics, glassware, and books. Rowena Colthurst, the daughter of the owners, was studying at Bristol University at the time. She later described the loss of Pitchford as "like a bereavement". Her husband James recalled people "sitting in a tent bidding for paintings by Reynolds, or the lumpy bed that Queen Victoria had slept in … And then a porter would just carry them to the front of the house to be put in vans and cars and driven away. It was surreal."[1] The house and land were sold to a Kuwaiti princess, who planned to use the estate as a stud farm. The new owner hardly ever visited, and the house sat empty and unloved.

Members of the Historic Houses Association knew only too well that Pitchford was just one of hundreds of houses that faced uncertain prospects as the country entered a recessionary economic phase. Writing in the winter 1990 edition of *Historic House* magazine, the association's president, the earl of Shelburne, drew attention to the two hundred and fifty houses that had been put up for sale in the previous decade. Each of these houses had been in the same family's ownership for two generations or more; their sale was an indication of how owners could no longer bear the financial burdens of managing this heritage. For Shelburne, government help was needed if a mass exodus of owners was to be avoided. One of the solutions offered was that of greater use of heritage maintenance funds: the vehicle first introduced by the Labour government of the mid-1970s, which permitted owners to invest income-generating assets into special purpose funds free of any capital tax charge, provided that the income from the fund was devoted to heritage preservation. Shelburne called for all income and capital gains tax on these

---

[1] Quoted in William Cash, *Restoration Heart: A Memoir* (London, 2019), pp. 34–35.

funds to be waived, and for owners to have greater freedom to move assets in and out of the funds without incurring additional tax charges provided any proceeds were reinvested in the repair and maintenance of heritage. The fact that full purchase tax (VAT) was payable on repair work was also considered something of an injustice for those obliged, by law, to keep listed buildings in good condition. An exemption was available for when approved alterations were being carried out, so why not widen this to repairs and maintenance too?[2] The official government response, at least from the treasury, continued to be sceptical of the grounds for state intervention. No major tax concessions would be forthcoming, despite the stark nature of the statistics. The philosophy underpinning Nicholas Ridley's approach was now clear. The government was not going to step in, except in the most extreme scenarios.

Perhaps, too, the government's view was that the new national lottery would solve many of the problems facing heritage. The creation of the lottery was a flagship policy for John Major, whose election victory in 1992 meant a continuation of the Conservative rule that had started in 1979. The victory gave Major five more years at the helm, before the landslide defeat inflicted on him by Tony Blair's New Labour in 1997. The national lottery idea, however, was equally embraced by New Labour. The lottery was indeed transformational in its impact on heritage, which in 1992 had been selected as one of five good causes on which the proceeds of the lottery would be spent, the other four being sports, the arts, communities, and projects to mark the new millennium. The lottery quickly proved an enormous success, generating more funds for heritage investment than had ever been thought possible. Within a matter of years, the Heritage Lottery Fund, a new public body administered by the trustees of the National Heritage Memorial Fund, was soon the biggest UK distributor of public support for heritage. Early controversies, such as over whether lottery money should have been used in 1995 to purchase an archive of prime minister Winston Churchill's papers for the nation, meant that the Heritage Lottery Fund received as much scrutiny in its choices as English Heritage had before it.

The row over the Churchill papers may also have diminished the enthusiasm of the trustees of the National Heritage Memorial Fund to actively embrace the idea that lottery funds might be used to support privately owned heritage. While the lottery rapidly became a primary source of capital funding for charities such as the National Trust and the national museums and galleries, private owners were denied the opportunity to apply for support under the

---

[2] 'The President's Page', *Historic House* 14:4 (Winter, 1990), 5.

terms of the founding legislation. Although it had made much of the Churchill papers controversy while in opposition, the Labour party gave assurances to the HHA that it would support a change in the rules that would permit private owners to receive lottery grants.[3] The legal change to permit this happened in 1997, but the Heritage Lottery Fund only changed its procedures to allow applications from private owners in 2002, almost a decade after the lottery was first established. Even then, private owners whose houses were open to public access were only given the chance to apply for funds up to a ceiling of fifty thousand pounds, a small fraction of the support that was being offered to their competitors in the major heritage charities. Although the cap was raised to a hundred thousand pounds in 2013, it remains in place today (at the time of writing). Meanwhile, the limit for charities when applying for major grants has recently been lifted to as much as ten million pounds, putting them at a hundredfold advantage over private sector applicants.

While lottery investments had a transformational impact on heritage sites across the country, privately owned houses tended not to see the benefit of this unless they were held in the form of charitable trusts. Private owners increasingly saw that the policy advantages they had gained in the late 1970s and early 1980s were starting to slip away. The hardening of the HHA's lobbying stance in the early 1990s, and the more muscular defence of the interests of landowning families, reflected the frustration that many private owners felt. The situation may also have played a part in driving something of a wedge between the HHA and other heritage organisations. Relations remained cordial, of course, but no longer was it so common for the likes of the National Trust or English Heritage to express publicly their support for private owners, since these same owners had now become so much more militant in the defence of their positions. Where the chief executives of the National Trust, English Heritage, and the HHA had met as a 'Group of Three' well into the 1990s, such meetings would soon come to an end as something of a conceptual distance emerged between the three organisations.[4] National Trust and English Heritage membership numbers continued to grow, with the National Trust recruiting its two millionth member in 1990. Tensions were starting to be voiced publicly, with the sale of the privately owned Brympton d'Evercy in Somerset in 1992 being blamed in part on the difficulty in attracting sufficient visitor numbers in an area of multiple rival National Trust sites.[5]

---

[3]   HHA, *Annual Report for 1994/95*, p. 1.
[4]   See the HHA's annual reports from the 1990s for this.
[5]   HHA, *Annual Report for 1991/92*, p. 21.

Nevertheless, the Trust's chairman, Roger Chorley, wrote to chancellor of the exchequer Kenneth Clarke in September 1995 to remind him that the National Trust already had its "hands very full", such that it was unlikely to be able to take on more properties. Moreover, private ownership remained the most cost-effective means for important heritage to be looked after, to the extent that those owners' services were given free.[6]

The victory of Tony Blair's Labour party in the 1997 general election would reshape political contours for a generation. This was a very different sort of Labour government to the one that historic house owners had come to know in the mid-1970s. Blair's political talent lay in triangulation: charting a third way that merged social democratic values and principles with essentially Thatcherite economic policies. Talk of wealth taxes was banished: the New Labour government claimed to be "supremely relaxed" about wealth accumulation, in the words of their leading spokesman Peter Mandelson. An early decision was to rename the department of national heritage as the department for culture, media and sport. Combined with invitations to rock stars and Young British Artists to attend receptions at Number 10, the impression was given that New Labour was deliberately turning its back on heritage and the past and putting more emphasis on the arts and creative industries. The 'Cool Britannia' moment did not last long, however. Labour's first secretary of state for culture, Chris Smith, was a seasoned politician who also had a doctorate from Cambridge (on the Romantic poets). When he spoke at the HHA's annual general meeting in November 1997, he sought to allay any concerns over signals that the departmental name change may have sent.[7] The loss of the word 'heritage' did not mean that the government was underplaying the significance of the built and historic environment. Rather, these were to be encompassed in a broader concept of 'culture', which "form part of our sense of who and what we are as a people". The government remained committed to protecting heritage, Smith insisted, but new thinking was needed about how best to conserve it, present it, interpret it, and bequeath it to future generations, "rather than simply have a retrospective view".[8]

It remained the case, however, that New Labour ministers were instinctively less excited about the preservation of the past than they were about

[6] HHA Archive, Letter from Lord Chorley to Kenneth Clarke, chancellor of the exchequer, 18 Sept. 1995.

[7] Since 1990 these meetings have been held at the Queen Elizabeth II conference centre in Westminster.

[8] 'Chris Smith's Speech', *Historic House* 22:1 (Spring, 1998), 9–11.

progressive visions of the future.[9] The celebrations of the new millennium were marked by the opening of the Millennium Dome in London: a strikingly modern construction built on derelict wasteland on the Greenwich peninsula. Work had already begun on the project under John Major's government, and it was enthusiastically embraced by Tony Blair. Although the cost of it all would attract criticism, the Dome was the most popular visitor attraction in the country in the year 2000, receiving six and a half million visits. The other signature policy associated with Chris Smith's time as secretary of state was that of free admission to the national museums and galleries, most of which were in London, but which also encompassed museums in Liverpool, Manchester, Bradford, and York. Where these museums had been encouraged to levy a charge on admission under Mrs Thatcher's government, New Labour made it possible for them to waive admission fees and yet still be able to reclaim the sales tax charged to their business costs. Significant year-on-year increases in visitor numbers at these national institutions would follow, further boosted by considerable new investments in museum and gallery buildings and facilities, often funded from the lottery.[10]

Conscious of the allure that museums, the arts, and the creative industries had for New Labour ministers, the diverse elements of the heritage sector sought once again to rally behind a common cause. This cause now was not so much the threat of outright destruction as had been highlighted in the early 1970s. Rather, the mission at hand was to make the case for government support for heritage and the historic environment in a new era of technocratic public sector management. Much emphasis was placed on access and audience diversity, which were themes in strategic documents such as *Power of Place* (2000) and *A Force for our Future* (2001). The aim was to highlight the economic, social, and cultural benefits of heritage, using as much evidence as was possible from new statistical digests such as the *State of the Historic Environment* report (2002), published annually from 2003 as *Heritage Counts* and a sort of successor to the English Tourist Board's former *Heritage Monitor*.[11] An early reminder for the New Labour government of the economic muscle exerted by heritage was provided in 2001 when an outbreak of foot and mouth disease in

[9] See the discussion in Robert Hewison, *Cultural Capital: The Rise and Fall of Creative Britain* (London, 2014).

[10] For more on this policy, see Ben Cowell, 'Measuring the Impact of Free Admission', *Cultural Trends* 16:3 (2007), 203–224.

[11] See also the discussion in Ben Cowell, *The Heritage Obsession: The Battle for England's Past* (Stroud, 2008), and Ben Cowell, 'Why Heritage Counts: Researching the Historic Environment', *Cultural Trends* 13:4 (2004), 23–39.

livestock led to the emergency closure of large parts of the English countryside. Incidents such as these shone a light on the fact that tourism was more important to the national economy than food and farming, and that heritage was the principal reason why Britain remained a sought-after tourist destination for international and domestic visitors.

Despite the growing awareness of the power of heritage to create jobs and bring economic rejuvenation to places, it remained something of a challenge to convince government of the case for fiscal incentives. New Labour showed no more enthusiasm than their Conservative predecessors for reducing the rate of VAT charged on repairs and maintenance, albeit that places of worship were able to benefit from a rebate scheme from 2001. Meanwhile, the Finance Act of 1998 significantly tightened the rules on the conditional exemption of heritage assets from inheritance tax. The effect of the changes was to strengthen requirements for public access to these assets, as well as to promote greater awareness of the undertakings that owners had agreed to meet. In addition, some owners were significantly affected by the abolition of the one estate election regime from 2001 onwards. This was the arrangement whereby the costs of repairs and maintenance to a mansion property could be set against the income received from other parts of a diversified rural estate, such as from farm or cottage rents or from forestry. The best the HHA could do was achieve a three-year delay to the implementation of the new rules.

The curtailment of the one estate election system was further evidence that the owners of country houses could expect no special treatment, or even any basic recognition of the rising costs of their endeavours. On the contrary, these costs seemed inexorably to rise year on year. Fiscal conditions continued to worsen in 2006, when the government announced its intention to tax most property-owning trusts as if they were discretionary rather than interest-in-possession trusts. The effect was to impose a ten-yearly tax charge (at a rate of six per cent) on all such trusts created from that point onwards. It was a severe deterrent to the use of trusts in relation to country house properties, even though these legal mechanisms had been an "essential element in helping houses and their contents survive", as James Hervey-Bathurst, HHA president, explained. Added to the continued application of VAT, the new requirements on conditional exemption, and the ever-rising costs of repairs and maintenance, it was "a dangerous cocktail for historic houses".[12] Meanwhile, the government continued to reject proposals from the association for a form of

---

[12] 'The President's Page', *Historic House* 30:3 (Autumn, 2006), 5.

heritage property maintenance relief that would give some fiscal respite for owners and encourage a regular and ongoing cycle of repair work.

Given these somewhat precarious fiscal and financial conditions, it was perhaps little wonder that the fate of country houses, and the schemes devised by owners for their protection and preservation, remained an ongoing topic of public fascination. A Channel 4 television show, which ran for four series between 2008 and 2012, took *Country House Rescue* as its theme. The show was hosted by Ruth Watson, a restaurateur and hotelier who owned and ran the hotel at Hintlesham Hall in Suffolk, and who had previously presented another popular show, *The Hotel Inspector. Country House Rescue* took a similar format, and involved Watson arriving at a different house in each episode to speak to the owners and provide her own advice on what they might consider doing with the property. Pentillie in Cornwall, Riverhill in Kent, and Elmore Court in Gloucestershire all received visits from Watson in this way, during which different commercial applications or suggestions were proposed, debated and, on occasion, implemented. The show brought to life the realities involved in the ownership and occupation of country houses, providing a counterpoint to another Channel 4 show, *Grand Designs*, where the focus was on new development, albeit that this sometimes also involved the restoration or dramatic reimagining of historic buildings.

The rescue and restoration of country houses continued to attract considerable media interest and publicity. Acts of direct government intervention were noticeable by their rarity. One such example was Apethorpe in Northamptonshire, an important Jacobean palace that had been converted for use as an approved school after the war, but which had sat empty and unused after its sale to a Libyan businessman in 1983. Here, the department for culture, media and sport took the highly unusual step in 2004 of forcing a compulsory purchase of the building to protect it from further dilapidation. Under English Heritage custodianship, a significant amount of restoration work was carried out until the property could be sold on again, to a private owner, in 2014.[13] The sale recouped only a small fraction of the public money that had been spent on the property, rendering Apethorpe a reminder of the conditions of market failure under which heritage typically operated.[14] Left to the market alone, there remained a significant conservation deficit of necessary investment that

[13] Kathryn A. Morrison (ed.), *Apethorpe: The Story of an English Country House* (London, 2016).

[14] The market failure concept was being explained by economists at this time in books such as David Throsby, *Economics and Culture* (Cambridge, 2001), and Alan

only the government was in a position to meet. The trouble was that the government was not able to afford too many houses of the significance and scale of Apethorpe.

Moreover, the separation of English Heritage into two distinct organisations – Historic England (the government's main adviser on heritage, inheriting the functions of the old historic buildings commission, including the ownership of the collection of national heritage assets) and English Heritage (now a stand-alone charity, existing purely to manage the commission's estate) – introduced a measure of uncertainty as to how future acts of country house rescue would be instigated by government in England. Would the new charity have the legal, political, and financial authority to act as a saviour 'of last resort' should circumstances require it? Or would such actions remain the prerogative of Historic England only, even though it no longer had a property-managing function? This question remains unresolved today, more than eight years after the two organisations were formally separated in 2015.[15]

National Trust ownership remained an option, but its appetite for rescuing country houses noticeably waned in the new millennium. Tyntesfield in North Somerset was purchased by the Trust in 2002 after the government had declined to get involved. A high-profile fundraising campaign and a significant contribution from the National Heritage Memorial Fund helped to secure the property for the nation. Since then, the Trust has taken on just one major house: Seaton Delaval in Northumberland, built by John Vanbrugh and acquired from the Delaval-Hastings family in December 2009 following an acceptance-in-lieu tax settlement. The Trust needed to launch a major fundraising campaign to raise an endowment for the property, which combined funds from its own reserves with those raised by the local community and a contribution from the regional development agency for the north-east. It proved one of the last acts by the regional development agency, which would be abolished by the incoming Conservative and Liberal Democrat coalition government a year later in 2010. It also proved to be the last truly significant country house to be taken on by the National Trust, notwithstanding the acquisition of Nuffield Place in Oxfordshire (the mansion property of William Morris of Morris Motors), and more recently Munstead Woods in Surrey (home of garden designer Gertrude Jeykll).

Peacock and Ilde Rizzo, *The Heritage Game: Economics, Policy, and Practice* (Oxford, 2008).

[15] Nor has English Heritage yet made a net surplus on its annual operations.

In the absence of intervention by the government or by the National Trust, the saving of important heritage buildings in recent decades has therefore depended much more on the persistence and energy of individual owners and enthusiasts. The HHA instigated a new restoration award in 2008, sponsored by Sotheby's auction house, to draw attention to heroic cases of country house rescue. The inaugural winner of the prize was Markenfield Hall in North Yorkshire, recognising the completion of the full-scale restoration of the moated medieval site by Lady Deirdre Curteis, widow of Lord Grantley, who had remarried the television director and dramatist Ian Curteis. The restoration award would be used to recognise truly ground-breaking acts of transformation in country house properties. An example was Wimborne St Giles in Dorset, a house that was inherited unexpectedly by Nicholas Ashley-Cooper after the murder of his father, the tenth earl of Salisbury, and the sudden death in succession of his elder brother, the eleventh earl. As twelfth earl, Ashley-Cooper was left with a house in a perilous state of disrepair, which led to the abandonment of his promising career as a DJ and club promoter in New York and a return to the Dorset countryside. The restoration of the house has been a triumph, and income is now generated by leasing it for weddings and other events.[16] A full list of the winners of the restoration award since 2008 can be seen in an appendix to this book, right up to the joint winners in 2022, Lytham Hall in Lancashire and Wolterton Hall in Norfolk.

The achievements of the owners of houses and estates have sometimes been accomplished in the face of challenging political circumstances. The drive for greater devolution that began under New Labour, with legislation creating a new parliament in Scotland and assembly in Wales, also saw an increase in interest in land reform. Anti-landlord tendencies in political discourse were fuelled by books such as Andy Wightman's *Who Owns Scotland?* (1996) and its counterpart south of the border by Guy Shrubsole, *Who Owns England?* (2019).[17] The ruling Scottish National Party (SNP), in command of Scottish politics since 2007, made a pledge to see a million acres transfer to community control by 2020. Land reform made it onto the statute books in Scotland with legislation that sought to promote the community acquisition of land, building

---

[16]   Earl of Shaftesbury and Tim Knox, *The Rebirth of an English Country House: St Giles House* (London, 2018).

[17]   Andy Wightman, *Who Owns Scotland?* (Edinburgh, 1996). An updated version was published as *The Poor Had No Lawyers: Who Owns Scotland and How They Got It* (Edinburgh, 2015). Guy Shrubsole, *Who Owns England?: How We Lost Our Green and Pleasant Land and How to Take It Back* (London, 2019).

18. Lytham Hall in Lancashire, joint winner of the Historic Houses / Sotheby's Restoration Award 2022.

19. Interior of Wolterton Hall, Norfolk, joint winner of the Historic Houses / Sotheby's Restoration Award 2022.

on the community right to buy that had been established in 2003. Powers were also introduced to reform agricultural tenancies to return more power to tenants over the owners of the largest estates. It was reported in 2015 that half a million acres had passed into community control in Scotland: falling short of the original aspirations, this nonetheless represented a significant shift in the equilibrium of land ownership. A land commission was established to keep the situation under review and promote the SNP's strategy for further land reform, now in the interests of achieving net-zero for carbon and in promoting the accumulation of natural capital.

Despite these less-than-promising conditions for landowners north of the border, a noticeable number of restoration award winners have come from Scotland, including Aldourie Castle (2011), Kinross (2013), Marchmont (2018), and Dunvegan (2019). The saga of Dumfries House provides another Scottish example of a long-running problem house that nevertheless has had a successful conclusion. The mansion was built for the earl of Dumfries by John Adam and his son Robert, who worked on the house before heading off on his grand tour, after which his business activity was mainly in London. The property passed to the earls of Bute in 1814 and stayed in that family for nearly two centuries. It was offered to, but eventually declined by, the National Trust for Scotland in the 1990s. In the early years of the new millennium, the seventh marquess of Bute declared that the house and its collection were for sale, citing the ongoing expense of maintaining the property. The importance of the grade A mansion, and in particular its furniture collection, led to calls for it to be rescued for posterity. Eventually, just before the furniture was about to be sold at auction, a consortium of supporters stepped in with a package worth forty-five million pounds in total. Most notable of these was the Prince of Wales (now King Charles III), whose own regeneration charity provided a loan worth twenty million pounds. The house opened to the public in 2008 and since then has been used to demonstrate how an estate can develop sustainable options for the future. Being owned by a charity has made it possible to secure philanthropic funding, but financial security was also envisaged to come from the development of Knockroon, a Poundbury-style settlement nearby. Support has come too from Morrisons supermarkets, which provided funds for the restoration of the farm associated with the estate. Visitor facilities and overnight accommodation have meant that the house has been able to attract paying guests. The rescue of Dumfries House has demonstrated how sustainable models are available to those houses that have sufficient financial backing. Although the financial crisis of 2008 created some uncertainty as to the viability of the model, the initial loan has now been repaid and Dumfries has become an exemplar model for how the country house can find a new role and purpose in the twenty-first century. With over a hundred employees, it shows how houses can develop serious social purposes while retaining their historical and artistic significance.

Pitchford Hall in Shropshire, where this chapter began, has also been successfully rescued from its former uninhabited state. Rowena Colthurst, who retained a significant part of the family estate, resolved that, should circumstances change, she would buy back the house and its grounds and restore her family's association with the building. It took until September 2016, but Rowena and her husband James Nason were able to fulfil their ambition and move their young family back into Pitchford after twenty-four years of the house sitting empty and unused. Some items originally from the house have now been returned, such as a silver engraved christening cup from 1877 and a set of copper jelly moulds featuring the crest of the earl of Rosebery (a relative of the family through marriage).[18] Since then, they have undertaken the painstaking work of updating the house for twenty-first-century use. A regular programme of bespoke tours of the property has helped to keep funds coming in, as has the installation of a solar array on nearby land.

Perhaps the most striking case of country house rescue in recent years has been that of Wentworth Woodhouse, near Rotherham in South Yorkshire. This substantial mansion, said to have the longest façade of any house in the country, was the ancestral seat of the earls Fitzwilliam. A visit from King George V and Queen Mary in 1912 saw several days of dinners and celebrations, including an assembly of thousands of people from the local area, including many of the miners from the Rotherham district who worked the Fitzwilliam coal seams. The minister for mines, Manny Shinwell, was widely considered to have committed an act of anti-aristocratic spite after the second world war, when he ordered open-cast mining to be conducted in the immediate vicinity of the mansion. Famously, the local miners objected to this, out of deference to the family. But the mining caused considerable damage to the landscape setting of the house, where Repton had once been involved in laying out a new design. Financially wounded by death duties and the nationalisation of the coal industry, the Fitzwilliam family searched for a solution that would somehow keep the house intact, even if many of its contents were sold off at successive auctions. Rather than see the property converted to social housing, the whole thing was leased as an educational establishment, first as the Lady

---

[18]   Anthony Lambert, 'Focus On: Pitchford Hall', *Historic House* 41:1 (Spring, 2017), 22–26.

20. The east front at Wentworth Woodhouse, South Yorkshire (Wentworth Woodhouse Preservation Trust).

Mabel College of Physical Education (named for the seventh earl's sister) and then, from 1979, as the geography and physical education departments of Sheffield City Polytechnic. This institutional use of the house lasted until 1988, at which point the Fitzwilliam family finally severed their connections with the property. It was sold, first to Wensley Grosvenor Haydon-Baillie, a businessman, and then to Clifford Newbold in 1998. The Newbold family made efforts to address the restoration needs of the house, which by this time stretched into millions of pounds. But the death of Clifford Newbold in April 2015 foreshadowed another change of ownership. The house was put back onto the market with an asking price of eight million pounds. A preservation trust dedicated to the rescue of the house ended up buying the property for seven million pounds in February 2016.

Since then, the Wentworth Woodhouse Preservation Trust has embarked on an ambitious programme of restoration, with a target of spending more than a hundred million pounds in total on the property. It has been boosted by grants from public sources. Chancellor of the exchequer Philip Hammond used his budget speech in November 2016 to grant an initial £7.6 million towards the trust's ambitions. It was another rare example, as had happened with Calke Abbey, of governments making a one-off payment to a heritage cause, with the side effect of generating some political capital. In his case, Hammond was able to use the announcement to make a political point about how the Conservative government was trying to make amends for the damage caused by the post-war decisions of Labour's Manny Shinwell. Since then, Wentworth Woodhouse has been successful in attaining lottery grants, and received substantial investment during the Covid-19 pandemic, when a culture recovery fund was established to ensure ongoing business for conservation companies. The priority at Wentworth Woodhouse has been to make the roof sound and watertight. Another project has been to restore the camelia house, while work has also begun to bring the stables back to active economic use. The house provides a ready example of how charitable ownership is one of the routes for house restoration, albeit that the property remains largely empty of collections and no longer functions as a lived-in home. Just as the support of the miners counteracted Shinwell's attempts, literally, to undermine the house in the 1940s, the significant support of local residents breathed new life into Wentworth Woodhouse in the twenty-first century.

Examples like Wentworth Woodhouse and Dumfries House were unique: major and important properties that required charitable capital injection. For most country houses, such solutions were never going to be either practical or affordable. Instead, country houses were rescued not by dramatic interventions, but by ongoing care and maintenance, funded through whatever business activity the house could sustain. Many of the same pressures that faced historic houses in the second half of the twentieth century continued into the first two decades of the twenty-first. Houses that dabbled in weddings might find themselves suddenly being classified as businesses by the valuations office, and therefore subject to business rates where previously they had paid domestic taxes. New forms of environmental controls, such as a requirement for energy performance certificates before any domestic properties could be leased, imposed new costs on owners. Meanwhile, the old enemies of country houses – fire, rot, burglary – continued to make their presence felt. Allerton Castle in North Yorkshire suffered a severe fire in 2005. Goodwood House and Arundel Castle in West Sussex have both suffered well-publicised robberies in the last ten years. A catastrophic blaze took hold at the National Trust's Clandon Park in Surrey in 2015 and it remains half burnt-out while plans are developed for its future.

While many houses today enjoy much better business prospects than fifty years ago, house owners remain only too aware of the challenges on the horizon. The confidence of country house economics must be balanced against continuing uncertainties. Taxation remains an ever-present issue. For country house owners, a tax on inherited wealth represented nothing less than an

existential threat. If forty per cent (or more) of an asset's value had to be sur-
rendered to the government at the point of transfer, then the likelihood was
that the asset, or substantial parts of it, would need to be sold. This was the
process that Gowers had identified in 1950 where the slow unravelling of an
entire estate might begin with the sale of parcels of land and part, or all, of a
collection to satisfy tax demands. Taxation therefore had serious implications
for the built heritage. At the same time, to be effective a tax policy needed to
treat everyone equally. Attempts to alleviate the damage caused to heritage by
capital taxation involved various heritage-related exemptions or concessions,
particularly where this protected the future of a heritage asset open to public
access: the conditional exemption of a significant property from the immediate
charge against inheritance tax, for example, or the ability to invest in a maintenance fund without incurring a capital tax charge. Critics of these heritage
concessions queried why country house owners should have such advantages.
But successive governments have determined that the alternative represented a far greater loss of public benefit. After all, were an owner simply to sell
a work of art to another private individual to meet a tax demand, all public
access to that artwork could be lost forever. A great many of the estimated over
twenty-one million visits made to privately owned historic houses in 2022 were
to houses that were opened because of conditional exemption undertakings.[19]
By bringing country house owners into a partnership with the state, owners'
private assets were bound into public access requirements that effectively
made them part of a national collection, especially so in the case of artworks
accepted-in-lieu-in-situ.

For much of the period under consideration, the prospects of any revival in
the Labour government's wealth tax idea of 1974 seemed a distant possibility.
Successive governments largely accepted the political orthodoxy established
under Mrs Thatcher, that the state should aim, as far as possible, to reduce
levels of taxation. Many influential thinkers on the Conservative side of politics
even questioned the merit of retaining the inheritance tax that Nigel Lawson
introduced as chancellor of the exchequer in 1986, to replace Labour's tax on
all capital transfers. Economists pointed to the relatively low levels of tax revenue generated by the inheritance tax, and the theoretical barrier it created to
wealth creation. It was widely understood that the wealthier someone was, the
more they were able to employ clever accountants and lawyers to find perfectly
legal ways of minimising any tax liability owed to the state.

[19] See <https://www.historichouses.org/policy-hub/infographics-library/> [accessed
10 Sept. 2023].

More recently, the idea of a wealth tax has seen something of a revival. The Liberal Democrats under Vince Cable first toyed with the idea in 2009, proposing an annual levy of half of one per cent on the owners of houses worth more than a million pounds. Under Ed Miliband, who succeeded Gordon Brown as Labour party leader after the party's election defeat in 2010, an annual mansion tax of three thousand pounds was proposed on the owners of properties worth over two million pounds, with an even higher rate for those with houses worth more than three million pounds. Such an idea has now been dropped as the official policy of the Labour party. But as concern deepens over social inequality, political parties may yet look again at attempting to use capital taxation for redistributive purposes. Thomas Piketty's *Capital in the Twenty-First Century*, first published in English in 2014, renewed the call for governments to be proactive in adopting redistributive tax policies through increased levels of inheritance tax. A UK enquiry into the option of a wealth tax that reported in 2020 suggested that such taxes rarely achieved the ends they set out to serve.[20] Still, the enquiry demonstrated that the idea remains firmly on the table, particularly for parties of the left. The consequences for heritage of such policies are rarely discussed: presumably it is seen as too niche or inconsequential a topic when set against the social transformations that the proponents of a wealth tax seek to effect. That is as maybe, but nonetheless the heritage problem remains unresolved. How will country house heritage – an assemblage of architecture, landscape, and collections – survive intact if it is subject to yet further fiscal incursions? An answer might be bespoke exemptions in return for those heritage assets remaining open to public access, but it would be as well to address the issue at the outset of the development of new fiscal instruments, rather than scrabble around for a solution to the problem after a finance bill has been passed.

Perhaps owners would be more willing to accept higher levels of taxation if the state reduced its intervention in areas such as planning. But at present this remains an equally unlikely scenario. New Labour pledged to reform the system of heritage protection. The plan was to make it more comprehensive, yet at the same time streamline the systems and processes involved. These were all good sentiments, but a proposed new bill failed to find sufficient parliamentary time before the New Labour era of government ended in 2010. Instead, commitments were made to making reforms that didn't require primary legislation.

---

[20]   Arun Advani, Emma Chamberlain, Andy Summers, *A Wealth Tax for the UK* (London, 2020).

Any progress on these reforms was stymied in the subsequent years, principally by those nervous at the implications of allowing controls to be relaxed.

Planning regulations governing listed buildings added considerably to the costs faced by the owners and custodians of such buildings. It was almost an inexorable law of the public sector that regulations would multiply unless there was a concerted effort to strip them away. The last few decades have seen a flourishing of regulatory measures, whether in the form of mandatory energy performance certification for buildings or the requirement for environment impact statements alongside development applications. Clearly, such regulatory measures serve entirely valid purposes, whether this is reducing carbon emissions or promoting positive environmental outcomes. But the cost of implementing them fell squarely on individual private owners. Far from enhancing the protection of historic buildings, such measures could serve to weaken the business model under which historic houses operated. The Enterprise and Regulatory Reform Act introduced by the coalition government in 2013 attempted to promote a more liberal regulatory system for listed buildings. It introduced the concept of a listed building consent order, a measure that would provide pre-ordained consent for works to a defined set of heritage assets, either at a local planning authority level or nationwide. Large parts of the heritage profession did not jump for joy at this new freedom, fearing a diminution in their own regulatory authority. Rather, they insisted that the consent order approach could only be used if it was first tested on a few small-scale pilots. At the time of writing, these pilots have stalled and not a single listed building consent order has ever been enacted nationally, more than a decade after the act was passed.[21]

The planning system represents an imposition on the freedom of action of private individuals, in the interests of a wider public good. Untrammeled development is clearly a sub-optimal outcome: a strong regulatory system puts limits on private action in the interest of attaining public benefits. Any major scheme of work now requires a multitude of environmental surveys, including specialist reports on heritage significance as well as the impact of any development on resident bat or newt populations. Undoubtedly, the planning system has helped to protect the historic interest in landscapes and settings, as well as the physical fabric of important buildings, at a time when demolitions are all-too tempting (given the advantageous rate of VAT that applies to new-build

---

[21] Some local authorities have introduced local listed building consent orders, for example to give owners the freedom to install solar panels on grade II-listed properties. Again, such moves often generate considerable resistance among heritage professionals.

over historic restorations). Owners of historic houses are well advised to make friends with their local planning officers, in case they should ever need an application to be given a fair hearing. All too often, however, hard-pressed local planning offices lack the capacity to deal with the multitude of applications coming their way, leading to delays in the resolution of cases.

The level of requirements on owners is now so great that it might be imagined that there will come a time when it is no longer viable to own a listed building. This seems the case for example in relation to energy efficiency measures. A joint survey undertaken by the CLA and Historic Houses (the trading name of the HHA) in late 2022 revealed that almost two-thirds of respondents – sixty-two per cent – had declined to apply for listed building consent, or had withdrawn applications for changes, due to the complexity of the heritage consent system. An even greater proportion – nearly ninety per cent – said that they thought the planning system was a deterrent to the introduction of energy efficiency measures at their historic properties.[22] The Gowers report advocated that the most sustainable solution for historic houses was for them to remain lived-in domestic residences. For houses to remain lived-in, they will need to adapt to the new conditions of the twenty-first century, especially in relation to climate change and the need for greater energy efficiency. This could well be the fault line on which owners and government will need to reach a resolution soon. So far, governments have proved reluctant to introduce the sort of reforming measures that might see, for example, the removal of the need for listed building consent to install an air-source heat pump on a listed grade II cottage. The more alarm bells ring about the need for urgent action in the face of the changing climate, however, the less this seems tenable.

[22]   DC Research, *Successes and Failures of Heritage Protection – a Survey of Members who Own or Manage Heritage* (London, 2023), <https://www.historichouses.org/app/uploads/2023/01/a192-historic-houses-and-cla-survey-final-report-011222-cf.pdf> [accessed 10 Sept. 2023].

The British country house today

Easter weekend is normally one of the busiest for those country houses that open as attractions. Places that target family groups will often advertise special events, such as Easter egg hunts or cream teas. If the weather is kind – which cannot be guaranteed for an event that could in theory fall as early as late March – then large crowds can normally be expected. Mothers' Day can also be another occasion that brings out lots of groups, to visit gardens or to enjoy a family meal. Mothers' Day on Sunday 22 March 2020, however, was an unusually muted affair. A few days earlier, the British prime minister had announced that cafes, restaurants, and pubs must close their doors because of the growing numbers of cases of a new coronavirus, Covid-19. A day later, on Monday 23 March, large parts of the economy ground to a halt as the first government-mandated nationwide lockdown was announced.

At the time, most hoped that such measures might only be needed for a matter of weeks. Things did not quite turn out this way. Three national lockdowns followed, each lasting several months. The period from March 2020 to early 2023 saw an unprecedented level of state intrusion into private life and activity. All sectors of the economy suffered, but the hospitality and attractions sectors were hit harder than most. Every time new public health measures were introduced in response to sudden surges in case numbers, social events such as wedding celebrations were hit with especially tight controls. At one point, the only type of wedding that could take place involved no more than six people, with no celebratory event of any kind afterwards. Symbolising the effect such measures had, the British monarch was photographed attending the funeral service of her late husband in 2021, sitting alone and isolated in the pews of the chapel at Windsor Castle.

Those country houses that depended for their income on wedding events, or on income from tourist visits, faced horrendous business conditions. Although the government moved swiftly to provide emergency incomes for millions of workers now no longer able to work, the medium- to longer-term financial outlook was bleak. Further government inducements to spend in restaurants once lockdown restrictions started to ease – an 'eat out to help out' scheme in England, and reductions in VAT – offered some mitigation, albeit at the risk of encouraging further spreading of the disease. Only with mass vaccinations was it possible to truly get the situation under control. The final regulations – a requirement for travellers to the UK from China to bring Covid testing kits with them – were only relaxed in April 2023, more than three years after the pandemic had first been declared.

At the start of the pandemic, in the spring of 2020, it was feared that the longer-term consequences of the disease would be dire. The HHA was already aware of redundancies having been made, because of lost income of nearly a quarter of a billion pounds in 2020 alone. Many houses took advantage of the furlough scheme and asked staff members to stay at home. This simply meant that routine repair and maintenance work was not carried out. Gardens went untended, except by the owners themselves, who were now photographed for special magazine features with headlines such as 'life in an English castle under lockdown.'

Despite these adverse conditions, the lockdowns highlighted the single factor that has been the main topic of this book: the resilience of British country houses. This collection of houses, that have lived through war and flood, fire and famine, could now add pestilence and disease to the list. Trading conditions were as tough as they had ever been in the calendar year 2020. But houses overall showed that they were able to cope with the disruption, and to leap at any opportunities that came their way. Many privately owned gardens opened their gates instantly once the government changed the rules to allow this at the end of May 2020.

Owners in many houses used ingenuity and enterprise to find ways to trade within the lockdown rules. Drive-in cinema experiences at Knebworth House in Hertfordshire allowed big screen entertainment, provided social groups remained seated in their own cars. Others used the same idea to host drive-in weddings, where couples' pledges of vows were filmed and relayed into car stereo systems. Pop-up temporary coffee kiosks replaced the catering on offer inside venues, and timed-ticket booking systems proliferated as houses anticipated changing consumer practices after the pandemic. By 2021 visitor numbers had recovered the ground they lost in the previous year. In 2022, over twenty-one million visits were made to Historic Houses member properties, a similar number as had visited National Trust mansion sites. The pandemic had seen a drop of nearly a third in the number of members of the public taking out membership of Historic Houses, but by 2022 the losses had been fully recovered, and membership grew to its historically highest level.

The Covid pandemic notwithstanding, it remains the case that a remarkable revival in the fortunes of British country houses has taken place over the last half century. This revival has been as emphatic as it was unanticipated fifty years ago, when the outlook for country houses was particularly bleak. The first-ever publication prepared for the newly formed Historic Houses Association in October 1974 speculated that, if trends continued, there might not be any country houses left by 2023. The few survivors would be those safely absorbed within the National Trusts (whether for England, Wales, and Northern Ireland, or for Scotland) and thereby shielded from the vicissitudes of life in the private sector. Only a minority could look forward to this; the rest faced a deeply uncertain future. Planning requirements from 1968 may have made it much more difficult to demolish country houses, but that did not stop them being 'lost' in other ways by having their purpose and meaning ripped from them: whether sold and transformed into offices, hotels, hospitals, or schools, or subdivided into apartments. Conversions such as these sometimes spelled the end of a country house as a living entity, and almost certainly meant the end of a link to any one family. Such scenarios were also likely to involve the sale of wider estate lands, and the loss of collections of furniture, tapestries, and artworks that had previously formed part of their unified ensemble.

Plenty of country houses met exactly this fate. But changing economic and fiscal conditions were sufficient to enable the greater proportion of houses to survive into the new millennium. The Labour government of the 1970s drew back from the wealth tax that it had proposed in its election manifesto of 1974. Of even more significance, perhaps, was the same government's decision to widen the range and number of assets for which it was possible to claim an exemption from capital taxation. While it had been possible since 1896 to claim an exemption of an artwork from death duties, it was only with the Finance Act of 1975 that it became possible to exempt buildings and their landscapes from the new capital transfer tax. As we have seen, that decision was probably somewhat inadvertent since it was originally intended merely as a temporary stopgap while the wealth tax proposal was being considered. After the wealth tax idea was dropped, the exemption option was effectively made permanent, and was rolled forward under the new inheritance tax regime introduced from 1986. Around three hundred country houses have taken the exemption route, meaning that all of them must now open to the public for a minimum number of days every year (usually twenty-eight or thirty, but sometimes many more). Effectively, it means that these houses are now part-owned by the state, or at the very least that the state has a substantial interest in their operation. The option for privately owned houses to establish heritage maintenance funds, also introduced in 1975/76, provided a further route for owners to attempt to keep afloat. By ringfencing the income from estate assets (whether land, property, or investments) for the purposes of keeping the house at the heart of an estate in good order, a property could achieve almost the same level of security as was enjoyed by those that had been absorbed by the National Trust. Improvements to the maintenance fund regime in 1980, to make it less of an inalienable allocation of assets, meant that many more house owners took up this option (although perhaps fewer than two hundred in total ever did).

UK economic growth in the 1980s favoured those houses prepared to embrace business diversification. The relentless increase in National Trust membership – it had reached a million by 1980 and would increase to more than five times this amount over the subsequent decades – was indicative of the latent public demand for country house experiences. Some houses became known for their ability to feed this demand, most notably Chatsworth with its farm shop, its restaurant, and its overflowing car parks on the busiest summer days. The duchess of Devonshire, like Lord Montagu, demonstrated an ability to generate significant publicity for her house through media-friendly interviews and publications. Not all houses were on the scale of Chatsworth, but many found it possible to generate significant incomes from day visitors as well as from special events in the park, such as Knebworth's rock concerts, Goodwood's motor race revivals, and Burghley's horse trials. Economic recovery after the recessionary years of the early 1980s meant that people had more disposable income, and a renewed appetite for experiences and tangible contact with history. These trends continued into the 1990s and early 2000s. New features opened at historic houses across the UK: restored gardens, adventure playgrounds, stable blocks repurposed as cafes and coffee shops. The demand for such things seemed insatiable, even while critics of the 'heritage industry' found it ironic that the field in which Britain had such a strong competitive advantage was arguably so nostalgic and backward-looking.

Government never fully credited the power of country house tourism, or indeed tourism more generally. It took a crisis like the foot and mouth disease outbreak of 2001 to demonstrate just how significant tourism was to the UK economy. During the outbreak of the disease the countryside was closed, and the perception of Britain as a destination suffered. Once the crisis was over, the government promised never again to underestimate the importance of tourism as an economic force. Historic houses and castles continued to score as one of the highest motivational factors for nearly half of all inbound tourists.

Nevertheless, country house owners could be forgiven for feeling embattled as the economic confidence of the 1980s and 1990s gave way to the political and commercial realities of the new millennium. While the foot and mouth outbreak had damaged the business prospects of those in the most affected areas, other developments gave private owners the impression that the influence they had so carefully cultivated in the 1970s was now on the wane. Although funding from the national lottery became, after 1994, the biggest source of grants for heritage, private owners were largely denied the chance to apply – at a time when the availability of grants from English Heritage and its equivalents in Scotland and Wales was steadily diminishing. The announcement of the abolition of the one estate election rules by New Labour in 1998 came as a hammer blow to those houses where income from farming or forestry helped to offset the losses incurred when opening a house for tourism. Although the HHA helped to ensure a three-year delay to the implementation of the change, the association was unable to do anything to prevent the end of one estate election, or indeed to persuade the government to put in place alternative provisions for maintenance relief.

Nor would the change of government in 2010 bring any renewed hope: in fact, prospects largely got worse. The new Conservative and Liberal Democrat coalition government proved just as deaf to the needs of historic houses and landed estates as its predecessor at times had been. In the name of clamping down on legalised tax avoidance schemes, George Osborne, the new chancellor of the exchequer, put a cap on the use of the sideways loss mechanism, to which many historic house properties had turned after the removal of the one estate election option. Under pressure to equalise rates of VAT for the repair and maintenance of listed buildings with the zero-rated exemption that applied to the building of new homes, Osborne took the decision instead to remove the surviving discretionary VAT relief for approved alterations to listed buildings. Henceforth, the repair, maintenance, and alteration of listed buildings would all incur a twenty per cent VAT charge. It might not make a difference for everyone (those that were VAT-registered could potentially reclaim VAT, after all), but for the HHA's 'typical' member (if there was such a thing), it meant yet another escalation in the cost of doing business. So too did the imposition in 2013 of yet another new tax on buildings owned by companies (the annual tax on enveloped dwellings, or ATED). The best that the HHA could do was to secure exemptions from ATED for those historic buildings opened to the public as visitor attractions or events venues.

Most of the revival in the fortunes of country houses in the last fifty years has happened despite, rather than because of, the actions of government. More usually, country house revival has happened because of strenuous efforts by individual owners to bring their properties into use and to diversify the commercial activities that were run from them. The liberalisation of regulations concerning wedding ceremonies in England and Wales in 1994 created a step-change in the number of country houses diversifying into weddings and other events. Suddenly, it was possible to have both a wedding ceremony, and the party afterwards, within the setting of a beautiful country house. Five hundred country houses, between perhaps a quarter and a third of the total number, are now active wedding venues, typically hosting an average of one wedding a month, but plenty having as many as two or three a week. Weddings and events were not the only sort of diversification to take root in a country house setting. Events meant that a ready supply of nearby overnight accommodation was also needed – so countless disused stable blocks and garden lodges were converted into self-catering units. These could now be leased out to other sorts of guests as well, leading to the growth of a vibrant market in country house holiday lets. The fact that most bookings are now taken online for this sort of accommodation was simply another demonstration of the way that houses have developed digital platforms to promote their businesses. Larger houses might also convert stable blocks or other ancillary buildings to other commercial uses: tea rooms, restaurants, shops. Another option was to convert such premises into commercial spaces for letting, whether for offices, studios, or workshops. Many houses benefited from contracts for film and television work, whether for the filming of period dramas such as *Wolf Hall* (at Broughton) or for contemporary shows such as *Bake Off: The Professionals* (at Firle Place). The fact that film and television crews were permitted to continue working during the Covid-19 pandemic lockdown of 2020–21 led to a great many new productions being made to satisfy the hunger of subscribers to digital streaming services. But after all, what better conditions could there be for filming than a historic house with no visitors?

Hopetoun House in Scotland, an example of a house now held within a charitable trust established with help from the National Heritage Memorial Fund in the 1980s, has benefited hugely from its association with the ongoing television drama *Outlander*. Hopetoun, near Edinburgh, is also a venue for corporate events and weddings, and has played host to successful electronic dance music festivals in recent years. Clive Aslet quotes Andrew Hopetoun, resident trustee at Hopetoun, on the somewhat surprising reinvention of what used to be called 'stately homes':

> People used to ask, 'What on earth is the point of these places?' Now they say what fantastic places these are. I think it is a very positive time. The older generation used to say – 'What! You live in the big house!' As though we

were either mad or eccentric. People of our age don't seem at all surprised that we should be living here.[1]

This attitude of mind has helped to deflect preconceptions about historic house owners, especially in Scotland where the government has pursued an active agenda of land reform in direct opposition to the interests of landowners.

The other striking political event to have happened in recent years was the UK's exit from membership of the European Union, in the process known as Brexit. Brexit officially occurred on 31 January 2021, while the UK was still battling with the presence of the coronavirus. Formal departure was the culmination of several years of negotiation and political uncertainty, prompted by the largely unanticipated result of the referendum of May 2016, which was narrowly won by those supporting 'leave'. Brexit is only relevant to the story of this book because of the dates involved. The period explored here has encompassed the entire forty-seven years of the UK's membership of the European Union (along with its predecessor entities). The establishment of the HHA in 1973 took place not long after the European Communities Act 1972 had committed the UK to joining the European Community. Arguably, much of the impetus for establishing an independent owners' association in Britain derived from the UK's new-found need to keep pace with other European countries. By 1973 there were already associations to represent private owners of historic family mansions in several other European states. The leading lights of the HHA in its earliest days were fully aware of this European hinterland of owners' organisations. The early HHA was an enthusiastic supporter of the European Architectural Heritage Year, hosting an international conference of historic house owners from across the continent in Oxford and York in July 1975.

It was perhaps unsurprising that owners of historic houses showed themselves to be such significant advocates of greater European collaboration. The country house, after all, has always existed in an international as well as local context. Houses in Britain were populated with items acquired by owners while on grand tours of Europe. Paintings, furniture, tapestries: all were sent home from dealers in France, Germany, Italy, and Spain to take residence in fashionable drawing rooms and saloons in British houses. Families might also have, and take pride in, close links to kinsfolk in other European countries. Lord Montagu showed much enthusiasm for building links with European partner associations and did much to curry favour with British politician Roy Jenkins

---

[1] Andrew Hopetoun quoted in Clive Aslet, *Old Homes, New Life: The Resurgence of the British Country House* (London, 2020), p. 183.

during his time as president of the European Commission. Nevertheless, the Brexit issue divided the nation, and members of the association were similarly split. For every passionate Europhile, there was someone on the opposite side – such as Sir William Cash, one of the most prominent of the parliamentary Brexiters and a longstanding HHA member at Upton Cressett. Given this split within its membership, the HHA has remained officially neutral on the principle of UK membership of the European Union but continues to show its solidarity with other owner organisations on the continent by remaining an active participant in the European Historic Houses Association.

The period of the Covid-19 pandemic also witnessed a measure of soul-searching about international relationships of a different kind: the links of heritage sites to colonial and imperial sources of wealth. Country houses arguably had a globalising influence on British society and culture. They were places that featured the latest architectural styles, often imported from continental Europe, while inside the house paintings from dealers in Rome or Paris could be seen alongside furniture, tapestries, and other objects imported from continental expeditions. The last fifty years has seen a greater understanding of the global connections of British country houses, and a growing pressure on owners to be more transparent about the origins of the funds with which houses were built and collections amassed. Since the turn of the twenty-first century there has been a growing chorus of interest in this line of critique, which seems only to have accelerated in recent years. Houses, so often depicted as being firmly rooted in their local setting, have been viewed instead as hubs within global networks of exchange. Whether or not a house was directly funded from wealth created through the slave trade, past international connections and interactions create dilemmas for owners and custodians in relation to how such networks are to be presented, if at all. As Oliver Cox notes, "for heritage organisations, and privately-owned country houses alike, the question of how to present and interpret these global histories is their biggest challenge at the start of the 2020s."[2]

A different 'way of seeing' country houses sought to expose the origins of these accumulations of property and chattels, adopting a similar critical gaze to that shown by John Berger in his 1972 television documentary of the same name.[3] Edward Said, author of *Orientalism* (1978), similarly foregrounded the

[2] Oliver Cox, 'From Power to Enslavement: Recent Perspectives on the Politics of Art Patronage and Display in the Country House', *Art and the Country House* (2020) <https://doi.org/10.17658/ACH/TE58> [accessed 16 Aug. 2023].

[3] John Berger, *Ways of Seeing* (London, 1972).

often unspoken but implicit imperialist assumptions of western society and culture. In one of his later essays, Said interrogated Jane Austen's *Mansfield Park* (1814), the action of which takes place while the owner of the eponymous estate is away from the property and inspecting his Caribbean investments.[4] None of this is an especially new perspective, of course. As Sathnam Sanghera has observed, the imperial roots of England's wealth and good fortune have long been made clear by writers such as George Orwell, who noted in *The Road to Wigan Pier* (1937) that anyone stepping into a taxi or eating a plate of strawberries and cream was unavoidably complicit in a global capitalist system that condemned a hundred million Indians to poverty.[5]

Sanghera's *Empireland* (2021) was a thoughtful account of the lasting impact of imperialism on English life and culture, by someone whose personal heritage was as a second-generation immigrant from Punjab. Sanghera visited Sezincote House in Gloucestershire, to reflect on the brief early-nineteenth-century architectural penchant for buildings that carried direct echoes of English predominance on the Indian subcontinent. Sezincote, designed by Samuel Pepys Cockerell in 1805, features a large domed roof, carvings of pineapples, and Hindu temples in the garden. Sanghera drew on Stephanie Barczewski's study of *Country Houses and the British Empire 1700–1930* in support of his assertion that "country houses were the favoured asset through which to launder colonial booty".[6] Barczewski produced an estimate that between six and sixteen per cent of British country houses "were at some point in this span purchased by men whose money came from the Empire".[7] Perhaps the greater surprise was that this figure was not higher. After all, some of the commentary produced during the decolonising moment in British historiography has taken it almost for granted that country houses were deeply implicated in the (somewhat different) businesses of colonialism and slavery. In her more recent work, Barczewski has noted that England's imperial entanglements have in fact left remarkably little imprint on the actual architectural design of country houses.[8] Sezincote was notable for drawing on overtly Orientalist motifs in its construction. More often, historians must dwell upon absences when seeking to expose

---

[4] Edward Said, *Culture and Imperialism* (London, 1993).

[5] Sathnam Sanghera, *Empireland: How Imperialism Has Shaped Modern Britain* (London, 2021), p. 259.

[6] *Ibid.*, p. 265.

[7] Stephanie Barczewski, *Country Houses and the British Empire, 1700–1930* (Manchester, 2014), p. 122.

[8] Stephanie Barczewski, *How the Country House became English* (London, 2023).

the colonial origins of the wealth that funded the building of country houses and estates.

The best of the recent writing on this issue has drawn on detailed new research to make explicit the previously hidden or obscured colonial connections of country house properties. The bicentenary of the abolition of the transatlantic slave trade in 2007 produced a flurry of work and public engagement which sought to highlight the degree to which the country house, and other kinds of heritage, were central to histories of imperial oppression and exploitation. The HHA responded with a special edition of its magazine that featured stories from houses that were willing to be open about links to the transatlantic slave trade. These houses included Harewood, near Leeds, where David Lascelles showed remarkable bravery in foregrounding the origins of his family's wealth – the slaves and sugar plantations of the Carribean. With Harewood operating as an educational charitable trust since 1986, Lascelles insisted that it was the duty of the estate to lay bare the facts of the matter. Archival material was digitised and made available online. Meanwhile, Harewood also hosted performances of *Carnival Messiah*, a reinvention of Handel's oratorio by Trinidad-born and Leeds-based musicologist Geraldine Connor. Lascelles' motivations were to "acknowledge the past, deal with the present, address the future", and in so doing he showed a great deal of foresight. He was one of the owners commended by the Jamaican high commissioner to the UK, Burchell Whiteman, who called for a continuation of efforts "to deepen the involvement in the world of history and heritage of those communities who have so far felt excluded from it".[9]

The bicentenary was the spark that led English Heritage to commission much research in this area, resulting in a volume of essays on the subject and a major review of the connections between its properties and the transatlantic slave trade.[10] Initial research by historian Miranda Kaufmann found that twenty-six of thirty-three English Heritage properties investigated had some connection to either slavery or its abolition. Further detailed surveys of four more sites – Bolsover in Derbyshire, Brodsworth in Yorkshire, Marble Hill in London, and The Grange in Hampshire – were subsequently commissioned. More information was also made available through the *East India Company at Home* project, which demonstrated the impact of imperial possessions on

---

[9]   'HHA Marks Bicentenary of the Abolition of the Slave Trade', *Historic House* 31:3 (Autumn, 2007), 28–33.

[10]   Madge Dresser and Andrew Hann (eds), *Slavery and the British Country House* (Swindon, 2013).

domestic life in Britain. The Centre for the Study of the Legacies of British Slavery created an online database of all those families that received compensation following the abolition of slavery in 1833. All this research added greatly to understandings of the close entanglements between country houses and colonial sources of wealth.

The National Trust was noticeable in not having joined the party sooner. But the Trust was working on a project of its own, conceived initially as a creative response to the issues, called 'Colonial Countryside: National Trust Houses Reinterpreted'. Leading the project was literary scholar and creative writer Corinne Fowler. For Fowler, the Colonial Countryside project was revelatory, since it involved paying attention to the responses of a diverse group of ten-year-old children to houses and collections maintained by the Trust. Those children could view objects and buildings, and immediately sense the connections to their own families' journeys to England from other parts of the globe. At the same time, the Trust commissioned a scholarly enquiry into the links between its properties and the eras of colonialism and the slave trade. This investigation found that ninety-three out of three hundred properties investigated had some link: a significantly higher proportion than was identified in Barczewski's earlier study. Admittedly, not all the links identified in the Trust's report were direct links with colonialism or the slave trade – Peckover House in Wisbech was listed because of its links to the *anti*-slavery movement.

A definitive version of the Trust's investigation has yet to be published, however. The murder of George Floyd in Minneapolis in May 2020 gave rise to protests across the world at racial prejudice and inequality. Black Lives Matter marches were held in the UK, and in Bristol in June 2020 a crowd of protestors toppled a statue of the slave trader Edward Colston – itself a listed structure – into the harbour. It was not long after this heated moment, with tensions running high, that the National Trust chose to publish an 'interim' version of its report.[11] Fowler's subsequent book, *Green Unpleasant Land* (2020), summarised the anger that the Trust's publication provoked for some, including high-profile members of the government, who felt that the Trust had strayed into overly political territory.[12] A subsequent investigation by the Charity Commission exonerated the Trust of any such charge. The Commission did,

[11] Sally-Anne Huxtable, Corinne Fowler, Christo Kefalas, Emma Slocombe, *Interim Report on the Connections between Colonialism and Properties now in the Care of the National Trust, Including Links with Historic Slavery* (Swindon, 2020).

[12] Corinne Fowler, *Green Unpleasant Land: Creative Responses to Rural Britain's Colonial Connections* (Leeds, 2020), p. 125.

however, criticise the Trust for not doing more to pre-empt or manage potential risks arising from the somewhat hasty publication of the interim report and
said that the charity "could have done more to clearly explain the link between
the report and the Trust's purpose".[13]

It remains the case that country houses are, for some, such an egregious
symbol of past wrongs that their present-day custodians are constantly at risk
of failing to show adequate cognisance of this history. The president of the
Royal Historical Society, Margot Finn, devoted part of one of her presidential
addresses in 2020 to critiquing the online presence of Combermere Abbey.
Finn was discomforted by the record of the first viscount Combermere, a slave
owner who served as governor in Barbados, commander-in-chief in Ireland,
and commander-in-chief of India. Surely, Finn argued, the plunder and loot
that came to the estate because of viscount Combermere's overseas engage-
ments were integral to the history of the house and its collection? Finn objected to the apparent present-day erasure of this history from the Combermere
Abbey website. She took issue with the way the wedding venue presented itself
within an essentially insular version of English history, "shorn … of references
to colonial wealth and imperial military exploits". Finn was critical of Combermere's marketing slogans, where the venue was described to potential couples
as being "Steeped in a thousand years of English history", without ever being
honest about the darker aspects of that history. Finn's preference was presumably for the wedding venue's advertising collateral, if it was to make an appeal
to history at all, to feature details of the imperial phase of that history in all its
brutality. Only in a footnote did Finn acknowledge that more than a century
had passed since the Cotton family, the descendants of viscount Combermere,
had owned or lived at Combermere.[14]

Had Combermere been demolished after all in 1975, as very nearly happened, its current custodians might have been spared the accusation of deliberately eliding or erasing aspects of its past in the pursuit of a sustainable business
model (in this case, a commercial wedding business). But Combermere Abbey
did survive, as did hundreds of other country houses. Clearly, there is no statute of limitations on a crime as pernicious as the transatlantic slave trade. But

[13] Charity Commission press release, 11 March 2021, 'Charity Commission finds
National Trust did not breach charity law', <https://www.gov.uk/government/news/
charity-commission-finds-national-trust-did-not-breach-charity-law> [accessed 10
Sept. 2023].

[14] Margot Finn, 'Material Turns in British History: Part IV. Empire in India, Cancel
Cultures and the Country House', *Transactions of the RHS* 31 (2021), 1–21.

do owners who today have no personal or familial connection with the people who were involved in this trade nevertheless carry a responsibility to in some way make amends for it? These controversies present a significant challenge to owners today, but perhaps especially where houses are open to day visitors (as perhaps around six to seven hundred of them are). How such houses respond to this 'global turn' in our understanding of culture, history, and heritage will be a critical issue in the years ahead. Some houses have deliberately taken steps to embrace their past where this was unquestionably bound up with abhorrent involvement in slavery and the slave trade. Others have positively explored other aspects of diversity, such as queer histories, to increase their inclusiveness and appeal to ever-more diverse audiences. There is surely room for a multiplicity of interpretative approaches to this issue to be adopted, as well as, if preferred, none.

One group of independent owners has gone further than most in making a visible commitment to reparative justice for past wrongs. The Heirs of Slavery group, launched in April 2023, comprises descendants of plantation owners, slave traders, merchants, and others integral to the transatlantic slave trade. They include David Lascelles, who had already done so much to direct the visitor experience at Harewood to his own family's history. Laura Trevelyan represents a family with investments in sugar plantations in Granada and pledged to give a hundred thousand pounds by way of reparations. Another member of the group, Alex Renton, published a full account of his own family's ownership of estates in Tobago and Jamaica, based on papers kept in the archives at Kilkerran House in Ayrshire, Scotland. Renton's realisation of the extent of his family's investments led him to conclude that owners had no other choice but to "put our privilege to work" by pursuing reparative justice of some kind.[15] Charlie Gladstone, of Hawarden Castle in North Wales, is the latest owner to have followed suit, by way of offering reparations for his great-great-great grandfather's plantations in the Caribbean.[16]

While country houses continue to be beset by age-old threats of fire, flood, or burglary, a more fundamental challenge to them these days might therefore be criticism of the silences within houses' interpretative schema. It is striking to note the absence of any earlier discussion of these issues among house owners, at least until the bicentenary of the abolition of the slave trade in 2007.

[15] Alex Renton, *Blood Legacy: Reckoning with a Family's Story of Slavery* (Edinburgh, 2021), p. 336.

[16] 'We want to make things better, rather than say this history is nothing to do with us', *The Observer*, 20 Aug. 2023, p. 14.

That anniversary was just the beginning of a new wave of questioning about the role and purpose of country houses. The challenge now, however, feels more fundamental. If it is true, as British historian David Olusoga has reportedly said, that younger generations visiting country houses today will be busy "on their phones Googling it to see where the money came from" while their parents are enjoying the gardens and a cream tea, then the decolonising turn in historical enquiry surely needs to be taken seriously by house owners who open to public visiting.[17]

By the same token, the age-old complaints of house owners, about oppressive rates of taxation or overbearing levels of regulation, continue to be heard. This is not without some justification: governments are too prone to forget the reality of life for smaller businesses, where changes in fiscal or regulatory conditions can make all the difference to profit margins. Historic Houses (the modern brand name for the HHA) continues to fight these causes. But other, potentially much more profound, challenges loom. The climate is warming because of human action. The effects are often noted at country house properties. Sudden deluges of rainfall can leave parks as waterlogged lakes, and guttering on houses might now need to be entirely replaced to accommodate such downpours. Many houses still rely on carbon-intensive oil-based heating systems, which surely will need to be replaced within a matter of years rather than decades. The climate challenge is one of the greatest threats that any generation has had to face. Typically, many country house owners have chosen to see it as an opportunity and have been early adopters of renewable energy technology such as solar arrays and ground-source heat pumps. Grade I Athelhampton House in Dorset is now entirely net zero, because of its heat pumps, solar panels, and Tesla battery units.

Fortitude and optimism in the face of a problem as large as the climate challenge attests to the resilience shown by British country houses over the last half century. Time and again, the owners of these houses have found ways for their buildings to survive. There was more than a little exaggeration in those claims being made in the early 1970s that the country house might have had its day. A combination of enterprise and initiative, with occasional acts of generosity on the part of successive governments, have enabled country houses to weather storms and emerge in as good if not better condition than

---

[17] 'National Trust working on policy on return of colonial loot, chair says', *Guardian*, 31 May 2023, <https://www.theguardian.com/uk-news/2023/may/30/national-trust-working-on-policy-on-return-of-colonial-loot-chair-says> [accessed 10 Sept. 2023].

they were in before. This is surely something to be celebrated, even while newer generations are determining for themselves what this slice of heritage might signify, exactly.

Appendix

HHA Presidents

1973–1978	Lord Montagu (Beaulieu)
1978–1982	George Howard (Baron Howard of Henderskelfe; Castle Howard)
1982–1988	Commander Michael Saunders Watson (Rockingham Castle)
1988–1993	The Marquess of Lansdowne (earl of Shelburne at the time; Bowood House)
1993–1998	Sir William Proby (Elton Hall)
1998–2003	The Earl of Leicester (Holkham Hall)
2003–2008	James Hervey-Bathurst (Eastnor Castle)
2008–2012	Edward Harley (Brampton Bryan Hall)
2012–2016	Richard Compton (Newby Hall)
2016–2020	James Birch (Doddington Hall)
2020–	Martha Lytton Cobbold (Knebworth House)

HHA Executive Officers

1973–1974	David Coleman (Executive Secretary, on secondment from BTA)
1974–1981	Richard Miller (role known as Secretary General from 1976)
1981–1996	Terry Empson (role known as Director General from 1983)
1996–2005	Richard Wilkin
2005–2015	Nick Way
2016–	Ben Cowell

Winners – Garden of the Year Award

1984	Heale House, Wiltshire
1985	Hodnet Hall, Shropshire
1986	Newby Hall, North Yorkshire
1987	Arley Hall, Cheshire
1988	Barnsley House, Gloucestershire
1989	Brympton d'Evercy, Somerset
1990	Parham Park, West Sussex
1991	Holker Hall, Cumbria
1992	Forde Abbey, Dorset

1993   Haddon Hall, Derbyshire

1994   Levens Hall, Cumbria

1995   Hever Castle, Kent

1996   Sudeley Castle, Gloucestershire

1997   Athelhampton, Dorset

1998   Iford Manor, Wiltshire and Mellerstain House, Berwickshire

1999   Pashley Manor Gardens, East Sussex

2000   Cottesbrooke Hall, Northamptonshire

2001   Exbury Gardens, Hampshire

2002   West Dean Gardens, West Sussex

2003   Kiftsgate Court, Gloucestershire

2004   Borde Hill Gardens, West Sussex

2005   Burton Agnes Hall, East Yorkshire

2006   Bourton House Gardens, Gloucestershire

2007   Houghton Hall, Norfolk

2008   Blenheim Palace, Oxfordshire

2009   Chenies Manor House, Buckinghamshire

2011   Castle Howard, North Yorkshire

2012   Abbotsbury Subtropical Garden, Dorset

2013   Dalemain, Cumbria

2014   Bowood House, Wiltshire

2015   Renishaw Hall, Derbyshire

2016   Caerhays, Cornwall

2017   Helmingham, Suffolk

2018   Miserden, Gloucestershire

2019   Newby Hall, North Yorkshire

2020   Mapperton, Dorset

2021   Gordon Castle, Moray

2022   Wentworth Woodhouse, South Yorkshire

Winners – Restoration Award

2008   Markenfield, North Yorkshire

2009   Chillington, Staffordshire

2010   Wilton House, Wiltshire

2011   Aldourie Castle, Inverness

2012   Boconnoc, Cornwall

2013   Kinross House, Kinross

2014   Norton Conyers, North Yorkshire

2015   Wimborne St Giles House, Dorset
2016   Combermere Abbey, Shropshire
2017   Glynde Place, East Sussex
2018   Marchmont House, Berwickshire
2019   Dunvegan Castle, Skye
2020   Iford Manor, Wiltshire
2021   Radbourne Hall, Derbyshire
2022   Lytham Hall, Lancashire and Wolterton Hall, Norfolk

Bibliography

Archival sources

Historic Houses Association archives (held at the association's offices):
    AGM minutes.
    Annual reports.
    HHA executive council minutes.
    Minute books of committees and other governance fora.
The National Archives:
    COU 3/676.
    LCO 2/5753.
    T 218/524.
    T 227/4421.
Parliament:
    HL Deb. 26 June 1974, vol. 352.
Victoria and Albert Museum archives:
    MA/28/243/1 (8/9 Oct – 1 Dec 1974).
    RP/1974/105 (1973–74) – files associated with the *Destruction of the Country House* exhibition.

Selected articles from *Historic House* magazine, presented chronologically

Hugh Tapper, 'Survey of Houses Open to the Public', *Historic House* 1:1 (Autumn, 1976), 15–16.

'The National Trust', *Historic House* 1:3 (Spring, 1977), 24–25.

'Mentmore for the Nation?', *Historic House* 1:3 (Spring, 1977), 29–30.

David Jacques, 'Restoring Historic Gardens and Parks', *Historic House* 2:3 (Summer, 1978), 13–15.

Stephen Weeks, 'Penhow Castle, Gwent', *Historic House* 4:1 (February, 1980), 23–25.

George Howard, 'Conserving Art in Houses', *Historic House* 5:1 (Summer, 1981), 18–19.

Peter Chubb, 'From Stately Home to Conference Centre for All Occasions', *Historic House* 5:2 (Autumn, 1981), 20–23.

'President's Review', *Historic House* 6:1 (Spring, 1982), 5.

'Organisation of Ancient Monuments and Historic Buildings in England', *Historic House* 6:1 (Spring, 1982), 19–20.

Michael Balston, 'The House and its Landscape', *Historic House* 6:2 (Summer, 1982), 14–16.

'How Bodysgallen Hall was Restored as a Country House Hotel', *Historic House* 6:2 (Summer, 1982), 17–19.

Gerald Maitland-Carew, 'A Secure Future for Thirlestane', *Historic House* 8:4 (Winter, 1984), 21–23.

Anthony Furse, 'Charitable Intention', *Historic House* 9:2 (Summer, 1985), 17–19.

Peter Rumble, 'Public Money for Private Houses', *Historic House* 10:1 (Spring, 1986), 13–15.

'Hospitality – Country House Party Style', *Historic House* 10:2 (Summer, 1986), 14–17.

'Kedleston: Secured for the Nation', *Historic House* 10:2 (Summer, 1986), 24–27.

'The Next Generation', *Historic House* 10:3 (Autumn, 1986), 30–33.

Neil Cossons, 'What *is* interpretation?', *Historic House* 11:2 (Summer, 1987), 16–18.

Merlin Waterson, 'Diversity and Dimension: Interpretation of Historic Houses', *Historic House* 11:2 (Summer, 1987), 20–22.

'President's Review', *Historic House* 11:3 (Autumn, 1987), 5.

'Lady Mexborough at Home', *Historic House* 11:3 (Autumn, 1987), 24–27.

Michael Saunders Watson, 'President's Review', *Historic House* 12:1 (Spring, 1988), 5.

Nicholas Ridley, 'The November Speech', *Historic House* 13:1 (Spring, 1989), 25–26.

Penny Cobham, 'Diversify or Bust?', *Historic House* 13:3 (Autumn, 1989), 18–20.

'The President's Page', *Historic House* 14:4 (Winter, 1990), 5.

'Food for Thought', *Historic House* 16:4 (Winter, 1992), 20–22.

Noël Riley, 'History According to Kentwell', *Historic House* 17:1 (Spring, 1993), 23–25.

'Filming at Historic Houses', *Historic House* 19:2 (Summer, 1995), 31–34.

'Securing the Future', *Historic House* 19:3 (Autumn, 1995), 20–24.

'Chris Smith's Speech', *Historic House* 22:1 (Spring, 1998), 9–11.

Giles Worsley, 'Country House Fires', *Historic House* 26:3 (Autumn, 2002), 31–33.

'Garden of the Year Award', *Historic House* 28:3 (Autumn, 2004), 26.

'Borde Hill', *Historic House* 29:2 (Summer, 2005), 24–26.

'Walled Garden at Scampston', *Historic House* 29:2 (Summer, 2005), 32.

'The President's Page', *Historic House* 30:3 (Autumn, 2006), 5.

'HHA Marks Bicentenary of the Abolition of the Slave Trade', *Historic House* 31:3 (Autumn, 2007), 28–33.

James Scott, 'Tax Update', *Historic House* 34:4 (Winter, 2010), 11.

'Location, Location, Location', *Historic House* 34:4 (Winter, 2010), 40.

Anthony Lambert, 'Focus On: Pitchford Hall', *Historic House* 41:1 (Spring, 2017), 22–26.

General works

Adams, Ruth, 'The V&A, the Destruction of the Country House and the Creation of "English Heritage"', *Museums & Society* xi (2013), 1–13.

Advani, Arun, Emma Chamberlain, Andy Summers, *A Wealth Tax for the UK* (London, 2020).

Aslet, Clive, *Old Homes, New Life: The Resurgence of the British Country House* (London, 2020).

Aslet, Clive, *The Story of the Country House: A History of Places & People* (New Haven and London, 2021).

Baigent, Elizabeth and Ben Cowell (eds), *Octavia Hill, Social Activism and the Remaking of British Society* (London, 2016).

Bailey, Catherine, *Black Diamonds: The Rise and Fall of an English Dynasty* (London, 2007).

Bannister, Freddie, *There Must Be a Better Way: The Story of the Bath and Knebworth Rock Festivals 1969–1979* (Cambridge, 2003).

Barczewski, Stephanie, *Country Houses and the British Empire, 1700–1930* (Manchester, 2014).

Barczewski, Stephanie, *How the Country House Became English* (London, 2023).

Bateman, John, *The Great Landowners of Great Britain and Ireland* (Leicester, 1971).

Beckett, J. V., *The Rise and Fall of the Grenvilles: Dukes of Buckingham and Chandos, 1710 to 1921* (Manchester, 1994).

Bedford, John Russell, duke of, *A Silver-Plated Spoon* (London, 1959).

Bedford, John Russell, duke of, *How to Run a Stately Home* (London, 1971).

Berger, John, *Ways of Seeing* (London, 1972).

Binney, Marcus, *Our Vanishing Heritage* (London, 1984).

Binney, Marcus, *SAVE Britain's Heritage 1975–2005: Thirty Years of Campaigning* (London, 2005).

Binney, Marcus and John Harris, *The Destruction of the Country House: 40 Years On* (London, 2014).

Binney, Marcus and Kit Martin, *The Country House: To Be or Not to Be* (London, 1982).

Byrne, Pauline, *Mad World: Evelyn Waugh and the Secrets of Brideshead* (London, 2010).

Camoys Stonor, Julia, *Sherman's Wife* (London, 2006).

Cannadine, David, *The Pleasures of the Past* (London, 1989).

Cannadine, David, *The Decline and Fall of the British Aristocracy* (New Haven and London, 1990).

Cannadine, David, *In Churchill's Shadow: Confronting the Past in Modern Britain* (London, 2002).

Cannadine, David and Jeremy Musson, *The Country House: Past, Present, Future* (New York, 2018).

Cash, William, *Restoration Heart* (London, 2021).

Chick, Martin, *Taxing Wealth: A Historical Perspective* (London, 2020).

Clifford, Helen M., *Behind the Acanthus: The NADFAS Story* (London, 2008).

Colvin, Howard, *Calke Abbey Revealed* (London, 1985).

Cooke, Robert, *Government and the Quality of Life* (London, 1974).

Cormack, Patrick, *Heritage in Danger* (London, 1976).

Cornforth, John, *Country Houses in Britain, Can They Survive?: An Independent Report* (London, 1974).

Cornforth, John, *The Inspiration of the Past: Country House Taste in the Twentieth Century* (London, 1985).

Cornforth, John, *The Country Houses of England, 1948–1998* (London, 1998).

Cowell, Ben, 'Why Heritage Counts: Researching the Historic Environment', *Cultural Trends* 13:4 (2004), 23–39.

Cowell, Ben, 'Measuring the Impact of Free Admission', *Cultural Trends* 16:3 (2007), 203–224.

Cowell, Ben, *The Heritage Obsession: The Battle for England's Past* (Stroud, 2008).

Cowell, Ben, *Robert Hunter: Co-Founder and 'Inventor' of the National Trust* (Stroud, 2013).

Cowell, Ben, 'Saving Country Houses and their Collections in the Twentieth and Twenty-First Centuries', *Art and the Country House* (2020) (www.artandthecountryhouse.com/).

Cox, Oliver, 'From Power to Enslavement: Recent Perspectives on the Politics of Art Patronage and Display in the Country House', *Art and the Country House* (2020) (www.artandthecountryhouse.com/).

Cragoe, Matthew and Paul Readman (eds), *The Land Question in England, 1750–1950* (London, 2010).

Dalton, Hugh, *High Tide and After: Memoirs 1945–1960* (London, 1962).

Daunton, Martin, *Trusting Leviathan: The Politics of Taxation in Britain, 1799–1914* (Cambridge, 2001).

Daunton, Martin, *Just Taxes: The Politics of Taxation in Britain, 1914–1979* (Cambridge, 2002).

DC Research, *The Economic and Social Contribution of Independently Owned Historic Houses and Gardens* (2015).

Delafons, John, *Politics and Preservation: A Policy History of the Built Heritage 1882–1996* (London, 1997).

Devonshire, duchess of, *Chatsworth: The House* (London, 2002).

Devonshire, Deborah, *Wait for Me!* (London, 2010).

Devonshire, Deborah, *All in One Basket* (London, 2012).

Dooley, Terence and Christopher Ridgway (eds), *Country House Collections: Their Lives and Afterlives* (Dublin, 2021).

Dresser, Madge and Andrew Hann, *Slavery and the British Country House* (Swindon, 2013).

Evans, Shaun, Tony McCarthy and Annie Tindley (eds), *Land Reform in the British and Irish Isles since 1800* (Edinburgh, 2022).

Fearnley-Whittingstall, Jane, *Historic Gardens: A Guide to 160 British Gardens of Interest* (Harmondsworth, 1990).

Feddon, Robin, *The Continuing Purpose: A History of the National Trust, Its Aims and Work* (London, 1968).

Fellowes, Jessica, *The World of Downton Abbey* (London, 2011).

Floud, Roderick, *An Economic History of the English Garden* (London, 2019).

Fowler, Corinne, *Green Unpleasant Land: Creative Responses to Rural Britain's Colonial Connections* (Leeds, 2020).

Fulford, Francis, *Bearing Up: The Remarkable Survival of the Landed Estate* (London, 1998).

Girouard, Mark, *Life in the English Country House: A Social and Architectural History* (New Haven and London, 1978).

Glen, Alexander, *Footholds Against a Whirlwind* (London, 1975).

Glendinning, Miles, *The Conservation Movement: A History of Architectural Preservation – Antiquity to Modernity* (London, 2013).

Gowers, Ernest, *Houses of Outstanding Historic or Architectural Interest* (HMSO, 1950).

Green, Simon and Jane Thomas, *Dumfries House: An Architectural Story* (RCAHMS, 2016).

Harris, John, *No Voice from the Hall: Early Memories of a Country House Snooper* (London, 1998).

Harris, John, Roy Strong, Marcus Binney (eds), *The Destruction of the Country House 1875–1975* (London, 1974).

Healey, Denis, *The Time of My Life* (London, 1989).

Hearn, Karen, Robert Upstone, Giles Waterfield, *In Celebration: The Art of the Country House* (London, 1998).

Hewison, Robert, *The Heritage Industry: Britain in a Climate of Decline* (London, 1987).

Hewison, Robert, *Cultural Capital: The Rise and Fall of Creative Britain* (London, 2014).

Hiskey, Christine, *Holkham: The Social, Architectural and Landscape History of a Great English Country House* (Norwich, 2016).

Hopetoun, countess of, Polly Feversham, Leo Schmidt, *Hopetoun: Scotland's Finest Stately Home* (Munich, 2020).

Hudson, Norman and Sarah Greenwood, *Film and Photography in Historic Houses and Gardens* (London, 1983).

Huxtable, Sally-Anne, Corinne Fowler, Christo Kefalas, Emma Slocombe, *Interim Report on the Connections between Colonialism and Properties now in the Care of the National Trust, Including Links with Historic Slavery* (Swindon, 2020).

Jenkins, Clive, *All Against the Collar: Struggles of a White Collar Union Leader* (London, 1990).

Jenkins, Hugh, *The Culture Gap: An Experience of Government and the Arts* (London, 1979).

Jenkins, Jennifer and Patrick James, *From Acorn to Oak Tree: The Growth of the National Trust, 1895–1994* (London, 1994).

Jenkins, Roy, *European Diary, 1977–1981* (London, 1989).

Jenkins, Simon, *England's Thousand Best Houses* (London, 2003).

Jones, Arthur, *Britain's Heritage: The Creation of the National Heritage Memorial Fund* (London, 1985).

Kennet, Wayland, *Preservation* (London, 1972).

Knox, James, *Cartoons & Coronets: The Genius of Osbert Lancaster* (London, 2008).

Knox, Tim, 'The Stripping of the Country House', *Emmanuel College Magazine* xcvii (2015–16), 32–44.

Lee, Geoffrey, *The People's Budget: An Edwardian Tragedy* (London, 2008).

Littlejohn, David, *The Fate of the English Country House* (New York and Oxford, 1997).

Lyon, Neil, *'Useless Anachronisms?' A Study of the Country Houses and Landed Estates of Northamptonshire Since 1880* (Northampton, 2018).

Lytton Cobbold, Chryssie, *Board Meetings in the Bath: The Knebworth House Story* (London, 1986).

Lytton Cobbold, Henry, *Great, Great, Great: Lines, Tracks and Happy Highways to Knebworth House* (Knebworth, 2022).

Mandler, Peter, 'Nationalising the Country House', in Michael Hunter (ed.), *Preserving the Past: The Rise of Heritage in Modern Britain* (Stroud, 1996).

Mandler, Peter, *The Fall and Rise of the Stately Home* (New Haven and London, 1997).

Matless, David, *About England* (London, 2023).

Middleton, Victor, *British Tourism: The Remarkable Story of Growth* (2007).

Montagu of Beaulieu, Lord, *The Gilt and the Gingerbread* (London, 1967).

Montagu of Beaulieu, Lord, *Wheels Within Wheels: An Unconventional Life* (London, 2000).

More-Molyneux, James, *The Loseley Challenge: The Story of Half a Century's Ownership of an Historic Estate* (London, 1995).

Morris, Rachel, *The Museum Makers: A Journey Backwards* (Tewkesbury, 2020).

Morrison, Kathryn A. (ed.), *Apethorpe: The Story of an English Country House* (London, 2016).

Mowl, Tim, *Gentlemen and Players: Gardeners of the English Landscape* (Stroud, 2000).

Musson, Jeremy, *English Country House Interiors* (New York, 2011).

Musson, Jeremy, *Romantics and Classics: Style in the English Country House* (London, 2021).

Nixon, Sean, 'Trouble at the National Trust: Post-War Recreation, the Benson Report and the Rebuilding of a Conservation Organization in the 1960s', *Twentieth Century British History* 26 (2015), 529–550.

Parker, Christopher, *Browsholme Hall 1975–1995: A Point of View* (1998).

Parker, Philippa, 'Lost Country Houses in Lancashire: Reappraisal and Analysis', *Northern History* 55:1 (2018), 111–123.

Parry, James and Elizabeth Ashcombe, *Sudeley Castle: Royalty, Romance & Renaissance* (London, 2021).

Peacock, Alan and Ilde Rizzo, *The Heritage Game: Economics, Policy, and Practice* (Oxford, 2008).

Pearce, Edward, *Denis Healey: A Life in our Times* (London, 2002).

Peill, James, *The English Country House* (London, 2013).

Peill, James, *Glorious Goodwood: A Biography of England's Greatest Sporting Estate* (London, 2019).

Probert, Rebecca, *Tying the Knot: The Formation of Marriage, 1836–2000* (Cambridge, 2021).

Raven, James, *Lost Mansions: Essays on the Destruction of the Country House* (Basingstoke, 2015).

Renton, Alex, *Blood Legacy: Reckoning with a Family's Story of Slavery* (Edinburgh, 2021).

Richardson, Tim, *English Gardens in the Twentieth Century* (London, 2005).

Richardson, Tim, *The New English Garden* (London, 2015).

Roberts, W. M., *Lost Country Houses of Suffolk* (Woodbridge, 2010).

Robinson, John Martin, *The Latest Country Houses* (London, 1984).

Robinson, John Martin, *The Country House at War* (London, 1989).

Robinson, John Martin, *Felling the Ancient Oaks: How England Lost its Great Country Estates* (London, 2012).

Robinson, John Martin, *Requisitioned: The British Country House in the Second World War* (London, 2014).

Said, Edward, *Culture and Imperialism* (London, 1993).

Samuel, Raphael, *Theatres of Memory* (London, 1994).

Sanghera, Sathnam, *Empireland: How Imperialism Has Shaped Modern Britain* (London, 2021).

Saunders Watson, Michael, *I Am Given a Castle* (Hindringham, 2008).

Sayer, Michael, *The Disintegration of a Heritage: Country Houses and their Collections, 1979–1992* (Norwich, 1993).

Scott, Ann, *Ernest Gowers: Plain Words and Forgotten Deeds* (London, 2009).

Scriven, Marcus, *Splendour and Squalor: The Disintegration of Three Aristocratic Dynasties* (London, 2009).

Seymour, Miranda, *In my Father's House: Elegy for an Obsessive Love* (London, 2007).

Shaftesbury, Earl of and Tim Knox, *The Rebirth of an English Country House: St. Giles House* (London, 2018).

Sherborn, Derek, *An Inspector Recalls: Saving our Heritage* (Lewes, 2003).

Stevenson, Hew and Leslie Geddes-Brown, *Columbine Hall: The Story of a House and Its Transformation* (2018).

Stone, Lawrence and Jeanne C. Fawtier Stone, *An Open Elite? England, 1540–1880* (Oxford, 1984).

Stourton, James, *Heritage: A History of How We Conserve Our Past* (London, 2022).

Strong, Roy *et al.*, *The Destruction of the Country House, 1875–1975* (London, 1974).

Strong, Roy, *The Roy Strong Diaries 1967–1987* (London, 1998).

Summers, Julie, *Our Uninvited Guests: Ordinary Lives in Extraordinary Times in the Country Houses of Wartime Britain* (New York, 2019).

Throsby, David, *Economics and Culture* (Cambridge, 2001).

Thurley, Simon, *Men from the Ministry: How Britain Saved its Heritage* (New Haven and London, 2013).

Tinniswood, Adrian, *The Polite Tourist: A History of Country House Visiting* (London, 1998).

Tinniswood, Adrian, *Noble Ambitions: The Fall and Rise of the Post-war Country House* (London, 2021).

Tree, Isabella, *Wilding* (London, 2018).

Waterfield, Giles, *The Hound in the Left-Hand Corner* (London, 2002).

Waterfield, Giles and Rebecca Parker (eds), *Looking Ahead: The Future of the Country House* (London, 2012).

Waterson, Merlin, *The Servants' Hall* (London, 1980).

Waterson, Merlin, *A Noble Thing: The National Trust and its Benefactors from 1940 to the Present Day* (London, 2011).

Waterson, Merlin and Samantha Wyndham, *The National Trust: The First Hundred Years* (London, 1994).

Weideger, Paula, *Gilding the Acorn: Behind the Façade of the National Trust* (London, 1994).

Wheen, Francis, *Strange Days Indeed: The Golden Age of Paranoia* (London, 2009).

Williamson, Tom, *Polite Landscapes: Gardens and Society in Eighteenth Century England* (Stroud, 1995).

Williamson, Tom, Ivan Ringwood, Sarah Spooner, *Lost Country Houses of Norfolk: History, Archaeology and Myth* (Woodbridge, 2015).

Worsley, Giles, 'Beyond the Powerhouse: Understanding the Country House in the Twenty-first Century', *Historical Research* 78:201 (2005), 423–435.

Wright, Patrick, *On Living in an Old Country: The National Past in Contemporary Britain* (1985; rev. edn, Oxford, 2009).

Unpublished theses

O'Brien, Susan, 'Attitude, Altruism and Adaptability: How Two Gentry Houses, Kiplin Hall (Yorkshire) and Browsholme Hall (Lancashire), Survived the Twentieth Century' (Unpublished MA thesis, University of Leicester, 2018).

Porter, Elena, 'National Heritage in Private Hands: The Political and Cultural Status of Country Houses in Britain, 1950–2000' (Unpublished D.Phil thesis, University of Oxford, 2022).

Index

Printed and bound by CPI Group (UK) Ltd, Croydon, CR0 4YY

16/05/2024

14503383-0002